A Civil Society?

A Civil Society?

Collective Actors in Canadian Political Life

MIRIAM SMITH

broadview
press

Library and Archives Canada Cataloguing in Publication

Smith, Miriam Catherine
    A civil society? : collective actors in Canadian political life / Miriam Smith.

Includes bibliographical references and index.
ISBN 1-55111-231-0

    1. Pressure groups—Canada.   2. Social movements—Political aspects—Canada.
3. Canada—Politics and government—1993—   I. Title.

JL186.5.S55 2005   322.4'3'0971   C2005-900489-4

Broadview Press, Ltd. is an independent, international publishing house, incorporated in 1985. Broadview believes in shared ownership, both with its employees and with the general public; since the year 2000 Broadview shares have traded publicly on the Toronto Venture Exchange under the symbol BDP.

We welcome any comments and suggestions regarding any aspect of our publications — please feel free to contact us at the addresses below, or at broadview@broadviewpress.com / www.broadviewpress.com

North America
Post Office Box 1243,
Peterborough, Ontario,
Canada K9J 7H5
Tel: (705) 743-8990
Fax: (705) 743-8353
customerservice
@broadviewpress.com

3576 California Road,
Orchard Park, NY
USA 14127

UK, Ireland, and
Continental Europe
NBN International
Estover Road
Plymouth, Devon PL6 7PY
United Kingdom
Tel: +44 (0) 1752 202300
Fax: +44 (0) 1752 202330
Customer Service:
cservs@nbninternational.com
orders@nbninternational.com

Australia and
New Zealand
UNIREPS
University of
New South Wales
Sydney, NSW, 2052
Tel: + 61296 640 999
Fax: + 61296 645 420
info.press@unsw.edu.au

Broadview Press Ltd. gratefully acknowledges the financial support of the Government of Canada through the Book Publishing Industry Development Program for our publishing activities.

Edited by Betsy Struthers.
Cover design and typeset by Zack Taylor, www.zacktaylor.com

Printed in Canada

Contents

Acknowledgements

I wrote much of this book as a guest of the Canadian Studies Program at University College, University of Toronto. I greatly enjoyed the friendly and collegial atmosphere as well as the luxurious library facilities. I would like to thank Paul Perron, Principal of University College, and Sylvia Bashevkin, Vice-Principal of University College and former Director of the Canadian Studies Program, for inviting me to spend my sabbatical at the University of Toronto. I would also like to thank Maureen Fitzgerald and David Rayside of the Sexual Diversity Studies (SDS) Program in University College for welcoming me as part of the SDS community. The book was revised during my first term as a faculty member in the Department of Political Studies at Trent University, and I would like to thank my new colleagues, especially John Wadland, for making me feel welcome.

Several colleagues provided useful commentary on early drafts of the manuscript including Jacqueline Krikorian, Kiera Ladner, Nanda Purandare, François Rocher, and Joerg Wittenbrinck. The anonymous reviewers for Broadview Press made valuable suggestions for improvement. Michael Orsini provided feedback on the entire manuscript and on the writing process. Jeffrey Canton, Joanne Edwards, and Gordon Smith provided diverse entertainment and encouragement. Substantial funding from the Social Sciences and Humanities Research Council of Canada defrayed some of the research costs, and this support is gratefully acknowledged. Betsy Struthers provided excellent copyediting.

Finally, I would like to thank Michael Harrison of Broadview Press for his patient encouragement and good humour. In a world of media conglomerates, Broadview Press is a refreshingly independent Canadian publisher. Long may it flourish.

ONE

Neoliberalism and Group Politics

In the 1990s, [the] old regime is being dismantled piece by piece and the scaffolding of what might replace it gradually emerges, although its eventual form is not yet completely identifiable. What is evident is that forms of access to and representation of interests within the state are changing fundamentally.... The legitimacy of group action and the desire for social justice are losing ground to the notion that citizens and interests can compete equally in the political marketplace of ideas. In the process, a new, individualized identity for citizens is emerging. Support for this emerging identity exists within civil society as well at the state, although, of course, the social forces to which it appeals differ from those which still support the terms of the postwar regime.

— Jane Jenson and Susan Phillips, "Regime Shift:
New Citizenship Practices in Canada," 1996

This book explores the role of social movements and interest groups in Canadian federal politics. Such groups provide a vehicle for public participation in collective decision-making in a democratic society. Collective action is an alternative to voting and participating in the electoral system and enables people to pursue and express a broad range of political interests and identities. Farmers, workers, peace activists, feminists, environmentalists, and the business community have all organized to influence public policy and public opinion. Whether it is large corporations buying advertising space on Canadian television to influence the debate over global warming or the anti-globalization protestors taking to the streets of Seattle and Quebec City, collective actors are at least as important as political parties and, arguably, even more important in offering venues for citizens to shape political debate and policy outcomes. Such actors deserve study in their own right as analytically distinct from political parties seeking public office.

Participation in collective action is central to democratic political life. The right to assemble freely was one of the first freedoms of the democratic revolution and remains a core element in democratic practice. The most recent wave of contestation and contention, centred in the anti-globalization movement, may convey the impression that the global era is one in which groups have more power than ever in the political process. The declining role of states may lead to the decoupling of democratic rights from the framework of the nation-state (Held, 1995; Soysal, 1994). Historically, the central framework of democratic group politics has been provided by the nation-state. While transnational and global organizing are important forms of collective action, there are a broad range of issues on which the domestic nation-state is still central to decision-making and to political outcomes. Many observers have pointed out that Canada's participation in free trade agreements with the US was a decision that was undertaken by business elites, using the Canadian state as their instrument (McBride, 2001). In this sense, the Canadian state has been a willing and eager participant in globalization and economic restructuring. This fact is recognized by anti-globalization and transnational activists who often target states and state policies in addition to other actors in the international system (Ayres, 2004; Keck and Sikkink, 1998). Furthermore, global and transnational arenas lack the framework of competitive elections and the rule of law; in them, collective action is aimed at diverse targets, ranging from corporations to international organizations and trade agreements in which (aside from democratic states) the individual has no formally guaranteed political rights or role. In contrast, in the domestic arena, democratic citizenship, even the most old-fashioned democratic citizenship of the eighteenth-century variety, presupposes that citizens have the right to pursue their interests and identities and, in so doing, that they have the right to assemble with others for that purpose. Whatever its faults, the domestic nation-state has furnished the dominant model of democracy and democratic political participation. While the nation-state may be headed for the dustbin of history, this book is premised on the assumption that it is not there yet. For these reasons, the role and function of collective actors at the level of the federal state in Canada is still centrally important to the quality of democratic political life and public policy.

In exploring the role of groups and social movements in Canadian politics at the federal level, I have chosen the widest possible definition of collective action. The very terms that are used to discuss group politics in themselves imply theoretical and normative assumptions about the role of collective action in politics. As I will discuss at length in Chapter 2, the term "collective action" often implies a rational choice approach, based on economics, in which the calculating self-interest of the individual is seen as the basis of collective action. The once common political science term "interest group" invokes a pluralist approach in which society is seen as composed of a large number of diverse groups that contend, more or less equally, for power. The term "pressure group" also implies a pluralist approach in which groups are seen as pressuring the state for their preferred policies and outcomes. Interest groups and pressure groups are sometimes defined as self-regarding, that is, out to pursue the interests of their own members and clients. In contrast, public interest groups are often defined as other-regarding, that is, as seeking to further a cause that is not directly connected to the interests of their own members, such as human rights or environmental protection. Interest groups are often distinguished from social movements in that social movements seek to transform social and political values or seek sweeping political change, while interest groups are more narrowly focused on obtaining selective benefits from the state. Others distinguish social movements and groups by their extent of organization, labeling formally organized and well-resourced groups as "associations" or "interest groups" and labeling smaller scale informal networks as social movements. Sociologists often distinguish contentious politics, such as demonstrations and protests which draw on informal activist networks and spontaneous action, from the formal associations to which such movements may give rise. For example, although the women's movement may engage in large-scale demonstrations, direct action or protests, the movement also comprises formal organizations, such as the National Action Committee on the Status of Women. Similarly, the environmental movement is larger than formally organized groups, such as Greenpeace. Still other observers have noted the rise in importance of the voluntary or charitable sector in Canadian politics. This refers to groups that undertake direct service provision or charitable work.

There are also a number of very different normative visions of the role of groups in democratic political life. Right-wing populists in Canadian politics have often defined certain forms of group activity as "special interests," a term that implies that such groups are illegitimate and undemocratic (Dobrowolsky, 2000b; Harrison, 1995; Patten, 1999). Right-wing populists have tended to label groups with the special interest label when they do not like their aims and goals (e.g., Brodie, 2002). Therefore, for example, First Nations, women's organizations, and gay and lesbian groups have often been labeled special interests, while groups like the National Taxpayers Association or the National Citizens' Coalition are defined by right-wing populists as legitimate and democratic representatives of the common good. Some argue that group politics undermines democracy by distorting the democratic will of the people as expressed in elections (Knopff and Morton, 1992). According to critics, such groups are not necessarily democratic and do not necessarily represent the views of the people they claim to represent. In contrast, observers on the left define class politics as the central form of collective action. The dominance of class politics on the traditional left as the lens for viewing the political world has posed challenges for the understanding of forms of collective action that seek progressive social change, such as the women's movement, and yet that do not fit easily within the lens of class politics (Fraser, 1995; Conway, 2004). Behind these debates about the worth and value of groups in the political process lies a concern with social stability. Collective action has the potential to threaten social, political, and economic order. Even the casual observer of the Quebec City protests will recall the demonstrators attacking the wall that was designed to protect world leaders from the protestors. Defenders of social order are suspicious of group politics for this reason. As I will discuss at length in later chapters, the currently dominant discourse on the importance of "citizen engagement," "social cohesion," and the "voluntary sector" reflects a concern among federal policy-makers with social and political stability (see Mayer, 2003).

While the distinctions listed above may be useful for various theoretical or normative purposes, in this analysis I use the terms interest group, interest organization, social movement organization, and collective action interchangeably. The purpose of the analysis is to break down distinctions between the organized interest association (and interest group) and social movement organizations. As I will suggest, the tools of social movement theory may be profitably used to analyze business associations, while many social movements, such as the women's movement, have spawned professionalized associations that look much like the interest groups of pluralist theory. The social movement is usually defined in Castells's sense as movements that seek to transform the values and institutions of society (Castells, 1997). The definition does not preclude right-wing groups or anti-system movements, although in general it has been used to describe progressive social movements. Supposedly, interest groups do not seek such radical transformation, in either ideological direction. Yet, as I will show, the actions and agency of the traditional interest group also contribute to social and political change. Interest groups are based on the constitution of common identities just as social movement may involve the articulation of interests, including material interests. For these reasons, I draw on these terminologies interchangeably in order to emphasize that there is much benefit in applying common approaches to all forms of collective action outside the party system.

Neoliberal Globalization

The analysis presented here places the recent evolution of group and social movement politics at the federal level within the broad context of the profound social, economic, and political changes that have remade Canadian politics over the last 30 years. It is based on the assumption that we are in the midst of an epochal shift in the nature of global capitalism, one that has entailed an accelerating globalization of economic, political, and social life. In Canada, globalization has been manifested by North American integration through the Free Trade Agreement (FTA) with the US and through the North American Free Trade Agreement (NAFTA) with the US and Mexico. Over the last quarter century, Canadian politics has undergone a transition from the policies and practices of the postwar Keynesian welfare state to the market-based neoliberalism of the global era. Neoliberal globalization entails much more than free trade agreements, free markets, deregulation, or privatization. It is not only that states have more or less capacity to undertake certain types of policy choices than they once had (Gill, 1995), but it is also that the patterns of group and social movement influence *vis-à-vis* the state have been fundamentally altered. The transition from one set of economic polices to another has entailed a shift in the paradigm of politics in Canada, one that has important consequences for democracy (Bashevkin, 2002; McBride, 2001; Jenson and Phillips, 1996). The means and methods of influence for groups and social movements have been altered in ways that have heightened the legitimacy of business groups while undermining certain social movements. As Sylvia Bashevkin points out in her analysis of social policy reform under Clinton, Blair, and Chrétien, "the language or rhetoric employed by politicians and other opinion leaders helps to set the tone of public discussion." She documents the political shift by which right-wing politicians sought to "drive a wedge between feminist, anti-poverty and other campaigners, on one side, and the boundaries of 'legitimate' political mobilization, on the other" (2002: 5). In the globalizing neoliberal citizenship regime, the collective efforts of citizens to improve their lot and to have a say about the political issues that affect them have been undercut. The legitimacy of collective action is under attack as never before. The individual consumer/client/citizen has become the privileged political actor.

The central argument of this book is that the terrain of group politics in Canada has been restructured by the transition from the Keynesian welfare state era to the era of neoliberal globalization. It is well understood that this political-economic transition, which began with the oil shock of 1973, has recast entire swaths of Canadian public policy and led to restrictive fiscal and monetary policies, a scaled-back welfare state, and growing social and economic inequality. However, the extent to which the transition to neoliberalism has entailed a restructuring of patterns of political action by collective actors has not been as comprehensively assessed. By situating the politics of groups and movements in historical perspective, the book demonstrates how the spaces of access and influence have changed in the neoliberal era. The analysis reexamines the patterns of influence between governments and organized groups across the political-institutional spaces of political parties, Parliament, policy communities, and courts as a part of an ongoing and historically situated process of neoliberal globalization. The restructuring of Canadian political institutions has closed down traditional avenues of access and influence and opened up others. Litigation as a political strategy and courts as a site of policy change are more important than ever before for collective actors. Legislatures and political parties are less important, while policy communities have been transformed by the decline of what Donald Savoie has called the traditional "bargain" between public servants and politicians (Savoie, 2003). While analysts of Canadian political institutions, such as Savoie, do not generally situate their analyses in terms of the structural shift to neoliberal globalization, their work provides plenty of evidence of the restructuring of the Canadian state in the neoliberal era. This book offers an amplification of arguments like Savoie's by placing political-institutional change within the context of long-term historical and socioeconomic change.

In order to understand the impact of neoliberalism, it is essential to develop the concept in a way that moves beyond its use as a term to describe public policies such as privatization, deregulation, tax slashing, and program cutting. While public policies of this type are the core of the neoliberal policy agenda, it is critically important to recognize that neoliberalism is a form of social and political practice. In this sense, neoliberalism denotes values, practices, and policies that embrace individualism, commodification, and marketization (see Larner, 2000; J. Brodie, 2003). As Beck has pointed out, individualism under neoliberalism means that responsibility has been placed on the individual to diagnose the cause and solution for his or her own problems (Beck, Ulrich and E. Beck-Gernsheim, 2002). Poverty, for example, is no longer defined as a political or social problem but, in a return to the nineteenth century (and before), is defined as a personal failing. Those who participate in the labour force are defined as deserving while those who are not able to participate in the labour force are defined as undeserving and as less than full citizens. In the neoliberal world, the market intrudes into the private realm, into the family and personal relationships and into community life as never before. As we will see in this book, even politics and political relationships are directly shaped by neoliberal practices and commodified in an unprecedented manner. From the branding of political parties to lobbying firms who dominate the corridors of influence in Ottawa, Canadian political choices have become products to be bought, sold, branded, and marketed. A new class of for-profit political professionals are the carriers of the neoliberal ethos in the practice of politics.

While analysts, such as Stephen Clarkson (2002), use the term neoconservative to describe contemporary changes and although this term has been used to describe right-wing politicians of the 1980s like Thatcher, Reagan, and Mulroney, who led the shifts in neoliberal policy in the UK, the US, and Canada (e.g., Pierson and Smith, 1993), neoconservatism also includes social issues. The influence of the evangelical movement in Canada and the US and the rise of the "moral majority" has politicized issues of gender, the family, and sexuality as never before and given rise to distinct camps of social liberals (feminist, favourable to lesbian and gay rights) and social conservatives (anti-feminist and homophobic). Neoliberalism is agnostic on the moral issues of social conservatism and plays a contradictory role in relation to social conservatism. For example, neoliberalism might favour the growth of consumer-oriented lesbian and gay communities and the right to marry for same-sex couples who act as responsibilized private individuals. Social conservatives, however, would oppose state-sanctioned same-sex marriage, for example, as violating fundamental moral values, whatever its economic and consumer advantages. For analytical purposes, it is useful to distinguish social conservatism from neoliberalism.

In the neoliberal era, collective action is redefined as citizen engagement, charity, and voluntary sector organizing, efforts that are seen as critical to social cohesion and trust. These new terminologies and concepts replace the democratic politics of choice, conflict, and contestation with a technocratic vocabulary of consumerism, commodification, and marketization (Mayer, 2003). Political choices become something akin to consumer choice. Choosing a political party or political values is like choosing a pair of running shoes. As politics is packaged and sold to voters and citizens through political consulting, the role of markets and marketing becomes more and more central to political participation. Citizen engagement is in part based on the models of marketing and polling, carried out by for-profit companies. Collective or solidaristic social values are defined as private matters for charity or voluntary sector participation, just as they were in the nineteenth century, before the rise of the modern interventionist state. Social cohesion and trust suggest that the goal of politics should be to create social unity; implicitly, these concepts devalue conflict and contestation. Trust and cohesion are depoliticizing concepts that encourage us to seek solutions in cooperation rather than in conflict. Yet, if we wish to challenge dominant structures of social, political, and economic power, we may need to put ourselves into conflict with those structures and with the people and groups that defend them.

In the next chapter, the exploration of this shift from the Keynesian welfare state era to the era of globalizing neoliberalism is situated within the context of a host of diverse social science theories on the role of groups and social movements in the political process. I present the main theories that have traditionally animated the study of the role of organized interests in politics and explore the ways in which these have been applied and developed in the Canadian context. The third chapter presents a historically grounded discussion of how groups and movements have most often organized and influenced Canadian politics. This chapter shows how group and social movement organizing emerged in Canada through the process of industrialization and state-building and discusses the most common trajectories of influence for organized interests in the political system from the colonial era to the present. The following chapters explore the state-centred sites of influence and access for groups and movements in Canadian politics, focusing first on political parties and Parliament as a venue for movement and group activity before moving on to explore the institutionalized relationships of mutual influence between organized interests and the state bureaucracy and the ways in which groups and movements have used courts as an increasingly important space for political action in the years following the entrenchment of the Charter of Rights and Freedoms (the Charter). I build on Jenson and Phillips' (1996) analysis of government policies towards interest and advocacy groups by reviewing the efforts of the federal government to re-engineer the institutionalized relationships between the state and organized interests through the deployment of policies that deliberately delegitimate political advocacy, recasting the citizen as a client and consumer of government services and as a volunteer in charitable organizations.

In Canada, globalization has entailed what Stephen McBride (2001) has called a "paradigm shift" that has seen a wholesale change in economic and social policies at the federal level. This paradigm shift—from the Keynesian welfare state to neoliberalism—has led to a less hopeful future for group influence and power. While the rise of protest and contestation may seem to suggest that globalization implies more power for interest groups and social movements, the paradigm shift to neoliberalism has entailed a fundamental restructuring of access to the state at the domestic level. The opportunities for interest groups and social movements to influence public policy at the federal level have been both transformed and diminished by the transition to neoliberalism. Just as neoliberal restructuring has shaped the politics of organized interests and social movements in the contemporary era, so too, the agency of collective actors—business organizations, environmentalists, feminists, and anti-globalization activists—has shaped the process of neoliberal globalization. The agency of political, social, and economic actors reconstitutes the structures of economy, polity, and society (Giddens, 1984). Neoliberalism cannot be fully understood by tracing the discourse and policies of states or by focusing on economic and social policies. State policies and economic shifts are part of the story but not the whole story. Neoliberalism is a political project that restricts the scope and legitimacy of collective agency and democratic politics. By focusing on groups and social movements, this aspect of the current paradigm shift is brought to the fore.

TWO
Understanding Group and Movement Politics

This chapter provides an overview of the main theoretical approaches to explaining and understanding the role of interest groups and social movements in Canada and in comparative perspective. In general, political scientists have had trouble in situating the politics of groups and movements in the broader context of political, social, and economic change. There is no agreement among political scientists specifically or social scientists in general about the best ways to study group and social movement politics. Rather, there are a plethora of theories that draw our attention to different facets of collective action. Each of these theories have clear normative and ideological implications. As we will see, pluralist theories have tended to legitimate the American political system (and, by extension, the Canadian political system), while political economy, Marxist, and social movement approaches have tended to provide a critical stance toward existing democratic institutions and to cast collective actors into specific roles as challengers to dominant social, economic, and political power. In the sections to follow, we will canvass the theoretical approaches that have provided the broad brush strokes for studying social movements and groups in comparative and Canadian politics and explore their normative implications.

Theoretical Perspectives on Groups and Movements in Politics

The study of group politics emerged in political science as part and parcel of the behavioural revolution that occurred just before and after World War II. Prior to this, political science was dominated by legal and historical descriptions of political institutions. The behavioural revolution emphasized the idea that political scientists should study the actual behaviour of political actors, rather than simply describe the institutional and constitutional framework of the political system. The use of quantitative methodologies reinforced the scientific approach to the study of political action and became increasingly widespread in the emerging fields of public opinion and voting behaviour (Easton, 1965; Farr, 1995). The behaviouralists developed interest group studies as the dominant depiction of the American political system (Baumgartner and Leech, 1998). While other social scientists, such as sociologists, had drawn on meta-theories like Marxism in order to understand collective action, the behavioural revolution in political science arose as an implicit or explicit critique of Marxism, a critique that became more and more important during the Cold War. As political science developed as a discipline, especially in the US, behaviouralists pioneered new approaches to collective action that provided a counterpoint and rejoinder to the Marxist emphasis on class politics.

In the behavioural tradition, scholars, such as Truman (1951), argued that, in democratic societies like those in the US and Canada, individuals belong to many different groups and that these cross-cutting cleavages prevent class politics from dominating the democratic process. Further developed by such well-known democratic theorists as Robert Dahl (1961) during the 1950s and 1960s, pluralism came under fire in the youth revolt of the late 1960s and early 1970s. The cultural revolution of the 1960s and the rise of new social movements—Black power, the women's movement, the anti-war movement—led to the resurgence of neo-Marxist political economy theorizing as well as social movement studies in sociology. In Canada, where the purported scientific theorizing of the behaviouralists had been less attractive to political scientists, this resurgence was based on the political economy tradition, pioneered during the 1930s and 1940s by scholars like Harold Innis (1954, 1970). This new generation of scholars developed what came to be known as the new political economy, which moved away from the analysis of groups and toward functionalist and structural views of the relationship between class interests and the state (Clement and Williams, 1989). The 1960s also inspired extensive theorizing about the sources of political protest, which led to new theories of social movement politics in political science and, especially, in sociology (McAdam, 1982; Tarrow, 1998). New social movement theories explored the rise of feminism and environmentalism as critiques of capitalism and patriarchy (Buechler, 2000).

During the 1980s, the impact of neo-Marxist and social movement theorizing in political science was undercut in the US by the rise of new theoretical currents: historical institutionalism and rational choice theory.

Historical institutionalism sought to "bring the state back" into political science by exploring the ways in which institutions structure policy development, policy debates, and representations of social interests (Thelen and Steinmo, 1992). Rational choice theory disregarded group solidarities and identities by emphasizing the role of the self-maximizing individual as the fount of political action (Olson, 1971). While institutionalist and rational choice approaches to group politics have been less influential in Canadian scholarship than in studies of American politics, they are included here in order to provide an analytical counterpoint to other theories and to draw attention to some of their potential for the analysis of Canadian politics. These theories will each be explored in turn, with specific reference to Canadian debates. We will begin with pluralism, because the pluralist approach has undoubtedly been the dominant approach to group politics in Anglo-American political science, and many of its assumptions are of enduring importance in empirical studies of social movements and organized interests.

Pluralism

For pluralists, society is composed of individuals. This may not seem like a controversial assertion; however, there is a key difference between pluralism and rational choice theory, which give methodological primacy to the role of the individual in politics, and Marxism or Canadian political economy, which emphasize the importance of groups and structures of power. Pluralists begin with the individual, who, in their view, has multiple loyalties, representing his or her diverse interests and preferences. Any of the individual's interests may form the basis for participation in a group that seeks to influence politics.

In Canadian society, for example, class, language, religion, region, socioeconomic status, gender, and ethnicity might all be considered important lines of political cleavage. Groups form when like-minded individuals join together in pursuit of their common interests and pressure or lobby government for policies that will favour their group. Pluralists usually describe such groups as interest groups or pressure groups. Because there are many potential political cleavages in complex societies, pluralist theory argues that no one group will ever dominate politics for long. If one group becomes too powerful, another will often rise to counterbalance its power (Bentley, 1908). The multiple interests of individuals mean that there are many possible groups and that society is characterized by cross-cutting cleavages along different lines. For example, a francophone working-class man may feel his interests are best reflected by a group representing francophones or by a group representing working-class people. Sometimes, there may be a group that represents francophone working-class men, and the two dimensions of individual identity may be brought together in one organization. Trade unions in Quebec have often represented the linguistic and class interests of workers in this fashion. However, there may not always be one group that represents all or both of these groups at the same time or over time. According to pluralist theory, the force of class politics—in this case, working-class organization—is blunted by the fact that the individual also feels a loyalty to another group—francophones. Society is not divided by class cleavages alone, but is also characterized by cleavages based on other definitions of the interests of the individual. Because of this, it is not likely that one cleavage will become dominant or that strong groups will go unchallenged.

Pluralist theory does not have any explanation of how groups form in society. Pluralists observe that groups form when individuals with common interests come together to influence politics. The theory takes the interests of individuals as given. That is, it assumes that the peoples' preferences are what they say they are, and it does not ask how people come to hold their preferences or how their preferences might have been shaped by social forces. For example, an individual's preferences or values may have been formed by a religious upbringing or by media influences. Pluralists do not explore how these factors form or influence the beliefs of individuals. As we will see below, other theoretical perspectives attempt to explain how individual and group preferences are shaped.

According to pluralist theory, political scientists should be interested in group politics because public policy is a reflection of the struggle between groups to secure advantage (Dahl, 1961, Polsby, 1963). For pluralists, manifest and open conflict between groups is the key to political conflict; cases in which conflicts are submerged or marginalized or cases in which power is exercised by structural forces cannot be subsumed under the rubric of pluralism (Gaventa, 1982; Lukes, 1974). In this respect, state actors, such as politicians and bureaucrats, do not play an independent role in the development of public policy as they are influenced by the contestation of groups (although see Almond, 1988). Pluralist theory is analogous to Adam Smith's idea of the "invisible hand" of the market economy, in which economic growth for the good of all is the end result of the self-interested struggle of individuals. Pluralist theory suggests that there are multiple access points to the political system for all citizens through group politics. Even if one group wins out in a particular conflict over public policy, the same group is unlikely to win all the time. Thus, just as the invisible hand will correct the market economy, so too, in pluralist theory, the invisible hand of group conflict will "correct" a political system that has tilted too far in the direction of a particular group.

Pluralists do not have a theory of structural social and political power. That is, they do not have a theory of society that provides guidance as to the most likely forms of political conflict. Unlike Marxists, who see economic structures as giving rise to specific class politics and class conflict, pluralists do not take structural power into account. In pluralist theory, power is exercised by the individual or by the individual political actor (e.g., the government or the interest group), but it is not exercised through political and social structures of patriarchy, racism, or capitalism. Ultimately, though, pluralists do not have a theory of why certain groups win and others lose. For them, this question must be resolved through case-by-case studies of group politics and public policy outcomes, and there are a large number of such empirical studies of group politics in the American political system (Baumgartner and Leech, 1998). Because of the nature of political power in the hurly-burly world of group politics, there will not be a consistent winner among the groups. Because pluralists have no theory of how individuals define their interests and because they have no theory of structural social power, they are not able to predict which groups will win out in any given policy conflict (Manley, 1983). By the same token, this focus on the theoretical middle range is what gives pluralist theory its power. The theory suggests that we focus on group conflicts in policy formation but leaves open the question of which group will win in a given conflict. Because of this flexibility, the pluralism and its successor, neopluralism, still provide practical strategies for researchers interested in group politics and public policy, despite the far-ranging theoretical and ideological critiques that have been made of this approach by many different critics over the years. It is easier for researchers to focus on open conflict between political actors because the evidence of such open conflicts is readily accessible and verifiable.

Governments and states play a passive role in pluralist theory. Governments are the object of group demands and are not defined as actively shaping and influencing politics and public policy outcomes. Again, this view of government and the state as the passive instruments of powerful groups reflects the relative weakness of the American state compared to the strong and centralized states of continental Europe in the nineteenth century. The separation of powers system, weak political parties, and the importance of the legislature in the decision-making process all provide numerous opportunities for group influence in the American system. On an ideological and normative level, pluralist theory suggests that all is well with democratic political systems and that Marxist approaches are empirically wrong in their emphasis on the importance of class politics.

Pluralism was most fully developed in the US, and it reflected both the Cold War struggle against communism as well as certain features of the American political system itself, which seem to be particularly well described and legitimated by pluralist theory. For example, the pluralists' idea of cross-cutting cleavages seemed more suitable for analyses of American society than for the class-based politics of Europe. The American separation of powers system seemed to foreclose the possibility of easy dominance for one group. Just as pluralist theory describes, political institutions in the US are designed to prevent this dominance of one group by dispersing power among three branches (executive, legislative, judicial) and two levels of government (federal and state). Pluralism has some appeal for Canadian scholars of group politics. Because of its theoretical focus on the case-by-case middle range of policy analysis, it lends itself to empirical study of group politics. Like American society, Canadian society is seemingly diverse and thus provides a good example of the pluralists' cross-cutting cleavages and groups. As Canadian scholarship was influenced to some extent by the rise of behaviouralism in the US, the pressure group approach to group conflict was used in some Canadian studies (e.g., Pross, 1975).

However, in the 1960s and after, pluralist theory was found wanting on several fronts. The social conflicts of the period suggested that not everyone has access to the political system. Some groups may be permanently marginalized, and some may indeed have more power than others. This point was brought home forcefully by the race riots of the 1960s, the anti-war movement, and the student movement in the US. In Canada, the rise of more powerful Quebec and Aboriginal nationalisms and the resurgence of anti-Americanism among youth in English-speaking Canada deepened the critique of a happy and benign group politics. These movements and the accompanying counterculture of the period suggested a more profound appraisal of democratic capitalism and called attention to structures of power in society such as racism and sexism. Just as the US was under internal siege from within during the late 1960s and early 1970s, so too the dominant pluralist approach in political science came under fire. The response to these critiques was the development and revival of other approaches including neo-Marxism, Canadian political economy, and neopluralism. The neo-Marxist critiques of pluralist theory in political science helped to spawn the neopluralist amendments of the original theory. Therefore, it is to neo-Marxism that we will now turn.

Marxism and Neo-Marxism

In contrast to pluralism, structural theories of the role of social forces in the political process stress that power relations are not the result of individual choices but of socially patterned behaviour, collective action, and institutional and organizational configurations. Individual choices are overwhelmed by the structural forces that shape behaviour. The pattern of group formation is affected by economic and social inequality, which create systematic obstacles for marginalized groups in the political system. While there are a number of such structural theories, the most elaborated by far is Marxism and its neo-Marxist variants (Seidman, 2004).

Unlike the pluralists and neopluralists who see social forces as individuals organized into groups or interest groups, Marxists understand social forces as organized into classes. Classes are not merely socioeconomic groupings, such as "middle class" or "lower class," but are specifically defined by their relationship to the means of production. For Marxists, the economic organization of society determines class relationships. In a capitalist economic system like Canada's in which property is privately owned, the means of production (land, labour, and capital) are owned by the capitalist class or bourgeoisie, and the working class or proletariat, which does not own the means of production, is forced to work in order to live. The capitalist class attempts to extract as much value from the labour of the working class as possible, and the working class, in turn, struggles to resist this exploitation. The conflict between capitalists and workers in a capitalist economy is termed the class struggle. In the Marxist view, political conflict centres on the class struggle between workers and capitalists (Panitch, 1995). This perspective constitutes a profound critique of the pluralist perspective on the role of interest groups. It suggests that the main cleavages in society are not based on multiple group memberships but on economic divisions rooted in the capitalist economic system. Groups are not all able to access the political system; rather, the system is profoundly unequal, and the subordinated classes face structural barriers to political influence and participation. There is no tendency toward equilibrium between groups in a capitalist society. Instead, the system is characterized by the contested domination of one class.

Within this perspective, there are a number of views of the relationship between classes and the state and the impact of class conflict on political debate. The classical division among neo-Marxist theories of the state draws attention to the distinction between the state as the instrument of capitalists and the state in a capitalist system as part of a structure of power relations in which, over the long run, the state will tend to guard the interests of the system. The first view, referred to as the instrumental view, is usually considered to be too simple as it does not provide for the possibility that fractions of capital may come into conflict with each other and that the state may not always do the bidding of the supposedly dominant class. In particular, developments such as the expansion of the welfare state, the extension of labour standards, and legislation to improve the health and welfare of workers have been opposed by capitalists since such policies appear to undermine capitalist interests (Mahon, 1977; Seidman, 2004).

In response to this, over the 1970s and 1980s, neo-Marxists built on and elaborated the original Marxist theory by emphasizing structural perspectives on the role of the state in capitalism, stressing that state policies tend to favour the maintenance and defense of capitalism as an economic system over the long term. Neo-Marxist theorist Antonio Gramsci's (1992 [1932]) work on the ideological hegemony of the dominant class, exercised through social institutions such as media, religion, and education, has also been important in opening up the field of culture to neo-Marxist analysis. Gramscian approaches are useful because they move Marxist debates beyond the role of the state in democratic capitalism to considering how an economic system that, according to Marxists, does not benefit workers is nonetheless maintained in part through the dominance of capitalist values and beliefs. As a structural theory of political and economic power, neo-Marxism is able to inquire into the ways in which collective beliefs and values are formed, arguing that these reflect the economic power of the dominant class or, as in the case of Gramsci, are secured through ideological institutions.

In the analysis of collective actors in the political process, then, neo-Marxism and pluralism begin at very different starting points. Pluralists view society as composed of individuals who have multiple interests that give rise to cross-cutting cleavages. Neo-Marxists view society as composed of classes, in which the dominant class exploits the subordinated class, thus giving rise to class struggle. Pluralists have a benign interpretation of the ends of power; in the long run, the struggle between groups will even itself out and no group will dominate politics in a democratic political system. The neo-Marxist views democratic political institutions as a cover or tool for capitalist class power and as an arena of class struggle. The pluralist does not inquire into the source of the individual's interests and preferences, while the neo-Marxist emphasizes the ways in which the common sense consciousness of everyday life is shaped by the class system. What these two perspectives do have in common, though, is their view of the state and of state institutions as relatively passive in relation to organized collective actors. While there are many different interpretations of the role of the state within Marxist theory and within the middle-range empirical studies of the pluralists, both perspectives tend to downplay political institutions and their effects on group politics and policy development. The pluralist sees the state as vulnerable to group influence, an unsurprising conclusion given that pluralist analysis has most often been applied to the American political system, a system which provides multiple points for group access. The neo-Marxist sees the state as fundamentally capitalist and thus sees its actions as structurally circumscribed by class power, the capitalist economic system, and even the consciousness of citizens, who may be taught to consent to their own exploitation.

Canadian Political Economy: From Old to New

While pluralist approaches to the study of pressure groups existed in Canada during the 1960s, the approach was not as dominant as it was in the US. Nonetheless, the benign assumptions of the pluralist approach about the nature of political power in capitalist democracies also came under fire in Canada. However, the Canadian critique took on a particular flavour. Students of Canadian politics of this period were influenced by the political economy tradition pioneered by Harold Innis during the 1930s.

The Innisian approach to understanding Canada had a profound influence on the younger generation of Canadian students of politics during the late 1960s and early 1970s who spearheaded a revival of his scholarship as well as that of other early Canadian scholars as part of the English-Canadian nationalist critique of American power and American perspectives in political science, history, and sociology. Some of the scholars in this tradition might be properly characterized as neo-Marxist (Naylor, 1972) while others drew upon political economy as a structural framework for understanding power relationships but without the specific Marxist focus on class conflict. This political economy approach became known as the new political economy, in order to distinguish it from the work of the Innisian generation of the 1930s and 1940, which was characterized as the old political economy.

The old political economy emphasized the staples approach to Canadian economic development. Through works on the fur trade and the fisheries, Innis (1970, 1954) argued that Canadian economic development was based on the exploitation of these staple commodities for metropolitan areas in the UK and the US and that the Canadian financial, transportation, and communication systems had been built around the exploitation of staples resources. Canadian manufacturing was underdeveloped as Canada failed to exploit linkages from resource development. During the 1970s, Innis's works were revived by a new generation of political economists, led by Mel Watkins (1977). The new political economy took up the theme of colonialism, specifically, the colonial position of Canada in relation to American political and economic power. However, the new political economy had an ambiguous relationship to capitalist class power. On the one hand, some analysts in this tradition, such as Tom Naylor, viewed the Canadian state as the instrument of capitalist class power, much as in the instrumentalist Marxist view outlined in the previous section. On the other hand, others bemoaned the weak position of Canadian capital as undermining Canadian sovereignty and economic independence (Levitt, 1970). Much of the new political economy was concerned with structures of economic power in Canada and Canada's position of relative underdevelopment, compared to other similar political systems (e.g., Laxer, 1989; Marchak, 1985), and did not have much to say about collective actors in politics. For example, a new political economy analysis of why Canada adopted free trade would focus on the position of Canada as a region or series of regions in the North American political economy and the role of the Canadian state in reinforcing north-south economic linkages following the demise of the

Keynesian welfare state. Similarly, recent attempts to bring gender and race into Canadian political economy explore such issues as the ways in which the labour market is gendered or racialized but do not explore the role of collective actors as agents in the political process (Vosko, 2000; Abele and Stasiulis, 1989). The new Canadian political economy then, is mainly a structural approach that focuses on the social and economic forces that limit the actions of political actors, but does not suggest an approach to the study of such actors.

Historical Institutionalism

In 1979, Theda Skocpol published *States and Social Revolutions*, a comparative study of the Russian, French, and Chinese Revolutions. The book was a noteworthy landmark in the study of revolution and launched Skocpol's critique of what she viewed as the traditional pluralist and neo-Marxist approaches to state-society relations. Her revival of the state-centred approach or what came to be termed historical institutionalism has become increasingly dominant in studies of American political development and comparative public policy. This approach offers many advantages for exploring the agency of collective actors in the policy-making process, in the definition of policy "problems" and their "solutions," and in shaping the dominant discourses of politics.

Skocpol argued that the main problem with both pluralist and neo-Marxist theories of state-society relations was that both assumed that the state's actions were driven by social forces, that state decisions reflected the power of the dominant forces in society, and that political institutions played almost no independent role in shaping policy and political outcomes. Pluralists and neo-Marxists disagreed over the nature of society and over the nature of the collective actors or groups that comprised the social forces driving the state. As we have seen, for pluralists, groups are the most important social actors, and their conflicts drive politics. For neo-Marxists, the pluralist emphasis on the group is an ideology that masks the importance of classes, whose conflicts drive politics. Pluralist analyses tended to legitimate American democracy (and, hence, indirectly, American power in the world), while neo-Marxist analysis tended to de-legitimate American democracy and American power. But, despite the profound theoretical, normative, and ideological differences between pluralists and neo-Marxists, in Skocpol's view, they shared an important theoretical similarity in their lack of attention to the independent causal power of states and state institutions.

In contrast, Skocpol argued for a return to the Weberian tradition in social science, meaning a return to the work of German sociologist Max Weber who pioneered the study of the rationalities of a variety of large-scale social institutions such as religion, bureaucracy, and the state. Weber developed a critique of bureaucracy as the "iron cage" of modern industrial society as well as taxonomies of states and the implications of their differences for political styles and outcomes (Seidman, 2004). The importance of Weber for Skocpol rested on the systematic attention in Weber's work to the understanding of states as independent and internally differentiated, an attention that Skocpol and many other critics found to be lacking in American political science scholarship during the pluralist period. As we have seen, pluralists largely viewed the state in terms of government, hence neglecting the state's permanent apparatus, most importantly, the bureaucracy. According to Skocpol's critique, pluralists tended to view government as the "cash register of group demands" rather than an independent player, while the neo-Marxists were unable to offer any explanation of the capitalist state beyond their claim that it *was* capitalist and that it would enact policies that protected the capitalist system. As Skocpol and the historical institutionalists rightly pointed out, a theory of the capitalist state that rests on the assertion that such a state will always protect capitalism and/or capitalists cannot explain the myriad of interesting differences between capitalist states, such as the low rate of American social spending compared to other capitalist democracies (Skocpol, 1985).

While some have disputed her characterization of pluralist theory as ignoring the state (Almond, 1988), there is no doubt that Skocpol's interventions signaled a "return to the state" among students of group politics. As elaborated by Skocpol and her followers through a series of works in the 1980s and 1990s, mainly on American political development, the chief tenets of a historical institutionalist approach focused on the capacity and autonomy of the state in relation to society. The autonomy of the state was a key point of debate between neo-Marxists and historical institutionalists, with institutionalists arguing for a zone of autonomous action for the state, while neo-Marxists viewed the state as always implicated in and shaped by the capitalist system. For historical institutionalists, state autonomy and capacity were qualities that could be measured and compared across cases. Some states were stronger than others; some states had capacities in some areas and not in others. For example, the claim that welfare state programs had been undertaken in opposition to the interests of capitalists was explained by historical institutionalists in terms of the autonomy and capacity of state institutions, directed by state elites, who made policy choices. Where neo-Marxists would see such policies as an inevitable functional requirement for the defense of capitalism or as the product of class struggle within the arena of the state, the historical institutionalist school emphasized that the state itself was a player in the formation of such policies and that state bureaucrats had their own institutional self-interest in the development of policies that would benefit them (Weir and Skocpol, 1985).

Time is a central variable in historical institutionalist analysis. Not only does the state have the capacity to act independently of pressure from classes or groups, historical institutionalism emphasizes that the decisions of the state or policies of the state in one historical period influence the evolution of policy in the subsequent time period. This theoretical grounding of state-society relations in historical method was key to the historical institutionalist approach, which, in subsequent studies, became most popular for explaining American political development (APD) and, in fact, helped spawn APD as a distinctive subfield of American politics and American political science (e.g., Skowronek, 1982). The key concept here for historical institutionalism was the policy legacy: policies that were put into place during one historical period shaped politics and policy development in the subsequent period (Pierson, 1993). The notion of path dependence captured the idea that choices made in one historical period foreclosed subsequent political and policy outcomes. Historical institutionalist analysis emphasized that broad political outcomes entailed feedback loops between historical periods in which outcomes in one historical period were self-reinforcing. To take a Canadian example, empowering courts under the Charter of Rights and Freedoms (the Charter) was the political outcome of the constitutional struggles of the 1970s and early 1980s. Once the Charter was in place, it shaped political debate and political action such that over time Canadian politics became more focused on rights. In this way, legal mobilization was strengthened as a political option (Smith, 1999).

Compared to the other approaches that have been described so far, historical institutionalists share with neo-Marxists the idea that the beliefs and values of collective actors are shaped through social processes. Unlike neo-Marxists, however, historical institutionalists open up the possibility that the values and preferences of collective actors are shaped by contingent policy processes (policy legacies) as much as by macrosocial forces (the capitalist economic system). While a neo-Marxist might ask why workers believe in and consent to a capitalist economic system, the historical institutionalist would explore why workers in one context argued for industrial policies while workers in another ignored industrial policies and demanded Keynesian macroeconomic stabilization (e.g., Hattam, 1993). The historical institutionalist largely works at the middle range of theory, rather than at the macro level. Furthermore, while a neo-Marxist views society as divided into classes, which exist in a relationship of class struggle with each other, and while pluralists view society as divided into cross-cutting cleavages and group politics, historical institutionalists do not have a position on the nature of social power. Hence, they describe collective actors as class-based, group-based, or both. Precisely because historical institutionalism focuses on the mid-range level of theory, it does not have a theory of history or an overall theory of social power. Therefore, in historical institutionalist analyses, class-based politics arising from capitalist exploitation may be acknowledged at the same time as group-based interests are also recognized.

Neopluralism

In response to the critiques of their approach by both neo-Marxists and historical institutionalists, pluralists amended their theory. They developed a new perspective, often called neopluralism (Lukes, 1974). In this approach, more attention was paid to the idea that government may influence the public agenda. The neopluralists conceded two important points to critics of the original pluralist theory. First, they acknowledged that democratic capitalist societies, such as Canada, might be characterized by persistent social inequality that would create barriers to the formation and influence of interest groups. For example, poor people are unlikely to have the economic and social resources to form effective interest groups, and their interests will not be reflected in the political system. The political system itself may mobilize bias; that is, certain types of political issues may be mobilized out of political consideration and debate. Another example is that of race. Until recently, the idea that Canadian society might be characterized by pervasive racism was not a subject of political debate. The issue of racism was simply ignored or denied by governments and powerful groups in the political system. Political debate was biased against consideration of the problem of racism in Canadian society and of how public policies could be designed to address it.

Second, in a variant of institutionalist analysis, neopluralists recognized that governments themselves could play an important role in the development of public policy. Governments were not simply carrying out the wishes of the strongest group; instead, politicians and bureaucrats were actively involved in the development of public policy and often used groups to communicate with particular constituencies of citizens to legitimate these policies. Groups might advocate their interests to government, but the bureaucracy also might develop institutionalized links with key groups and consult them regularly on the formation of policy. This type of analysis draws on historical institutionalism but is less theoretically ambitious and relies more on public policy analysis than on the grand questions of comparative politics. Studies of policy communities and policy networks are important in the studies of Canadian public policy. For example, Coleman and Skogstad (1990) analyze the role of policy networks and policy communities as institutionalized linkages between collective actors and the state, as will be fully discussed in Chapter 4.

Social Movement Theory

Another approach to the analysis of groups in the political process is provided by social movement theory, which was mainly developed by sociologists. In part, it is based on the experiences of the 1960s when a number of new movements arose that posed profound challenges to the status quo. The rise of the women's movement, the environmental movement, the gay liberation movement, the peace movement, the student movement, and the civil rights movement suggested that all was not well with capitalist democracies. New left movements, as they were sometimes termed, engaged in mass protests and demonstrations and generated a culture of transformative and liberation politics. These spontaneous mass protests seemed to be fundamentally different from the well-organized and institutionalized interest groups of pluralist theory and from the class politics of neo-Marxist theories.

Much like political science, sociology's dominant perspective on social movements had a reigning wisdom that was unseated by new theories. The dominant paradigm in the study of social movements in the wake of World War II understood them as forms of protest motivated by grievances and

had been developed to explain such mass movements of the interwar period as fascism, movements that were viewed as fundamentally irrational.
In contrast to this collective behaviour approach, two new theories were
developed which attempted to account for the prevalence of social protest
during the 1960s in the developed capitalist democracies and to justify the
legitimacy of such protests. These two new theories were the new social
movement theory, developed mainly in Europe, and resource mobilization
theory, developed mainly in the US. A third approach—the political process model—synthesizes these two theories. The political process model
deals with many of the same issues as political science models of group
behaviour, as we will see below. First, we will look at some of the common elements in the analysis of social movements across the three most
recent theories—new social movement theory, resource mobilization, and
the political process model—followed by a look at some of the distinctive
features of each of the three approaches in the order in which they arose.

What is a social movement? The broadest definition, offered by Manuel
Castells, is: "purposive collective actions whose outcome, in victory as in
defeat, transforms the values and institutions of society" (Castells, 1997:
3). For political scientists and sociologists who encountered the social
movements of the 1960s, a series of traits was thought to distinguish the
"new" social movements from organized interest and advocacy groups.
First, social movements challenge the traditional boundary between state
and society, public and private. In pluralist and neopluralist theory, there
is a clear distinction between state and society; societal groups form and
then attempt to influence government. Although groups may develop institutionalized links to government, there is still a clear distinction between
public and private. Social movements challenge this distinction, arguing
that "the personal is political" and bringing issues that were once defined
as private into the sphere of public debate and discussion. For example,
violence within the family was once an issue that was not discussed in the
public arena. The women's movement politicized the issue of violence
against women, in general, and violence in the family in particular. Social
movements may also challenge the public/private divide by demonstrating
how the private sphere is imbued with power relationships or politics. The
gay liberation movement challenged the heterosexual assumption of the
public presentation of sexuality. The women's movement pointed to power
relationships within the family as profoundly political. The environmental
and animal rights movements have challenged human dominance over the

natural world and animals, recasting economic issues as environmental concerns and injecting completely new issues, such as animal testing, into public consciousness.

Second, social movements may emphasize the creation and reinforcement of identity and the promotion of certain values over the pursuit of material interests. As such, social movement goals may be primarily aimed at society rather than the state. The second wave of the women's movement often engaged in consciousness-raising in which small groups of women would meet to share their experiences. In the process, women realized that their problems and experiences were not unique, that many women had had similar experiences, and that their problems had social and political causes. In this way, a common bond of solidarity was created among feminist women, and a new identity was formed which, in turn, provided the base for women's mobilizing. Many of the goals of the women's movement, such as ending violence against women, aim at changing the definition of socially acceptable behaviour or, as Alberto Melucci has put it, challenging the dominant "codes" of society (Melucci, 1996). Although state policies may also be targeted, state policy alone cannot effect changes in social behaviour. Similarly, the environmental movement encourages people to "reduce, reuse, recycle," thus targeting the dominant cultural codes and social practices of consumerism.

Third, social movements are often said to engage in strategies and tactics that are more radical than those used by interest groups. While interest groups may attempt to influence government policy through the conventional means of lobbying in one form or another, social movements often engage in direct action tactics. For example, the environmental movement has often chosen to confront its opponents directly rather than to work with government. The dispute over clear-cut logging is an example. Environmentalists have spiked trees and chained themselves to trees to prevent clear-cut logging. Such direct action tactics are often particularly useful because they create dramatic media footage that can be used to promote the values of the movement. Large-scale disruptive demonstrations and protests may also be used to force government action and to capture media attention. Social movements are also said to have a more decentralized and democratic organization than interest groups. They often form as networks of activists, with little formal organization, and even where formal organizations exist, they are often highly decentralized. The new left explicitly rejected bureaucratization and majority rule as oppressive and often operated by direct democracy, task rotation, and consensus decision-making, in which each member of the group could veto group decisions and in which tasks were rotated among members.

In reality, social movements may not conform to this ideal typical picture. Some have been quite well organized, at least during certain periods, and may seek to influence government through participation in consultative exercises or policy communities. Unlike traditional interest groups, social movements usually form networks of smaller groups instead of well-organized and hegemonic organizations. Rather than conforming to the ideal type description of social movement political behaviour, many movements may follow a dual strategy of influencing the state and influencing society. For example, environmental groups may lobby government while engaging in activities that are designed to influence public opinion and to change social attitudes (Wilson, 1992). In practice, social movements pursue diverse strategies. Further, distinguishing collective actors on the basis of their regard for their own material interests is also problematic. As we shall see, the tools of social movement analysis work well for understanding business militancy of the 1980s and 1990s, despite the fact that such groups pursue the material interests of their members. Social movements that are thought to be part of identity politics—ethnocultural groups, gay and lesbian groups, or women's groups—may also have important material interests at stake in their organizing.

The lesbian and gay movement is a good example of a modern social movement, whose loose structure and diverse tactics exemplify the less formal models of political contestation found in social movement politics. The movement began in small homophile organizations in the 1960s, organizations that brought together gay men and lesbians who were principally interested in countering the stigma of homosexuality in society and in overturning the criminal definition of same-sex sexual behaviour. During this period, the police routinely raided lesbian and gay gathering places such as bars, rounding up the clientele and sending them off to the police station to be charged with "gross indecency" or "buggery." The RCMP's "fruit machine" weeded out lesbians and gay men from government service, especially in the military and diplomatic services, where their presence was thought to undermine moral and state security (Kinsman, Buse and Steedman, 2000). Many lesbians and gay men socialized with each other in private networks, meeting only in each other's homes for fear of discovery; hiding their relationships and sexual lives from their families, co-workers, and communities; and living a veritable double life, in some cases, for all of their lives. Homosexuality was illegal, shameful, and hidden.

The first step in the creation of a modern lesbian and gay social movement was for lesbians and gay men to define themselves as such and to realize that they shared a common social identity. If lesbians and gay men were afraid to come out, even to themselves or to each other, they could not construct a common identity. However, once this step was breached, as it was increasingly in Canada during the 1960s, 1970s, and 1980s, lesbians and gay men were able to claim a sense of political and social identity and to form organizations and groups to advocate for their interests. The movement created its own means of communication through the lesbian and gay media, just as today many social movement networks use the Internet as the infrastructure of their communication. Lesbian and gay organizations were established to serve a broad array of purposes, including pressuring governments in favour of anti-discrimination measures. Most of these organizations were very small, locally based in Canada's major cities, and funded through individual donations. Informal networks of lesbian and gay activists, based in urban areas, were very important to the building of the movement, and there was substantial overlap between individuals who were active in service organizations in the lesbian and gay urban communities and those who were active in political organizations. In the early period, services such as the "gay line" (an information line for lesbians and gay men) were highly political because of the contested and stigmatized nature of gay and lesbian life. Holding a gay or lesbian dance was a major political event in the early 1970s and, as such, a political statement that challenged the dominant political and social codes of Canadian society. In this way, the movement surged forward as an informal network of small groups.

The diverse tactics of the lesbian and gay movement also demonstrate the range of social movement activities. The movement has engaged in direct action, like demonstrations and zaps (kiss-ins), as well as spontaneous protests, like those against the Toronto bath raids of 1981. Over the last 20 years, the movement has also spawned mainstream advocacy organizations that have supported and intervened in litigation before the courts on same-sex rights issues. Yet, overall, the organizational weight of the movement rests at the urban level, not at the national level. The lesbian and gay movement is strongest in Canada's big cities, where it draws on the density of lesbian and gay "villages," networks, and organizations across a range of cultural and social sectors. In this sense, the movement takes the form of a diverse and decentralized sector of informal activist networks, rather than a large, formalized association at the pan-Canadian level.

Why do social movements arise, and what are the most important factors that influence their success and failure? The three theories of social movements have different answers to these questions. According to resource mobilization theory, social movements mobilize pre-existing grievances. For example, African Americans living under segregation evidently had grievances; however, systematic political mobilization around these grievances did not emerge until the 1950s. Thus, according to resource mobilization theory, it is not the grievances that are new but the resources that movements can bring to bear to press their demands (Jenkins, 1993). The success and failure of social movements is determined by their ability to bring diverse resources—money, organization, sympathetic allies, and expertise—to bear in their struggles. Resource mobilization is analogous to pluralist theory in political science because it focuses on organized groups that attempt to influence government and that are viewed as competing on a relatively level playing field (Mayer, 1995). In fact, many of the same critiques that were made of pluralist theory have been made of resource mobilization, particularly with respect to the extent to which the theory ignores both preference and value formation and structural sources of social power.

The new social movement approach argues that social movements are increasingly a feature of developed capitalist democracies as the older class-based politics has declined. According to this view, the developed democracies are increasingly post-materialist, that is, their political cultures are increasingly oriented around non-material political issues such as identities and values. Post-materialist values emphasize issues like quality of life and political participation rather than the material questions of who gets what, when, where, and how. This political cultural change sets the stage for the rise of movements that stress identity and non-material goals (Offe, 1985; Inglehart, 1997). These changes are associated with a particular class politics. The new social movement approach is post-Marxist in that it argues that the traditional class struggle is no longer dominant in the politics of advanced capitalist societies; rather, the new social movement theory stresses the rise of the new middle class of professional knowledge workers, who break with the old division between worker and capitalist and who are carriers of post-materialist values (Touraine, 1981).

The political process model brings together elements of resource mobilization and the new social movement approach, drawing from the former a focus on the social movement organization and the organizational networks that underpin such groups and from the latter a focus on identity and on the cultural processes through which movements construct their activism. However, in addition to this, the political process model, found in the work of scholars, such as Sidney Tarrow (1998), brings together these elements with a focus on the broader political environment within which social movements operate. The broad context of politics in relation to the goals of the social movement is what Tarrow terms the "political opportunity structure," which he defines as "consistent—but not necessarily formal, permanent or national—dimensions of the political environment which either encourage or discourage people from using collective action. The concept of political opportunity structure emphasizes resources external to the group" (Tarrow, 1998: 18). Tarrow specifies these elements as: 1) the degree of openness and closedness of the polity; 2) the stability or instability of political alignments; 3) the presence or absence of allies; and 4) divisions among elites (Tarrow, 1998: 18). The concept of political opportunity encompasses the institutions of the state and the ways in which political institutions provide points of access to social movements or block them. In a sense, the core chapters of this book on the central political institutions of Canadian politics at the federal level provide an exploration of the structure of political opportunity for interest groups and social movement organizations. Changes in the political opportunity structure for interest group and social movement organizing shape the negotiation of collective identities, the strategies of collective actors, and the policy outcomes of group and movement organizing (Orsini, 2002). In turn, these shifts feed into the universe of political discourse, privileging certain forms of collective identity and political strategy over others.

Rational Choice Theory

Rational choice theory arose in political science over the course of the 1980s, and, in American political science, it has become one of the dominant approaches to the study of collective action. In a recent review of the state of the discipline in political science in the US, the three dominant approaches were defined as behaviourism (the analysis of observable political behaviour as in pluralist analysis), historical institutionalism, and rational choice theory (Pierson and Skocpol, 2003). Class analysis, political economy, and social movement theory were nowhere to be found as distinctive approaches to politics. Rational choice theory is much more marginal in Canadian political science. To date, there have been very few works that have attempted to apply this perspective to the study of group behaviour in the Canadian context. The few works that have appeared are not the strongest exemplars of the rational choice tradition (e.g., Flanagan, 1998). Despite the weaknesses of Canadian work on rational choice, the approach has important implications for the study of group politics.

The seminal work in the development of rational choice theory and group politics is Mancur Olson's The *Logic of Collective Action* (1971 [1965]). Drawing from economics, Olson based his theory on the individual as a rational self-maximizer. Each individual seeks to maximize their own "utility" or seeks benefits for themselves. Economic theory is based on the assumption that the individual—whether a consumer or a firm—will seek to maximize utility. For example, a consumer is more likely to make a purchase if the price of the desired item drops. Firms are less likely to hire if the price of labour increases. Rational choice theory, then, is based on the idea that society is composed of individuals who seek their own advantage. Moreover, they seek advantage based on rationality, that is, there is a logical relationship between the ends sought and the means used to reach the ends. The ends sought by the individual are labeled "preferences" by rational choice theorists. Preferences are rank ordered, meaning that some are considered to be more important than others. When buying a car, for example, I might value price above interior space or size above gas mileage. We can imagine the same kinds of rank orderings in politics. When voting, I might value a party's position on abortion above its position on the economy, or I might value a party's ability to represent my regional interests more highly than its capacity to represent my economic interests. Rational choice theory is similar to pluralist theory in its methodological individualism. The focus on the collective as the sum of the individual is quite different from the neo-Marxist, political economy, and institutionalist traditions, which are structuralist in their interpretation of individual action.

The individual's pursuit of her own best interests through rational self-maximizing behaviour makes collective action difficult. A goal or a "good" (in rational choice parlance) may be such that the benefit cannot be restricted to the individual. One example of such a good would be clean air: the benefit of clean air cannot be restricted to a single individual. The same applies to many other types of goods, which, by definition, benefit a group of individuals. Higher wages, for example, benefit all workers in a given workplace. Resources for student activities and clubs on a university campus benefit all students. Rational choice theory labels these types of goods "public goods." In contrast, "private goods" are the property of the individual and the benefit accrues to the individual alone.

Much of politics is about the pursuit of public goods. According to Olson, the problem of collective action arises from the fact that the individual has no incentive to pursue a public good. The individual will benefit from the achievement of the goal (cleaner air, higher wages, better student activities on campus) as long as she is a member of the class affected by the public good (human beings, workers, students). Therefore, why should the individual waste his time in pursuing these public goods? Why should the individual join together with other individuals in pursuit of the goal? Why should workers join a union to push for higher wages when they will receive the benefit of the higher wages regardless of their contribution to the collective effort? Why should students push for better student activities or student services when all students will benefit from any gains that are made? Why not let someone else do the work and run any risks that may be entailed? This behaviour is called "free riding" in rational choice parlance.

According to Olson, the rational self-maximizing individual will tend to free ride on the efforts of others in the pursuit of public goods. This, for Olson, is the "problem of collective action," which is the central contribution of rational choice theory to the study of group politics. According to this view, individuals are not naturally inclined to sociability and group life. Such behaviour must be explained, rather than assumed, by the analyst. Here, rational choice theory parts ways very fundamentally with pluralist analysis. The pluralists saw society as composed of groups, which, in turn, were made up of individuals with diverse interests. Rational choice theory views society as composed of individuals with diverse interests. The pluralists never gave a thought to the process by which groups form. They assumed that, by default, people with common interests would form groups. Rational choice theory assumes that, by default, individuals will not form groups.

How then do groups come into being in society, according to rational choice theory? The solution of the problem of collective action is "selective incentives"—benefits that are restricted to members of the group. You must join the group in order to receive information from the group. You must join the group to receive access to governmental decision-makers who may affect your business. You must join the group in order to receive insurance benefits through a group scheme. All of these are examples of selective incentives.

Groups may also form through coercion and regulation. Most universities in Canada, for example, require students to join the student society and to pay a student activity fee as part of tuition. The public goods provided by the student society are deemed to be of benefit to all students, and all students are forced to pay for them as a condition of entry to the university. In Canada, the Rand Formula requires all the employees in the bargaining unit of a workplace to pay union dues, even if they do not choose to belong to the union. This law was passed in 1945 at the urging of the labour movement, which argued that unions would be in an untenable position if workers were left to choose for or against union membership. Free choice in this respect might lead employers to favour workers who chose not to join the union. From the perspective of rational choice theory, the Rand Formula is a form of coercion, which overcomes the collective action problem. Workers who will benefit from gains negotiated by the union may not free ride on the actions of union members, but, in accordance with the Rand Formula, are required to support the union by paying dues in a unionized workplace.

According to rational choice theory, the groups that are most likely to be able to offer selective incentives are those that are most likely to form. These will be groups that are able to offer economic incentives of some kind. Some rational choice theorists (including Olson) argue that politics will tend to be dominated by narrowly defined group interests because these are the groups that will be able to organize themselves successfully using selective incentives (M. Olson, 1982). Rational choice theory is particularly concerned about groups that are very large, such as taxpayers and consumers. It is difficult for such broad groups to form because of the problem of offering selective incentives to encourage organization. In the view of rational choice theory, all taxpayers would benefit from lower taxes, but it is unlikely that taxpayers will be able to organize to achieve this because of the problem of collective action. Similarly, although consumers would benefit from lower food prices, it is unlikely that consumer interests will be represented in debates over farm policy. Farmers' groups are much better able to organize and to offer selective incentives. In Europe, Canada, and the US, farmers' organizations have succeeded in negotiating important subsidies and tax breaks that greatly enhance profitability at the expense of consumers.

Just as pluralist theory implies liberalism and neo-Marxist theory implies socialism, so too there are important ideological implications to rational choice theory. The theory tends to lend very strong support to the neoliberal political project, that is, the restructuring of state-society relations around the rolled-back state, the retrenchment of social programs and social obligation, and the primacy of the choice and responsibility of the individual. By placing the self-maximizing individual as at the heart of the analysis, rational choice theory supports the central tenet of neoliberalism—the primacy of the individual in the market. Rational choice theory's pessimistic view of collective action mirrors the neoliberal distaste for groups and provides a justification for skepticism toward group claims. Rational choice theories suggest that group claims are undemocratic. Because groups comprised of most of society's citizens (e.g., taxpayers) are unlikely to be able to provide selective incentives, the groups that do form will tend to represent narrow and selfish interests. In this way, rational choice theory provides a theoretical justification for neoliberal discourse.

Neoliberalism and Group Politics

Of the approaches surveyed above, this book draws mainly from political economy, social movement theory, and historical institutionalism. From the political economy approach, I draw the idea that social movement and group politics will be shaped by broader changes in the political economy, such as industrialization or the transition to post-industrial capitalism. However, the political economy approach does not provide methodological or theoretical guidance to the student of group and movement politics beyond the suggestion of the centrality of class politics and the impact of economic change on political action. While political economy is concerned about social transformation, it does not offer the most useful theoretical approach for the exploration of the agency of collective actors (e.g., Carroll and Coburn, 2003). Instead, I have drawn more from macrosociological approaches such as historical institutionalism and from social movement theory because these suggest that large-scale social and political processes such as urbanization and state-building will play a crucial role in the creation of different types of contentious politics. Further, these approaches specifically explore the process of state restructuring and the interaction of social forces with political institutions and the policy process. Focusing specifically on political-institutional changes and the ways in which these changes have shut down and restructured the access of groups and social movement organizations to the state is a critically important analytical project, especially because of its implications for de-democratization (Jenson and Phillips, 1996). As we will see in detail in the next chapter, each historical period is characterized by typical repertoires and trajectories of political access and influence that reflect the macrohistorical characteristics of the time. While sociological, political, and economic change generate different types of collective action and contentious politics, collective actors also participate in the constitution of the discourse, practices, and public policies of their time (Jenson, 1989).

The transition to a new era of post-industrial globalizing capitalism has generated a new set of policies, practices, and discourse that has been labeled neoliberalism. Neoliberalism is characterized by a preference for markets over states and a preference for the individual over the collective. As government policy, neoliberalism entails retrenching the role of states, privileging market-based policies, and valorizing individual consumption. As a set of values and social practices, neoliberalism seeks the commodification of everything in its path, including access to the political process. As we will show, politics in Canada is increasingly commodified through the rise of professional lobbyists, pollsters, and consultants. This commodification of politics shapes group and social movement politics in important ways. Neoliberalism must be seen as more than simply a label that refers to a right-wing political ideology or as a descriptor for pro-market state policies. Rather, neoliberalism expresses itself in social values and social practices. While many groups and movements oppose neoliberal policies, the prevalence of neoliberal practices in society means that even progressive groups and movements may be caught up in or influenced by neoliberal discourse and values (McKeen and Porter, 2003).

In order to understand how this change occurred, we will begin in the past, by exploring the history of group and movement political activity in Canada. The historical overview will provide an introduction to the most significant groups and movements that have influenced Canadian politics. More importantly, it will provide an overview of the main repertoires of collective action or the typical discursive and political strategies that groups and movements have used to influence Canadian society and the state. This material will provide a historical baseline and backdrop for understanding the transition to neoliberalism and the consequences of this transition for group and movement politics.

THREE

Historical Trajectories of Influence
in Canadian Politics

Most of the theoretical approaches examined in Chapter 1 are based on the assumption that time is as important as space in understanding the meaning of contemporary political patterns. In the political economy approach, Canada's place in the international political economy and its pattern of staples and natural resource exploration are viewed as shaping state-society relations. In the institutionalist approach, the policy legacies and institutional patterns of one period are assumed to play a key role in influencing political debates, policy choices, and interest group politics in subsequent historical periods. In social movement theory, the growth of resources available to social movements and the changing political opportunity structure create openings for movement politics. In all of these cases, the patterns of social development and collective action can only be understood in historical context.

This chapter draws on these three approaches: political economy, historical institutionalism, and social movement theory. I argue that, in order to understand contemporary patterns of collective action in Canadian politics, it is necessary to understand the patterns of the past. As both political economy and historical institutionalism suggest, macrohistorical factors—industrialization, colonialism, urbanization, and state-building—create structures of political, economic, and social power. In turn, these structures throw up different forms of collective action over time. Industrialization and urbanization set the stage for the emergence of early social movements such as temperance, social purity, and the first wave of feminism. The process of industrialization led to the political mobilization of workers. State-building and European immigration to Western Canada gave rise to populist farmers' organizations. In a similar vein, the transition from the Keynesian welfare state to the era of neoliberalism has generated new forms of collective action. The new business militancy and the anti-globalization movement are both linked to the transition to neoliberalism in Canada. Changes in political institutions have created new challenges for democratic politics as collective action has been delegitimated and the role of the individual consumer/citizen is increasingly valorized.

In turn, contemporary patterns of collective action are influenced by the legacies of earlier political struggles. Collective actors play an active role in creating, reinforcing, and sustaining the dominant political discourse of the day. Although they may be limited by social, political, and economic structures, at the same time, collective actors also reproduce and constitute social structures. For example, the labour movement may be profoundly influenced by the particular form of capitalism in the Canadian economy. The highly regionalized nature of Canadian economic development helped shape a working-class politics that, historically, was very different in the coal mines of Cape Breton than in the factories of southern Quebec and Ontario or the logging camps of British Columbia. At the same time, the labour movement in Canada also shaped capitalism itself through its activism. Struggles with employers and governments helped bring about social reforms that, as in other developed capitalist economies, changed the nature of capitalist industrialism profoundly, especially over the first half of the twentieth century. But collective actors are not just mobilized in and out of politics by the structures of the economic, social, and political systems. They also participate in the mobilization of bias through the ways in which they make choices about values, ideologies, and strategies. They may contest the prevailing political wisdom of the time—as in the rise of second wave feminism, which challenged the traditional place of women in the home—or, they may reinforce dominant ideologies and beliefs—as in the impact of business organizations organizing in favour of free trade.

Political identities created by waves of contention and activism or reinforced by organized collective action help to define the common sense of our political landscape. Giddens (1994), Castells (1997), and other theorists of globalization have emphasized that we live in an area of reflexive modernization, meaning that identities are no longer given at birth by ethnicity, religion, nationality, and class status; instead, identity has become a set of life-choices or a process through which we (reflexively) choose identities. Cycles of collective action in Canadian politics have left identity choices behind them in the political culture, options that are there to be picked up by succeeding generations. For example, prior to the rise of the modern environmental movement, the political identity of "environmentalist" was simply not an option in Canadian politics. One might have been a conservationist or a nature-lover, but environmentalism did not exist as a collective political identity. Cycles of contention by group and movement actors produce new and alternative political identities and shape the universe of political discourse for succeeding generations.

In the succeeding sections, I provide an overview of the main cycles of collective action, including business organizing in the early period of Canadian state-building. I move on to discuss the early social movements from below, such as temperance and movements of the emergent urban middle class (social purity and the first wave women's movement). Then I explore the effects of farmers' and workers' political mobilization in forming the backdrop for the Keynesian era. Finally, the chapter explores the new social movements of the 1960s, the breakdown of the Keynesian era, and the new forms of collective action that have been produced in the neoliberal era—business militancy and the anti-globalization movement. These cycles have provided templates of collective identity and organizing for group and movement organizing.

Historical Overview

The legacies of collective action in politics may be seen in some of the earliest forms of protest politics in colonial Canada. The rebellions of the 1830s pushed the process of democratization in the colonies and constituted political identities that defined French-Canadian nationalism in Quebec and reform liberalism in Ontario. The impact of the nationalist heroes of the *Patriots* in Quebec and the Grits in Ontario sparked discursive constructions of citizenship and political identity that influenced politics long after the short-lived rebellions. Movements such as temperance, social purity, and women's suffrage at the end of the nineteenth and beginning of the twentieth centuries helped the rising middle class express and consolidate its sense of political and social identity. As Canada developed economically, business elites sought influence through the establishment of business associations, which provided the first models of the organized interest group in Canadian politics. Populist movements among Canadian farmers created new political parties of the left and right. Union activism across Canada shaped modern labour law and the welfare state in the Keynesian era, while business militancy in the last quarter-century has pushed forward the neoliberal agenda. The anti-globalization movement has contested the received wisdom of the economic and political elites of neoliberalism.

Trajectories of influence in Canadian politics follow models that are common to other similar societies, especially other developed capitalist democracies. Many of the key moments in the constitution of the universe of political discourse were similar to other democracies and, in some cases, directly shaped by templates of contention that were pioneered elsewhere. The close links between business and governments and the use of party politics, patronage, and lobbying are common in democratic capitalist countries. Farmer populism in the Canadian West is both similar to and influenced by farmer populism in the American Midwest. Subnational movements, such as Aboriginal nationalism and Quebec nationalism, are common in other countries, and the new social movement organizing of the 1960s and afterwards, as well as the contemporary anti-globalization movement, draw on templates that are explicitly cross-national or transnational.

Business, Political Parties, and the State

Most depictions of the history of interest group organizing in the US and Canada have argued that the modern interest group arose in the late nineteenth century with the transition from traditional agricultural societies to modern industrial and urban societies. The expanded role of the state in managing the modern industrial economy required new types of intervention, which, in turn, sparked the drive for enhanced political representation beyond the party system. While parties continued to act as an important vehicle for the representation of citizens' interests, the increasing complexity of the modern economy and society and the expanded role of the state in managing this complexity led to the formation of organized interest groups, especially those representing the business community, producers in specific economic sectors, trade unions, and occupational groups. This traditional depiction of the growth of groups representing "sectors" of society, rather than political parties which represent "spaces" of society, highlights the structural impact of the transition to industrialism and urbanization, the disadvantages of political parties as vehicles for increasingly specialized societal interests, and the growth of the state as key variables which give birth to the modern interest group (Pross, 1992; Walker, 1991).

In Canada, industrialization took place in the late nineteenth century, and urbanization occurred in Ontario and Quebec by 1920. Industrialization took on the distinctly Canadian pattern of the "branch plant" economy, with the most dynamic sectors of industry developing as branch plants of American industry. Primary production—mining, fishing, farming, and forestry—continued to play a critical role in the Canadian economy, even after industrialization and urbanization. Primary industries were organized around the production of commodities for export, whether in fishing, wheat farming, forestry, or mining. The emerging manufacturing industries of the late nineteenth and early twentieth centuries were mainly concentrated in southern Ontario and Quebec. The economy was highly regionalized, as some parts of the country were industrialized, while others continued to rely on traditional primary industries.

In post-Confederation Canada, political parties provided an important vehicle for elite and business interests. The Conservative and Liberal Parties of the period 1867-1914 were loosely organized electoral machines that relied on patronage to grease the wheels of party politics. The parties, especially the Conservatives, the dominant party from 1867-96, allocated jobs and contracts to party supporters. The parties were leader-driven, with weak formal organization beyond their parliamentary representatives. They lacked a broad program or principles, and their electoral appeals were designed to bring together the diverse sections of the country under a party label. In a society of agriculture and primary resource production and in an era of small government, the winning party controlled many of the most important positions in government, such as appointments as judges or tax collectors.

As the historian Gordon T. Stewart has explored at length, patronage was a key element in the emergence of Canadian democracy and became an important dimension of Canadian political culture, in comparison to the US and the UK in the same period (Stewart, 1986). The transition to responsible government in the 1840s meant that parties needed to be able to build solid majorities in order to sustain the stability of the executive power. The block in the political system that prevented the creation of such majorities in the legislature of the Canadas was one of the primary domestic political factors behind Confederation itself. This blockage was in part overcome through the creation of stable parties with solid electoral bases. According to Stewart's analysis of John A. Macdonald's leadership, Macdonald rewarded those who supported the Conservative Party and punished those who did not. Unlike the older model of the Chateau Clique and the Family Compact, positions were not given based on birth and connections, but on

Macdonald's own version of the merit principle, namely, hard work and contributions to the Conservative Party. Although government was small by modern standards, its role and powers were expanding over this period as the new Canadian state was established and as the Western provinces entered Confederation. By dispensing jobs and positions, Macdonald marshaled his troops and was able to produce stable majorities. This model was then emulated by the Liberals, first by Sir Oliver Mowat in Ontario and, in the 1890s and after, by Sir Wilfrid Laurier for the federal Liberals (Stewart, 1986).

This leader-centred style meant that parties were unlikely to embrace radical change or even to commit themselves to a party program that might limit the leader's leeway in negotiating with the major regional and linguistic blocs. However, the parties also worked as a vehicle for political influence for other types of groups in Canadian society. Because power in the party rested with the leader, early Canadian political parties developed close relationships with the economic elites who had driven the project of Confederation in order to further trade, commerce, and the lucrative exploitation of the natural resource industries. Business elites in Canada shaped the colonial and post-Confederation states in ways that would facilitate a transcontinental exploitation of Canada's natural resources as part of the British imperial system. Staples theory suggests that natural resource exploitation was the core of the Canadian economy during this period.

During the late nineteenth and early twentieth century, business elites enjoyed close links with party leaders and were able to influence the course of government policy more than any other group in Canadian society. The Conservative government of John A. Macdonald put into place the protective tariff for Canadian manufacturers and built the railway that solidified east-west communication and economic links. These close ties were demonstrated during the Pacific Scandal of 1872, in which Macdonald was alleged to have taken bribes from railway magnates in return for the contract to build the Pacific railway linking Central Canada to British Columbia. Although this scandal drove the Conservative government to defeat in 1873, they were soon reelected with Macdonald at the helm.

As industrialization took hold, business elites soon found that they required other forms of organization in order to exercise political influence rather than simply relying on ties to the two major political parties. As Michael Bliss and other historians of Canadian business have noted, despite the fact that "the late nineteenth and early twentieth centuries were the Golden Age of the Canadian business enterprise ... the business class as a whole perceived itself to be operating in a hostile environment" (Bliss, 1972: 175). Labour organizing brought pressure to bear on the business community to organize itself. Specialized organizations were established to represent the interests of different sectors of the economy. The first of these was the Ontario Manufacturers' Association, which was founded soon after Confederation in 1871. Renamed the Canadian Manufacturers Association (CMA) in 1877, this group is one of the most important business organizations in Canadian political history. The CMA represented Canada's emerging manufacturing industries, and it is no accident that it grew out of an Ontario business group since southern Ontario and Quebec were the centres of Canada's manufacturing.

The most important issue for the CMA in its early years was Canadian trade policy. The organization was founded to represent the interests of manufacturers to government, especially on the tariff issue. The CMA demonstrated one of the most important functions of interest groups in the political system, namely, the aggregation of interests or the bringing together of a large representative group that could claim to fairly represent a particular sector. Organized groups that can claim to represent their sectors have more legitimacy with the governments and with the general public than individuals or, in this case, even individuals who are members of the business elite. The formation of the CMA meant that governments had no doubt as to what manufacturers thought about Canada's trade policy. It wanted to maintain the protective tariff on Canadian manufactured goods in order to retain competitive advantage in the Canadian domestic market. By banding together, members of the CMA were able to exert more influence with more credibility than any individual manufacturer could have mustered. Further, the CMA's position in favour of Macdonald's National Policy, which included the protective tariff, helped the government to win favour with the public for its economic policies. In so doing, the CMA helped to create the universe of political discourse in which the interests of capitalists were equated with the interests of all Canadians, and the interests of Canadian manufacturing were equated with the interests of Canadian business. Therefore, there was a profitable exchange of legitimacy and credibility between the organized interest group and the state.

Another important variable, which is mentioned in traditional accounts of the origins of interest groups, is the growth of government. In the nineteenth-century agricultural societies of the British North American colonies, the tasks of the state centred on military defense, expansion, and policing; the provision of transportation, communication, and trade links; encouraging and organizing European immigration and settlement; and providing for the defense of private property and the rule of law. In this context, governments played an important indirect economic role in providing the infrastructure of the economic system; however, the direct impact of government was minimal. The size of the colonial government administrations and the later provincial and federal government bureaucracies was relatively small by modern standards, although they grew exponentially over time with the expansion of the Canadian state into the West. However, most civil servants were appointees of the party in power, hired for their party loyalty, not for their policy expertise.

The transition to industrialism entailed important changes to the structure of the state. By the early twentieth century, the federal and provincial governments began the long transition from the clientelistic bureaucracy of the patronage system to a merit-based civil service. This shift required not only an expansion of the numbers of civil servants and the overall size of the civil service at federal and provincial levels, but also an increase in the capacity of governments to extract resources from society through various forms of taxation and to administer increasingly complex regulations. In the federal government and some of the provinces, the civil service was greatly expanded and professionalized over the period just prior to World War I. Although the civil service had been theoretically guided by the idea of merit from its inception and even by competitive examinations as of 1882, in practice the patronage system of the nineteenth century meant that the rules were circumvented in practice and that appointments were based on the patronage principle (Stewart, 1986).

The transition from a civil service based on the patronage of the major political parties to a professional civil service organized around the merit principle began in earnest with the *Civil Service Act* (1908). This Act strengthened the Civil Service Commission (later, the Public Service Commission), which was responsible for managing and hiring personnel for the federal civil service on the merit principle, thus ending recruitment through patronage in the federal government. Following the expanded role of government in wartime, the Civil Service Commission's powers to implement the transition to the merit principle were strengthened by the 1918 *Civil Service Act*, which established competitive examinations for entrance into the public service. However, it took a generation for the patronage-appointed employees to work their way through the system, and it was not until World War II that the civil service at the federal level completed the transition to the merit principle. The ideal of the merit-based civil service reached its apogee in the World War II generation of powerful civil servants who presided over the expansion of the state during and after the war (Granatstein, 1998). In the provinces, the transition took place somewhat later and extended over a longer period, beginning in Ontario in World War I and running through to the Quiet Revolution in Quebec of the 1960s, which greatly expanded the size of the Quebec government. In some smaller provinces, patronage in provincial government appointments is still defended as a better system than the merit principle for certain types of jobs. In Prince Edward Island, for example, the small size of the province has reinforced the principle of party loyalty as a prerequisite for certain government appointments to this day.

The transition from agricultural to industrial society explains some of the growth of government in Canada, as in other developed capitalist economies. The processes of urbanization and industrialization created new social classes—urban workers, the new professional middle class, the industrial capitalist—that shaped Canadian politics and created new political identities. These processes created more complex modern societies, which required more regulation and intervention from the state. However, the requirement for state intervention was shaped by political struggles and by competing ideas about the appropriate role for government in economic and social life. The interventionist state did not follow automatically from these processes of social change but, rather, emerged over a long period, from the first formulation of the merit-based public service in the 1908 Act. There were certain critically important moments in the expansion of state power and capacity, notably, the two world wars and the advent of Keynesianism in the postwar period. This expansion of the capacity of the state and the withdrawal of parties from direct interference in the personnel management of the public service had important implications for the emergence of the modern interest group system.

The organized interest group provided a more focused and targeted means of formulating and expressing the political views of the diverse con-stituencies of the business community. Nevertheless, if business was suc-cessful in achieving its aims through the party system, what was the purpose of the establishment of complex, bureaucratic interest groups at federal and provincial levels? A political economy approach suggests that part of the answer may be found in the specific form of capitalism that predominated in Canada over this period. Canadian industrialization took place in tandem with American development, as many American companies dominated the most dynamic sectors of industry through the use of branch plant production. This pattern weakened the export capacity of Canadian industry and strengthened the relative weight of mercantile capital (e.g., banks) in the Canadian business community. Primary resource exploitation continued to play an important role in the Canadian economy. The complexities of the business community were reinforced by the gradual growth of government regulation and the importance of commercial and fiscal policies for business development. The creation of organized associations reflected these diverse interests. They provided a means for businesses to communicate with each other to define the common interests of the business community.

The establishment of the formally organized interest group and the exercise of influence through the party system constituted a model of conventional collective action that has been followed by many other groups, as we will see below. Beyond its impact on other collective actors, however, this model of collective action had other important effects. Like the other models discussed here, it had certain implications for the universe of political discourse. The process of exerting influence through political parties and the establishment of interest groups reinforced the Canadian state by defining a specifically Canadian space for politics and political debate. The formation of such interest groups suggested new forms of political participation, which were specifically state-focused, as alternatives to voting. Government was an object to be influenced by powerful social groups and a tool to be used in the service of societal interests. By using the party system and by directing the claims of organized interest groups against the state, this model of collective action generated a discursive politics in which organized interests cast their claims in terms of the public good, attempting—explicitly or implicitly—to mask their own interests behind the veil of national interest. Interest group politics of this type provided an alternative vehicle for citizen participation in politics, but one that was profoundly unequal as the "out" groups were marginalized from influence in the dominant parties and lacked the resources to create national-level interest groups of their own. This model also privileged bureaucratic and elite forms of group organization and the development of expert social knowledge produced by and for the group.

Finally, this trajectory of political influence, like the other models suggested below, was based on the construction of a certain type of individual citizen and helped to create new political identities for citizens. While identity politics is not usually considered to be a feature of business organization, this elision is in itself a result of the extent to which the dominant role of the white English-Canadian businessman constitutes the normalized picture of Canadian social, economic, and political leadership. Yet, the dominant position of these seemingly natural business leaders is a political identity created, reinforced, and valorized in part through collective action.

Early Social Movements

While business was the best organized and most influential group in the project of Canadian state-building, a number of early social movements played an important role in creating the political and discursive space for challenges to the status quo. These early social movements stretch back to the pre-Confederation period and provide direct evidence that contentious politics was a feature of agricultural society in Canada. These developments also demonstrate the ways in which social movements contributed and reacted to the processes of urbanization and industrialization.

Three important early movements were the temperance movement, the social purity movement, and the first wave of the women's movement. These movements were linked in themes, and their personnel often overlapped. The first to arise, in historical order, was the temperance movement, whose goal was to eliminate alcohol consumption. Its key features reflect those of contemporary social movement politics, despite the fact that temperance first arose in the colonies of British North America in the 1820s. Built on a sense of personal political identity, the movement aimed to fundamentally transform social practices, drawing on new forms of political communication such as newspapers and utilizing a broad range of tactics and strategies. Studies of the movement in the Canadian context have also shown the ways in which it was gendered and territorialized. Just as new social movement theory emphasizes the role of the post-materialist new middle class in the social movement politics of the 1960s and after, so too the temperance movement drew on the new middle class of the nineteenth century, that is, the professionals, doctors, lawyers, and clergy.

The temperance movement began in the 1820s as the first mass protest movement in the British North American colonies and, in different forms, continued until the Depression. Over time, the movement changed in organization, political strategies, class, and territorial bases, as well as in gender and racial politics. The British North American colonies were pre-industrial and rural, but, like the US, they enjoyed a relatively high rate of literacy and a relatively broad white male franchise compared to European countries of the same period. Similarly, Benedict Anderson's (1983) analysis of modern nationalism also emphasizes the importance of the emergence of printing technology and literacy to the development of a subjective sense of national identification and hence to the political and social construction of nations. The communication and transportation systems of the nineteenth century, as well as the political organization of the colonies in the pre-Confederation period, meant that the temperance movement was focused on the local level, but it diffused throughout the colonies in part through broadsheets and newspaper.

The appeal to temperance was closely tied to religious beliefs that provided the frame through which temperance activists appealed to their following. Its activists were clergy, and their main political strategy was the sermon, the speaker, and the temperance newspaper. Masses of followers were converted to abstinence by signing the pledge not to drink. Noel describes a movement that started out in ideological radicalism in the 1820s and that, like many social movements, moderated its appeals over time (Noel, 1995). The initial religious impulses were drawn from millennialism (both Protestant and Catholic), which was based on the belief that drinkers would go to hell and that judgment day was close at hand. Like some of the more recent social movements, the temperance movement was based on the construction of a collective identity, which was intensely personal and which called upon the individual to live life according to certain precepts drawn from the meaning frame of the movement as well as to work to spread the gospel of temperance and, eventually, to work for changes to public policies such as prohibition.

Most literature on temperance movements in North America stresses the connections between the movement and the class politics of the day. Beginning with Gusfield's classic study of American temperance (1963) and through a large number of Canadian studies, it has been asserted that the temperance movement in Canada was strongest where urbanization and the transition to market agriculture had taken hold. In this sense, the movement was in part a response to rapid social and economic change (Warsh 1993). Class politics was linked with racism and racial definitions of citizenship.

Many temperance leaders put forth the idea that drink was a threat to the educated (white) Protestant citizenry. These ideas also had a strong middle-class base. Protestant liberty, based on Christianity, was tied to the importance of literacy, self-improvement, and sobriety. One historian has suggested that the growth of temperance clubs in previously Loyalist areas of Ontario was a defensive strategy against Protestant Irish immigration in the 1830s and 1840s, which had led to the growth of the Orange Lodges and the displacing of Americans in the province (Lockwood, 1993). The temperance movement drew on the middle class, the respectable working class, and, most importantly, farmers, during a period of economic and social transition. Noel tells us that, during the nineteenth century, the causes of temperance, abolitionism, universal education, and free trade made up the platform of liberal reformers. The solutions to the problem of poverty were redemption, conversion, abstinence, hard work, and Protestant Christianity. As such, many of the key strands of the temperance movement were strongly opposed to the rise of ultramontane Catholicism in Quebec, which they associated with an undemocratic assertion of the power of the Church hierarchy (Noel, 1995).

The temperance movement was gendered in complex ways. It provided scope for women to participate in a mass movement. Women played vital supportive roles and provided much of the mass membership of the movement. The ideal of temperance itself was gendered, as the male was defined as dangerous and drunken while the female was associated with the "the selfless angel of the home and the innocent victim of male vice" (Noel, 1995: 101). Furthermore, temperance constructed gender roles in ways that further restricted women to the domestic realm and charged them with the moral education of children as their special task. In this way, the temperance movement shaped and reflected the changing gender roles of the mid-nineteenth century and prepared the way for the ideal of bourgeois domesticity that would underpin the shift from rural to industrial society. Specifically, temperance helped cement the idea that women did not belong in the work force (Noel, 1995).

The social purity movement, which emerged in the middle class of the cities of English-speaking Canada at the turn of the century, grew out of the temperance movement and overlapped with it. Like the temperance movement, the social purity movement defined a social and political problem and proposed a solution for it. While the former defined alcohol consumption as a problem with a personal solution (abstinence and salvation), the reformers of the social purity movement proposed changes in social mores and practices as well as public policy changes. Again, like temperance, the social purity movement was closely connected with reform Protestantism or the social gospel movement (as it was called in English-speaking Canada) and with the suffrage movement.

The politics of the social purity movement has been described in the seminal work by Mariana Valverde. At the turn of the century, the social purity movement described itself as principally concerned with morally uplifting the working class in Canadian cities (Valverde, 1991). As such, unlike the temperance movement, it was clearly the product of industrial society. Like temperance, however, it was also led by clergy and other middle-class professionals, doctors, teachers, and community workers. Unlike temperance, which, in the nineteenth century, had inspired almost one-third of the population of the province of Canada (Ontario and Quebec) to sign the pledge abstaining from alcohol, the social purity movement did not have a mass base. Nonetheless, its leaders formed a network of like-minded activists who sought to change social practices and, at times, to change policing practices and public policies at the municipal, provincial, and federal levels.

According to Valverde, the social purity movement was mainly concerned with sexual and moral regulation (prostitution, illegitimacy, divorce, obscene literature) and with providing resources for broken families and "fallen" women (Valverde, 1991). The sexual purity advocated by the movement was aimed at what Valverde calls the production of the self, that is, the movement viewed disciplined and morally pure citizens as national assets. "[T]he relentless scouring of the soul and shaping of individual character" (Valverde, 1991: 28) was aimed at producing citizens of the democratic state and at constituting and differentiating the new middle class from the working class. By making the working class into the object of middle-class philanthropy and aid, the movement helped to assert and identify the new middle class and eventually contributed to the formation of the modern social science disciplines of sociology and social work. Like the temperance movement, the social purity movement also contributed to the recasting of gender relations, both through female participation and in regulating the sexuality of women, especially, the "fallen" woman (Valverde, 1991).

This was the context for the emergence of the suffrage movement in Canada, which was successful in obtaining the franchise for most Canadian women in 1918. The suffrage movement was based on maternal feminism, which, in turn, had obvious links to social purity and temperance. It did not advocate women's equality with men in the social and economic spheres but, rather, emphasized the particular family responsibilities of women that were essential for the maintenance and development of the nation (Errington, 1993). Proponents of the suffrage, like members of the social purity and temperance movements, questioned industrialization and urbanization with their attendant ills of poverty and urban squalor. Suffrage advocates, like moral purity and temperance advocates, tended to see the family as the cornerstone of society and felt that giving women the vote would enhance the impact of traditional family values on politics. Moreover, many of the members of the suffrage movement were also members of the social purity and temperance movements and came from relatively high status professional backgrounds. Unlike the early temperance movement or the farmers' movement, the suffrage movement was not very large, and, as Bacchi (1983) points out, its successes came easily compared to the struggles in other countries such as the UK.

The suffragettes were not in favour of women's participation in the labour force or other goals that we would today consider feminist. They demanded the right to vote as part of the role of mothers and of women in family life, not as independent career women (Bacchi, 1983). Although both women and men belonged to the suffragette movement, educated elite women formed its core. These women often belonged to the reform associations that dotted Canadian towns and cities at this time or to clubs like the Young Women's Christian Association (YWCA) or the National Council of Women (Bacchi, 1983; Cleverdon, 1973 [1950]). The Protestant churches also provided a base for suffrage activities.

New opportunities for women in the late nineteenth century explain in part the rise of the suffrage movement. In particular, female labour force participation increased, and education opportunities opened up for women. The processes of industrialization and urbanization reinforced existing attitudes on issues such as temperance and sparked the creation of moral purity movements that fed into suffrage (Bacchi, 1983). Social reform was dominant in the movement and displaced the feminists who wanted to question the role of women in society. For social reformers, "woman suffrage provided the means to implement their larger reform programme and to give woman's maternal influence a wider sphere of action" (Bacchi, 1983: 32-33).

Regional issues also were important in the suffrage movement. It had its easiest successes in the prairie provinces, where the farmers' movement played a major role in opening up the idea of equality for women. The role of women's labour in pioneer farmer households appears to have been a major factor in determining women's right to vote in prairie communities on both sides of the Canada/US border (Cleverdon, 1974 [1950]). Further, like the social purity movement, parts of the suffrage movement were quite racist, calling for voting for white English-Canadian women who were thought to have more intelligence and education than natives or immigrant groups (Bacchi, 1983). Similarly, in Quebec, votes for women and women's potential involvement in politics were thought to potentially undermine national survival, as women would be drawn away from their important role as child-bearers and nurturers of the next generation. While in English Canada the role of women in the home was an argument in favour of suffrage, in French Canada their role augured the other direction. In Quebec, the Church strongly opposed women's suffrage, in keeping with the conservative nationalism of the period. The Church identified women's suffrage with an Anglo-American process of urbanization and industrialization that threatened the survival of French Canada. In these ways, the women's suffrage question was integrated with the nativist, racist, and nationalist ideas in both English and French Canada of the period, although in very different ways (Cleverdon, 1974 [1950]).

Farmers' Movements

As we have seen, the business community used informal links to the dominant parties as a means of exercising influence over governments before forming interest organizations of its own. This method was quickly countered by a competing model: the establishment of parties that were explicitly designed to represent and defend the interests of collective actors. In the UK, for example, in the early twentieth century, trade unions formed the Labour Party in reaction against a court ruling that limited union power. The solution to political powerlessness for British unions was to form a party that would compete with the others for electoral dominance and political influence. This model was a relatively successful one for the British labour movement. Similarly, in many European countries, peasants and small farmers formed peasants' parties or farmers' parties. Other farmers' groups sought influence within conservative or religious parties (e.g., Christian Democratic parties). As we will see in more detail below, farmers and labour in Canada formed mass parties of both the right and left that competed with the dominant Liberals and Conservatives. Some of these parties gained power at the provincial level—United Farmers of Ontario, United Farmers of Alberta, the Cooperative Commonwealth Federation (CCF), Social Credit, the New Democratic Party (NDP)— although they failed to break through at the federal level (e.g., Progressive Party, Social Credit, CCF-NDP).

The creation of a social movement of farmers in Canada in the late nineteenth and first half of the twentieth century was by no means unusual. Farmers' movements played a key role in shaping the politics of many other comparable countries, such as the US, over the same period. Comparative historical sociologists exploring the social origins of democracy in European politics have found that the evolution of peasant and farmers' parties is one of the key variables that shaped political systems in the twentieth century. Collective action by peasants and farmers may be channeled to the left or right of the political spectrum. In the US and Canada, farmers' movements have supplied populism on both extremes (Lipset, 1950) while in northern Europe, farmers' movements allied with emerging labour and social democratic movements to push for democratization and left policies (Esping-Andersen, 1985; Moore, 1966). If the temperance movement has been characterized as the first mass movement in the Atlantic provinces, Ontario, and Quebec, there can be no doubt that the farmers' movement was the first mass movement in Western Canada. Farmers' political activism also shaped the politics of Ontario and Quebec in the early part of the twentieth century. A farmers' government was formed in Ontario in 1921, while farmers provided strong support for the emergence of the *Union Nationale* party in Quebec.

Prairie populism, in part stemming from the US and reinforced by American immigration to Western Canada, especially to Alberta, was a mass movement that sought to assert the collective power of farmers against the impersonal forces of the market. The movement stemmed from the common economic and political interests of farmers. The regionalized development of the Canadian economy, in which Western Canada was viewed as a hinterland to be exploited by Central Canada, helped to produce conditions for collective action. At the same time, at the beginning of the twentieth century, the newly created prairie provinces were dominated by farmers. From the beginning, the fact that farmers dominated governments in the prairies created different political dynamics than prevailed in Central Canada.

At the turn of the century, farmer organizing swept the prairie provinces, in part inspired by the example of the farmers' associations in the American Midwest. The Grange, the Grain Growers' Association, and the United Farmers of Alberta, among others, were established in the first decade of the twentieth century and quickly developed an organizational infrastructure throughout Western Canada. Like other social movements, the farmers' movement of this period spread partly through the print media. The *Grain Growers Guide* was the movement's bible and was read throughout Western Canada. The farmers' organizations quickly took on deep and broad associational forms, from the local group through provincial and regional assemblies across the Western provinces. As W.L. Morton states in his classic work on farmer activism, "the primary purpose of the new organizations was to educate their members in collective action" (1950: 11).

Like other social movements, farmer activists identified conditions they wanted to improve, such as the economic vulnerability of the prairie wheat farmer. The movement clearly identified its opponents as the "Eastern" economic and political interests that controlled the Western transportation system, freight rates, tariffs, and other economic policies that militated against the interests of farmers. Like the temperance, moral purity, and women's movements, prairie populism was strongly influenced by the evangelical Protestant social gospel movement (Allen, 1971). The movement tended to construct the farmer as a figure of virtue and purity contrasted with the corruption and greed of urbanites in the East. In Quebec, farmer activism was centred in a different framework, influenced by religion and conservative Catholic nationalism. However, as in Western Canadian populism, the farmer was cast as the figure of bucolic virtue against the corruption of the anglo forces of urbanization and industrial capitalism. In Quebec, farmers' political activism was channeled by Catholic elites who turned it to the defense of the culture, history, and heritage of francophones. Under the *Union Nationale* party, party elites continued to defend the farmer as the primary figure of French-Canadian political and cultural virtue well into the 1950s (Monière, 1977).

The farmers' movement in Western Canada had a profound influence on the shaping of regional political identity, an influence that resonates in the Canadian party system to this day. Farmer activists founded the

Progressive Party, a left-populist party whose breakthrough in national politics in the 1921 election was the first demonstration of the distinctiveness of Western Canadian farmer politics and the first time a left-wing party had achieved any significant political support in a federal election. The Progressives championed the reform of parliamentary political institutions; opposed party discipline; favoured initiative, recall, and referendum; and argued that the Member of Parliament (MP) should primarily represent his constituents. On economic policy, the Progressives represented farmers' interests, especially on issues such as freight rates and tariffs.

The Progressive Party had largely disbanded by the early 1930s, but its experience gave rise to two successors—the CCF and the Social Credit Party. The CCF represented the tradition of what S.L. Lipset called "agrarian socialism" or the left radicalism of wheat farmers in Saskatchewan. Agrarian radicals combined with socialists from the parliamentary ginger group of socialists of the period, such as J.S. Woodsworth, to form the CCF in 1933 with some support from labour. However, the Depression also encouraged the populism of the right in Alberta with the collapse of the United Farmers' government in 1935 and the election of Social Credit. Social Credit was a political party, but also a protest movement, whose leaders used the new media of radio to reach the increasingly desperate Alberta farmers who had been decimated by the impact of drought and Depression.

The agrarian movements of Western Canada in the first part of the twentieth century helped to constitute Western Canadian political identity. While these movements created a sense of collective political identity for farmers, they also created a regional political identity. They were relatively successful in asserting the interests of farmers in the party system, and, during the 1930s and during the war, farmers succeeded in obtaining a range of policies that increasingly insulated the individual family farm from the vicissitudes of the market. While the decline of the family farm and the transition to large-scale food production have altered the economic and political interests of farmers, the impact of these movements on constituting a Western Canadian political identity has been enduring. The Reform Party of the 1980s and 1990s with its slogan "The West Wants In" was a direct successor of the agrarian revolt of 1921.

The Labour Movement

Of the social movements considered here, the labour movement is the one that most directly rose as a result of economic change. Although there had been many periods of radical protest from landless labourers and urban workers prior to industrialization (Greer, 1993), the urbanization and industrial development in Canadian society, particularly in Ontario and Quebec, and the accelerated exploitation of natural resources in British Columbia, northern Ontario, and Quebec in the mining and forestry industries in the late nineteenth and early twentieth centuries, gave rise to a large-scale working class, which formed the basis of the labour movement.

Several features of the Canadian labour movement are quite distinctive and have had long-standing consequences for the position of labour in Canadian politics: its relative weakness compared to labour movements elsewhere. This weakness is one of the factors that reinforces the territorial and market biases in the Canadian political system in the contemporary period. The comparative analysis of labour movements suggests that once labour incorporation into the polity has been established in a certain way, it is very difficult to roll back the clock (Collier and Collier, 1991). The development of strong social democratic trade unions tied to a left labour or social democratic party has played a key role in the development of solidaristic forms of capitalism in northern Europe. The idea that unions would found their own political party to protect their political interests, as in the case of British unions and the Labour Party, was familiar to Canadian trade unionists. At the same time, however, internal divisions in the labour movement from an early stage of industrialization meant that labour's party, the CCF, was a relative latecomer to the Canadian party system.

Among Canadian unionists, there were several competing political traditions including internationalism, business unionism, labourism, socialism, and syndicalism. American unions organized locals and branches in Canada as "international" (or American) unions. Because American unions were dominated by "bread and butter" unionism (or business unionism), which focused on short-term material gains for workers, this philosophy had a profound effect on both the structure and politics of Canadian unions. International unions reinforced the business unionism of early central Canadian craft unionism and conspired against class-based politics both directly and indirectly. Internationals created political divisions among Canadian unionists by their very presence in Canada; there has always been a competing and much weaker confederation encompassing Canadian unions. In Canada, the incipient apoliticism of craft unionism was reinforced by the overwhelming weight of business unionism within the American Federation of Labor (AFL). Labour historians have documented the strength of labourism as a political ideology among Canadian unions; repeated attempts to form a labour party foundered on lack of funds and, in some cases, outright prohibitions on party organizing from American headquarters (Heron, 1984; Horowitz, 1968; Piva, 1979; Robin, 1968). Financially, the close ties between the AFL and the central organization of Canadian and international craft unions, the Trades and Labour Congress of Canada (TLC), undermined labourism as a practical strategy. From the influx of the internationals, the consequent decline of the Knights of Labour, and the Berlin Congress of the TLC, the central organization of Canadian unions had little financial or organizational independence from the AFL (Babcock, 1974). Quebec unions were further alienated by internationalism; while European experience suggests that Quebec workers might well have favoured Catholic unions in any case, the influx of the internationals favoured the Church-backed establishment of Catholic and national unions in that province (Rouillard, 1989). In contrast, on the West Coast, internationalism meant socialism and syndicalism. The labour movement was highly gendered and racialized, and employers were successful in using non-white labour or women workers to undercut the price of labour for white male breadwinners. While these traditions were swamped by the numerical predominance of the more moderate Ontario unions on the national scene, they contributed to the fear that political divisions would weaken unions for the industrial struggle.

Thus, Canadian unionists were divided by internationalism, divided again by Quebec nationalism, and divided once more by their attitude toward the relationship between political and industrial goals. With respect to the latter, it is important to note that business unionism, labourism, and syndicalism share an important characteristic: a deep attachment to free and unfettered collective bargaining. In addition, business unionism and syndicalism share the belief that political goals can be achieved by industrial means: business unionism by arguing that unions have very few political goals beyond the achievement of a higher wage, and syndicalism by contending that socialism and workers' political power can be achieved through the use of the strike weapon (Bercuson, 1978; McCormack, 1977). On the other hand, labourists and socialists favoured the creation of political parties to ensure the representation of workers and to secure political gains.

One of the key political traditions of Canadian labour in politics was represented by the trade union confederation, the Trades and Labour Congress (TLC). While it eschewed electoral politics, it sought its mandate in political lobbying and annual "cap in hand" sessions with the federal government. Although this occasionally involved ties to one of the old political parties (Ostry, 1960; Ostry, 1961; Horowitz, 1968), its main purpose was the representation of the interests of labour at the national level regardless of factionalism, ideological divisions, or the political stripe of the party in power.

With the advent of industrial unions during the 1930s and 1940s, the split between craft and industrial unions in the US was replicated in Canada with the founding of the Canadian Congress of Labour (CCL). The CCL had somewhat more independence from the American Congress of Industrial Organizations (CIO) than did the TLC from the AFL, but, nonetheless, the largest and most powerful industrial unions of the postwar period were to be internationals (Abella, 1973). While the agrarian radicals were the key force in the founding of the CCF, this occurred when labour was still divided. Unlike the Labour Party or European social democratic parties, however, the CCF's organizational and financial links to organized labour were weak. From the start, the CCF departed from both the labourist and the pure social democratic models of the relationship between the party, the unions, and the working class. In particular, the CCF drew support from prairie farmers and, in fact, achieved its first provincial electoral victory in Saskatchewan in 1944. While the CCL unions were powerful carriers of a labourist or social democratic position on electoral politics—they endorsed the CCF, and several of them contributed to CCF coffers—there were no official ties between the union and the party. The anticipated massive influx of CCL-affiliated locals into the CCF did not occur. The CCF remained a farmer-labour coalition in which unions were conspicuous by their absence (Lipset, 1950; Whitehorn, 1985; Young, 1969; Zakuta, 1964).

This absence affected the party and the future chances for a social democratic alternative in Canada in several ways. The lack of union affiliations not only indicated the ideological orientation of the labour movement during this period but critically influenced the party's capacity to develop class consciousness, build effective organizations, win elections, generally propagate a class-based understanding of politics, and thus combat the defensive business unionism of the TLC unions. The party's poverty was notorious and, in itself, rendered it helpless at critical junctures. When the CCF topped the polls in 1944, its lack of funds contributed to its inability to withstand the counterattack launched by the mainstream parties (Caplan, 1973). The weakness of the CCF in national politics was both cause and consequence of the well-entrenched cleavages of the Canadian party system. Party politics revolved around linguistic, ethnic, and regional cleavages, rather than class divisions (Alford, 1963; Clarke *et al.*, 1986; Wilson, 1968).

In 1956, the AFL and CCL unions came together to form the Canadian Labour Congress (CLC). Although the CLC supported the newly formed NDP, it was not able to transform this support into votes at election time. The NDP was founded in 1961 with the idea that the labour movement would overcome its previous weaknesses and solidify trade union support, but this change never materialized. The model of trade unions establishing a social democratic, socialist, or labour party that would represent the interests of unionized workers in elections did not work in Canadian politics. Although the NDP enjoyed institutionalized ties with the union movement, these ties came under stress when the party held power provincially, most notably in British Columbia and Ontario, where NDP governments confronted their trade union allies in conflicts over the public wage bill and collective bargaining rights in the public sector. Similar conflicts have occurred in Quebec between unions and the *Parti Québécois* (PQ) governments. In both English-speaking Canada and Quebec, although unions have maintained precarious alliances with political parties, especially the NDP and the PQ, they have also undertaken socially focused strategies in alliance with other social movement actors such as the anti-globalization movement. The failure of Canadian trade unions to influence public policy has turned them away from state-focused strategies and toward strategies of influence through social movements.

Social Movement Protest: The 1960s and Their Aftermath

During the 1960s, a wave of youth protest throughout the world gave rise to a number of new social movements, including the student movement, the second wave of the women's movement, the peace movement, the environmental movement, and the lesbian and gay movement. The strategies of these new movements included direct action, demonstrations, and civil disobedience. Scholars of social movements claim that these movements were fundamentally different from those that had gone before in a number of respects, including their strategies, their ideologies, and their organization. In Chapter 1, we outlined some of the key features that are usually attributed to social movements. In some cases, they are more loosely organized than the formally organized interest association, they are often comprised of informal activist networks, and they often use disruptive and contentious tactics. They often aim to achieve broad social change and may not be striving to influence public policy *per se*.

The movements of the 1960s produced new forms of politics that broke with the Keynesian postwar conflicts over class and redistribution. For European students of new social movements, the break with the class politics of the postwar economic boom was quite marked. In the Canadian context, where class politics had never been that strong, the social movements of the 1960s were nonetheless successful in placing new issues on the agenda of both polity and society and reflected a number of important sociological changes in family structure, the decline of both Protestant and Catholic church influence (especially in Quebec), increasing female labour force participation, the expansion of higher education, the increasingly multicultural and multiracial character of Canadian society, and the gradual shift to post-industrial capitalism.

Social protest in Canada during the 1960s and 1970s took on different forms than the civil rights and anti-war movements in the US. Although there were anti-war protests in Canada, a number of other movements were also important, especially the women's, environmental, and lesbian and gay movements. Social protest of the period was also closely tied to nationalism in English-speaking Canada, French-speaking Quebec, and Aboriginal communities where important nationalist movements overlapped with other social movements, such as youth protest, anti-war protest, and the rise of the women's movement. In Quebec and, to a lesser extent, the rest of Canada, the 1960s and 1970s were also a period of relative radicalism among trade unions; in Quebec in particular, desecularization of trade unions led to a strongly Marxist and nationalist phase, which intersected with the nationalist movement and the women's movement. In English-speaking Canada, left nationalism was important among youth, as evidenced in the Waffle arm of the NDP. The Waffle challenged the NDP leadership on the issues of American domination of Canada and socialism. According to the Waffle, the existing NDP leadership had moved too far toward the accommodation of liberal capitalism at the expense of the goals of socialism and Canada's independence from the US. Among Aboriginal people, the 1960s saw the rise of transnational Aboriginal movements, not only the American Indian Movement but also the formation and solidification of new pan-Canadian Aboriginal organizations like the National Indian Brotherhood, which would later become the Assembly of First Nations.

The women's movement in Canada took off in a major way in the late 1960s with organizing around issues such as reproductive freedom, anti-violence, and pay equity. The movement evolved in a number of small, local organizations across Canada, many of which provided services to women. Women's shelters and rape crisis centres were established in local communities. Some sectors of the movement used more radical tactics drawn from long-standing repertoires of contention in Canada and elsewhere. An excellent example is the abortion caravan of 1970 in which the Vancouver Women's Caucus organized women to travel across Canada to Ottawa to highlight the lack of access to legal abortion. The cross-country caravan as a social movement tactic has been used many times in Canada, most famously by unemployed men during the Depression who marched to the nation's capital in the "On to Ottawa Trek." When they arrived in Ottawa, the protestors chained themselves to the visitor's gallery of the House of Commons, echoing the British suffragettes who chained themselves to the gates of the British Parliament. While movements such as the abortion caravan drew attention to the issue of women's equality, other sectors of the movement focused on changing public policies through conventional means. The appointment of the Royal Commission on the Status of Women in 1967 and its report, which documented the widespread inequality between women and men in Canadian society, was an important turning point in state-focused activism at the federal level. The Royal Commission report led to the establishment of the National Action Committee on the Status of Women (NAC), a federation of grassroots women's organizations (Vickers, Rankin, and Appelle, 1993).

Another important social movement of the time was the environmental movement. Like the women's movement, the environmental movement challenged the public/private divide. While the women's movement politicized issues such as reproductive freedom and sexual assault, the environmental movement questioned everyday social practices that contributed to pollution and environmental degradation. It also questioned the commitment to economic growth on which the postwar boom had been constructed and linked the agendas of environmentalism and peace through protests against nuclear power. One of the most important environmental non-governmental organizations (NGOs) in the world today is Greenpeace, founded in Vancouver in 1971. Greenpeace pioneered direct action tactics in environmental activism through its challenges to American and French nuclear testing in the Pacific, the whale hunt, the multinational oil companies, and destructive fishing and logging practices. The direct action tactics of Greenpeace have been used by environmental organizations throughout Canada and the world on a broad range of targets, including corporations, governments, and international organizations (Dale, 1996). At the same time, like many of the organizations of the women's movement, Greenpeace has become an institutionalized and well-organized group. As we will discuss in detail in Chapter 5, environmental organizations are relatively well integrated into the policy-making process on certain public policy issues. The environmental movement is a good example of a new social movement that has worked successfully on the outside and on the inside of the policy process. Further, the movement is an important precursor of later waves of transnational and anti-global organizing because it was one of the first to deploy direct action across borders.

The lesbian and gay movement of the 1970s and 1980s also provides another example of new social movement organizing that has had a broad range of effects on other movements. Like the other movements described here, it used a mix of direct action and conventional tactics and targeted both society and the state. Direct action tactics included occupations, demonstrations, and "zaps" (e.g., public kiss-ins). Like the women's movement, the lesbian and gay movement built local organizations to serve its communities with gay phone lines, lesbian and gay social spaces, and health services (Warner 2002). With the onset of AIDS, groups such as AIDS Action Now in the US and Canada engaged in direct action tactics (e.g., inverting the "kiss-in" to "die-in") and sophisticated media strategies to target drug companies and governments for their failure to act on the crisis. AIDS organizing made an important contribution to building up new repertoires of contention that would later be tapped by the anti-globalization protestors in the late 1990s and beyond (Shepard, 2002; Wood and Moore, 2002). Critically, both the environmental movement and the lesbian and gay movement contributed to the move towards targeting corporations, rather than states, a move that significantly foreshadowed the anti-globalization movement(s). Similarly, both movements combined the conventional and the unconventional—direct action and participation in litigation and lobbying activities—in ways that suggested that the old borderlines between organized interest groups and social movements were crumbling.

All of these movements—the women's movement, the environmental movement, and the lesbian and gay movement —questioned the existing institutions of society in different ways. They challenged everything from sexuality to the family to education and the health system and, in this way, broadened the very definition of politics. The universe of political discourse was fundamentally altered by the rise of the cycle of contentious politics. Politics was no longer confined to questions of states and markets, but had expanded to include questions of gender, sexuality, and the environment.

The New Business Militancy

In the wake of the protests of the 1960s, the accelerating shift to a new form of post-industrial global capitalism was underway. This change sparked a new wave of business militancy that paved the way for neoliberalism. Business militancy arose not only in opposition to the cycle of contentious politics of the 1960s, but also in reaction to the strains on the Keynesian welfare state paradigm that resulted from the first oil shock of 1973. As we have already seen, business elites and business associations have been important collective actors throughout the history of Canada. Yet, as Charles Lindblom has pointed out, business in capitalist market systems enjoys a privileged position. The market system reinforces business power without any action on the part of the business community. This structuring power of the market works through what Lindblom calls the automatic punishing recoil. Governments that fail to conform to the demands of business may be punished through a capital strike as investors flee for more friendly jurisdictions (Lindblom, 1977). Cross-national analysis of business associations demonstrates that they typically form when business feels its power is threatened, especially by the rise of labour. As Korpi (1983) and other comparative analysts of business power (Coleman, 1988) have demonstrated, business is most tightly organized in countries in which labour power is strongest. In northern Europe and, to a lesser extent, in the UK, where unions made substantial inroads, business organization tended to be highly organized at the national level. In contrast, in Canada and the US, labour was weak and divided, which opened the way to business dominance. Cross-national studies also show that, in countries with patterns of business dominance, such groups that do exist will tend to form a pluralist associational system, that is, a pattern of group organization in which there are a plethora of groups, which are poorly coordinated and not able to act in a concerted fashion (Coleman, 1988).

The Canadian business community has formed a large number of specialized associations, but central organizations of Canadian business have never been as tightly organized as have employers in many European countries. Nonetheless, over the last quarter century, business elites have played an important role in the discursive, political, and economic shift to neoliberalism. During the 1970s, the Canadian business community underwent a significant organizing spurt in reaction to some of the interventionist policies of the Trudeau era (Richardson, 1992). This resulted in the establishment of new business organizations, most notably the Business Council on National Issues (BCNI), which was modeled on the Business Roundtable in the US, and a major new think tank, the Fraser Institute. The BCNI brought together 150 of Canada's largest corporations, spanning the manufacturing, resource, and financial sectors (Langille, 1987). Multinationals held the dominant position within the organization. Doran and Marchildon describe the importance of business organizing in the origins of the Canada-US free trade agreement of 1987:

> The reality of impeded access to the American market in the early 1980s had jarred the Canadian business community into some fundamental rethinking of its attitude towards trade. Probably, the most fortuitous factor in the whole free trade calculation was the conversion of Canadian "big business" to support of free trade. Throughout the 1970s, corporate Canada had been groping its way back to an effective consensus. Confronted by the need of a common stand on public issues ranging from competition policy to tax reform, big business had come together in the Business Council on National Issues. (Doran and Marchildon, 1994: 110).

A new generation of savvy business elites pioneered a new strategy for the Canadian business community: the systematic exploitation of media to shape public discourse on economic, social, and political issues.

This strategy deliberately focused on changing public opinion in order to increase support for markets over government intervention. In explaining its own history, the Fraser Institute commented that, at one time in Canada, "people believed that central planning activities undertaken by government were the key to economic growth and development" (1999: 4). The Institute's history states, "[i]t was thought that government was a better agent of economic change and development because it was thought not to be subject to the same frailties as the private marketplace. Because government had no need to earn a profit it was also thought public services could be provided more cheaply, and that extensive public ownership of the economy would lead to greater well-being for Canadians" (1999: 4). It diagnosed the problem as one of flawed ideas: "Since the problem was incorrect ideas, the solution would depend upon an effective educational institute to inform Canadians about the consequences of particular courses of policy action" (1999: 6). Research would reveal the "crucial role" of markets and help to correct the "incorrect ideas" championed by those who favoured "central planning." The Fraser Institute's first booklet was called *Rent Control: A Popular Paradox*. As the Institute proudly recounts, after its publication in 1975, "rent control as a policy was dropped in almost every major jurisdiction" (1999: 8).

At the same time, in the early 1980s, the BCNI undertook a major media campaign in favour of free trade with the US. In 1985, it called for the establishment of a new disputes settlement resolution mechanism with the US and for a forum for bilateral free trade. BCNI leaders were important in convincing the Macdonald Commission on the Canadian Economy, which reported in 1985, to support free trade. They appeared in the media extolling the virtues of a free trade deal and testified before key parliamentary committee hearings that considered Canadian trade policy in the mid-1980s (Dymond, Hart, and Robinson, 1994). The BCNI laid the groundwork for free trade by breaking the taboos against discussion of it. For much of the twentieth century, it was assumed that Canada-US free trade was unthinkable because Canadians would not support such a close economic relationship with the US. By urging public discussion of the issue and by appearing in the media vaunting the idea of free trade, BCNI and Fraser Institute leaders put the issue onto the public agenda, which was the first step toward its acceptance. The BCNI also pushed for a number of other neoliberal policies, including deregulation, privatization, and tax cuts (Clarkson, 2002). During the 1988 election on the free trade issue, the BCNI formed a coalition in favour of free trade with other business groups. The coalition spent $4.2 million on political advertising during the election campaign, substantially outspending and outgunning the anti-free trade forces. In 2001, the BCNI changed its name to the Canadian Council of Chief Executives (CCCE, 2004).

The trajectories of business and labour influence in Canadian politics, then, have been based not only on the shaping power of the capitalist market system on the state, but also by the agency of political actors, such as those in the business community who have actively organized in pursuit of their goals. Influencing public opinion and shaping the universe of political discourse has been one of their main methods of influence. Convincing citizens of the new common sense of politics—a common sense that denies any challenge to global capitalism—has become a centrally important business strategy.

The Anti-Globalization Movement

Just as business has actively pursued an agenda to shape public opinion and the universe of political discourse, its efforts have been contested by the emergence of the anti-globalization movement, which has pioneered new forms of activism in Canadian and global politics. In Canada, the anti-globalization movement has its roots in the left nationalism of the 1960s in English-speaking Canada. As we have already seen in the discussion of the rise of Canadian political economy within political science during the late 1960s and early 1970s, the nationalist movement of the period gave rise to concerns on both the right and left that Canada was losing economic and political sovereignty. The left nationalists played an important role in the NDP and founded new groups (e.g., the Council of Canadians) and think tanks (e.g., the Canadian Centre for Policy Alternatives). During the free trade debate, left nationalists, trade unionists, the women's movement, and environmental groups came together in an anti-free trade coalition, the Pro-Canada Network (Ayres, 1998).

The cycle of militancy that culminated in the free trade election of 1988 slowly died off through the debates on NAFTA in the early 1990s, but organizations like the Council of Canadians survived to become key Canadian players in the anti-globalization movement later in that decade. Left nationalists had long critiqued American dominance of the Canadian economy, some from a Marxist perspective, others from a broad non-

Marxist political economy direction. Left nationalism offered a critique of neoliberalism from its inception, highlighting the retrenchment of the welfare state, and the reinforcement of restrictive monetary and fiscal policies and of policies such as privatization and deregulation (Cameron and Drache, 1985). The continuing moves toward continental and hemispheric free trade and changes in international trading regimes with the transformation of the General Agreements on Tariffs and Trade (GATT) into the World Trade Organization (WTO) in 1995 all fit with the left nationalist analysis of the decline of Canadian sovereignty, the Americanizing of Canadian economic and social policies, and the race to the bottom in economic and social policies.

Since the free trade debates of the 1980s, Canadian left nationalists and trade unionists continued to draw attention to the links between trade policies and other spheres of social policy such as the environment, health care, and education. These links had also been drawn in a number of other countries, especially through the debt crises of the 1980s and 1990s, the imposition of structural adjustment programs in developing countries, and moves by the WTO into the regulation of whole new swaths of economic and social policy through proposed regulations on investment and intellectual property. The acceleration of globalization and the diffusion of new forms of communication and information technology strengthened the capacity for groups to organize transnationally. International and transnational NGOs began to play a more important role as did People's Summits, which were held in tandem with meetings of heads of state, such as Asia Pacific Economic Cooperation (APEC), the Free Trade of the Americas Association (FTAA), and the proposed Multilateral Agreement on Investment (MAI). This organizing exploded in street protests and massive demonstrations against neoliberal globalization at Seattle in 1999 and Quebec City in 2001.

A large number of preexisting organizations and networks have contributed to the anti-globalization movement. In Canada, these include trade unions, women's organizations, environmentalists, and left-nationalist groups such as the Council of Canadians. These groups have challenged the inevitability of neoliberalism and argued that human rights, labour standards, and the environment must be integrated into global regulation of economic rules. As Jeffrey Ayres has documented, there was an intense battle between the elite press and movement activists over the label "anti-globalization" because many movement activists framed their opposition in terms of neoliberalism, rather than as anti-globalization *per se* (Ayres, 2004). That is, the movement questioned the hegemony of the ideology and practices of the untrammeled free market, rather than the virtues or inevitability of globalization itself. In fact, the anti-globalization movement is the preeminent global movement, itself a product of heightened economic, political, and communication links across borders.

The anti-globalization movement represents a new trajectory of influence in Canadian politics, one that brings together trends in social movement politics that have been apparent since the 1960s. First, the movement spans borders and has highlighted the problem of de-democratization that is entailed by the shift to neoliberalism. While transnational movements are not new, they have greatly expanded their scope and influence, and Canadians have been active participants in them. Many other Canadian-based social movements are involved in global and transnational organizing, especially in the areas of Aboriginal politics, the environment, and human rights. Second, the anti-globalization movement highlights the shifting targets of group politics and political activism through its deliberate targeting of media messages and its attacks on corporations and international trade organizations as well as states. While the Canadian state may be the target of activism through the strategies of transnational organizing, the global movement may also pressure the Canadian state to carry its message into state-based international venues. The Canadian state itself may be irrelevant to the targeting of certain forms of activism since the target may be another state, international organization, or corporation. Third, the anti-globalization movement in North America has drawn on repertoires of contention drawn from the social movements of the 1960s and after in the use of mass protests, demonstrations, "die-ins," and other such actions. Less hierarchical organizations, flatter networks, informal organization, and the use of the Internet and cell phones as means of mobilization are all new techniques that build on the traditions of democratic participation and consensus decision-making pioneered by the new left, the women's movement, and the gay liberation and AIDS movements (Shepard, 2002).

Trajectories of Influence in Canadian Politics

This chapter has provided a survey of the typical trajectories of group and movement influence in Canadian politics. Repertoires of contention for collective action arose in reaction to such macrohistorical changes as the transition to urbanized and industrialized societies, the process of state-building, the shift to post-industrial capitalism, and the rise of globalization. At the same, however, such trajectories helped to constitute the dominant political discourse in each of the periods in which they occurred, as well as leaving important legacies for the future. Collective actors contest the rules and norms that govern the political process and the types of claims that are deemed to be legitimate (or illegitimate) in political discourse. In the process, they assert political interests and political identities. In some cases, groups and movements are asserting newly emerged interests and identities, as was the case with early trade unions; in others, they are championing the interests of long-standing groups that have been politicized in new ways, such as farmers in Canadian politics at the turn of the century. Sometimes, they are declaring class interests and identities, as in the case of the social purity movement, which helped to constitute a new sense of class consciousness and class identity for middle-class urban Canadians. In other cases, they are claiming a nationally based identity, as in the case of Aboriginal nationalism. Group and movement militancy creates, solidifies, and reinforces a menu of identity choices for citizens as well as repertoires of contentious collective action. In Canadian politics, there are a set of typical identities that constitute a range of respectable choices for the citizen in politics. Business elites, trade unionists, suffragettes, moral reformers, and farmer activists all left their mark on Canadian politics before World War II and shaped the universe of political discourse of their time. In addition, however, they provided examples of movements in action that defined the possibilities for Canadian citizens of the postwar years, however uninformed many Canadians may be of the early history of social movements. Collective actors and collective action predate the establishment of the Canadian state. Colonial era movements such as temperance have left legacies of action, ideology, and strategy that have profoundly influenced subsequent movements like contemporary feminism and environmentalism.

We have now explored how collective actors have constituted themselves in Canadian politics over time, from the colonial era to the contemporary period. The next chapters will explore how group and social movement actors access the Canadian state, focusing on the central institutions of the federal government. The transition from the Keynesian welfare state to neoliberalism has gone hand in hand with changes in the structure of the state, changes that have made the Canadian state less democratic and that have created obstacles to influence by collective actors. The focus on the restructuring of the state is critically important to understanding how neo-liberalism has shaped the central political institutions of the federal government. Discussions of political institutions have been neglected in Canadian explorations of the neoliberal shift, as most analyses have focused on changes in public policy rather than on changes in political institutions. Yet, most group and social movement actors in Canadian politics still target the state in at least some part of their activism and activities. To the extent that groups and movements are moving away from targeting the state, they are doing so in part because of the ways in which political institutional changes are shutting down access to the federal government for many groups. We will begin with an exploration of the central representative institution of the state—Parliament—and the relationship between political parties, interest groups, and social movements.

FOUR

Arenas of Influence:
Parliament, Parties, and Elections

The transition from the Keynesian to the neoliberal era has reinforced the obstacles created by the Canadian Westminster system of governance to the influence of groups and social movements on legislatures and the party system. These obstacles are strengthened by the fusion of legislative and executive authority at the heart of Canadian political institutions and the highly disciplined nature of political parties. As we will see below, the Canadian party system is dominated by the "brokerage" model with respect to party organization and electoral strategies, and the Canadian voter is fickle and volatile (Clarke *et al.*, 1986). The volatility of the voter, the brokerage nature of the major parties, the first-past-the-post rules of the electoral system, and the rules of party and election financing create a legislative system dominated by the governing party. This dominance is the major barrier to group influence through the individual Member of Parliament (MP) or the opposition parties under most circumstances.

The nature of the dominant parties is reinforced and exacerbated by the increasingly important role of the media in election campaigns. As Alexandra Dobrowolsky has argued, the transition to neoliberalism has entailed a dumbing down of politics and political debate (Dobrowolsky, 2000a). Even in countries with a strong labour or social democratic tradition, such as the UK, left parties have undertaken "third way" policies that have brought them closer than ever to neoliberal politics of privatization, deregulation, welfare state roll-backs, and the attack on social solidarity and collectivism. New media technologies, such as the 24-hour news cycle, the rise of cable, and the impact of the Internet, have tended to marginalize substantive policy debate (Taras, 2001). Corporate concentration of media at the global level has restricted information and choice, even with the new technologies available to the public (Bagdikian, 1992). In turn, this militates against the involvement of non-territorial group and movement organizations in election campaigns and increases the volatility and indifference of voters. Because of the importance of media, political parties everywhere are in decline as social and political organizations, their functions increasingly taken over by party professionals, spin doctors, and professional lobbyists. Proposals to reform Canada's legislative politics—for example, through citizens' assemblies, proportional representation, or citizen engagement— reinforce the neoliberal emphasis on the individual and undermine the legitimacy of group and movement politics and contestation.

A Disciplined Arena

In 1988-89, the Mulroney government attempted to craft a compromise over abortion policy. Pro-choice groups argued that the government should not criminalize abortion, while pro-life groups argued that the government should make abortion more difficult to obtain. In addition to the pro-choice women's groups and fundamentalist pro-life groups, religious organizations and other stakeholders, such as physicians, also intervened in the debate. The Mulroney government's compromise legislation satisfied neither side. While party discipline prevailed in the House of Commons, the Senate, dominated by Liberals, proved more open to group influence. The stakeholders in the abortion debate furiously lobbied senators in the lead-up to the vote on the bill. It was a tie, which, under the Senate's rules, means that the bill was defeated. This was widely seen as a victory for the pro-choice movement because the result was that abortion was decriminalized, and the acrimonious debate surrounding the issue meant that the Mulroney government would be unlikely to reintroduce the bill (Brodie, Gavigan, and Jenson, 1992).

What is interesting about this episode is not that groups on both sides of the debate tried to influence the government's bill regulating access to abortion but, rather, that groups succeeded in influencing the legislative outcome. In Canada's parliamentary system, it is relatively unlikely that groups will be able to successfully exploit legislative opportunities to shape policy outcomes. The abortion bill episode stands as a famous exception rather than as a rule in the conduct of parliamentary business. This forms a stark contrast to the American system in which groups play a major and visible role in lobbying Congress and contributing to election campaigns of legislators. Why are organized interests largely shut out of Parliament in the Canadian system?

The Westminster parliamentary system creates a particular incentive structure for the institutionalized group or social movement organization that wishes to influence government policy. This incentive structure stems from the fusion of authority in the parliamentary system, a fusion that ties the fate of the executive to the fate of the legislature. The government must have the support of the legislature or the government will fall. The principle of parliamentary supremacy in the Westminster system appears to make the legislature powerful by giving legislators the final word on who will form the government. In contemporary parliamentary systems, including Canada's, the strength of political parties in the legislature and their disciplined method of functioning means that it is very unlikely that governments will fall or that the individual legislator will have a meaningful choice in supporting the government. For the most part, the legislator is a cog in the machinery of producing a stable government. By supporting her or his own party, the MP ensures that the party with the most seats will form the government of the day. The functioning of modern political parties and electoral machinery means that this support is normally not in question. The legislature becomes an electoral college that translates support for particular parties into a stable government.

The impact of fusion on shutting out groups and social movement organizations from the legislative arena is particularly strong in the Canadian parliamentary system (Young, 2000). The level of discipline among Canadian parties is high, compared to other Westminster political systems (Franks, 1987). This poses challenges to organized groups that wish to influence legislative outcomes (Pal and Weaver, 2003). Lobbying individual MPs will not be of much use under most circumstances because the MP must follow his or her party's line. For MPs in the opposition parties, it is unlikely that they would be able to garner support to bring a bill forward successfully in the legislature unless the leadership of the governing party decides to support the bill. Nonetheless, there are some mechanisms for group influence in the legislature: minority government, free votes, the caucus, and parliamentary committees.

Opportunities for Legislative Influence

In a situation of minority government or in a situation in which party discipline has been loosened by the party leadership for some reason, it may also be possible for groups to mobilize to influence the outcome of issues that are before the legislature or to influence the policy agenda of the government through the legislature. There have been ten minority government since Confederation, and these have all been important in terms of policy innovation; for example, the Mackenzie King Liberals introduced old age pensions under pressure from the Progressive Party in 1927. From 1972 to 1974, the Liberal government was in a minority position, supported by the NDP and had to respond to the NDP's policy agenda in order to maintain its support in the House of Commons. This gave the NDP an unparalleled opportunity for policy influence. Indeed, the Liberals' vulnerability to defeat in the legislature provided a political opportunity for groups and movements to influence the federal legislative agenda through the NDP. This period was one of the most fruitful for new legislation, resulting in measures such as the creation of Petro-Canada. In the case of Ontario in 1985, the Progressive Conservative (PC) party won slightly more seats (52-48), and the Liberals and PCs were tied in popular vote (37.9 per cent for the Liberals and 37 per cent for the PCs). In this situation, the Liberals, led by David Peterson, were able to strike a bargain with the NDP, leading to a situation of minority government that lasted two years (Williams, 2001). However, at the federal level, minority governments are not the norm; there was not a single minority government over the 25 years from 1979 (the Clark Progressive Conservative government) to the 2004 election. The minority government elected in June 2004 may usher in a period of legislative innovation, as did the Trudeau minority of 1972-74.

Party discipline may also be loosened by the decision of party leaders because of the nature of the political issue under debate. At one time in Canada's history, certain issues were defined as matters of conscience, and, out of respect for the religious beliefs of individual MPs, they were subject to free votes in the legislature; that is, the individual MP was not required to vote along party lines. Capital punishment, abortion, lesbian and gay rights, stem cell research, and same-sex marriage have sometimes been defined in this manner. For example, on the issue of capital punishment, in 1976 the Liberal government of Pierre Trudeau permitted a free vote. The last executions had taken place in Canada in 1962, and a moratorium on capital punishment had been in place since 1967. MPs voted to abolish it. However, with the rise of right-wing populism in the 1980s, the issue resurfaced on the policy agenda, especially within the PC caucus. In response to this pressure, the Mulroney government permitted a free vote on the return of capital punishment in 1987; the measure was defeated by

148 to 127 votes. The Mulroney government's abortion bill, detailed at the start of this chapter, is another case in which MPs were allowed a free vote on an issue defined to be one of moral conscience (Wearing, 1988).

However, the question of whether a policy issue is defined as moral is in itself a product of the political debate. Jenson's concept of the universe of political discourse reminds us that what is defined as political reflects the boundaries of political debate in a given period. Over time, as Canadian political culture has moved in the direction of rights, reinforced by the advent of the Charter, many issues that were previously defined as moral have come to be defined as questions of rights. For example, in the debate following the Ontario Court of Appeal decision legalizing same-sex marriage in 2002, some commentators suggested that the government might hold a free vote in Parliament on the issue, allowing the individual MP to express his or her personal views (Laghi *et al.*, 2003). In that case, as with abortion in 1988 and capital punishment in 1987, we might have expected to see furious lobbying by groups on both sides of the issue in order to influence the views and votes of MPs. However, the impact of the court decision and the political mobilization of the lesbian and gay movement have been successful in putting forth an alternative conception of lesbian and gay issues, one that defines these as a matter of rights, rather than a matter of individual conscience or religious belief. In any case, the definition of issues as "moral" only serves to obscure the fact that the government may choose to open up legislation to a free vote when it wishes; in reality, governments have used free votes to shirk the burden of making decisions when public opinion is divided. By converting a hot button issue into one of conscience, the government may seek to evade the problem (on blame avoidance, see Pal and Weaver, 2003). The role of the courts in adjudicating rights issues has permitted governments to transfer responsibility for such issues to the courts.

In considering how much influence can be exercised by MPs and, by extension, the potential opportunities for group or social movement influence through MPs in the legislature, the party caucuses are a critically important site of political debate. Because of the relative secrecy surrounding them, much of what goes on in caucus meetings must be inferred by comments made to the media or by the actions of party leaders. Again, the hot button issues of abortion, capital punishment, and lesbian and gay rights have occasioned debates in caucus and warnings to party leaders and, especially, leaders of the governing party, about how to proceed. At times, organized groups of MPs have emerged within the caucus to push for particular policy directions. For example, during the 1980s, under the Mulroney government, a Family Caucus of MPs organized within the PC party and pressured the government on issues such as gay rights. The existence of such groups inside the caucus provides opportunities for organized groups and social movement organizations to leverage pressure for a particular policy direction. In fact, Paul Thomas's study of caucuses found that outside pressure was particularly important in influencing the outcome of pressure on the party leadership through the caucuses. As Thomas summarizes his findings, "[w]hile the caucus seldom initiates policy, it does contribute to setting the agenda of government and to the parameters of policy choice. In addition to helping shape the climate of opinion in which legislation is drafted, caucus discussion can lead to delay, modification and even the abandonment of bills presented by ministers" (Thomas, 2001: 223-23).

At the same time, Canada, compared to other Westminster-style systems, does not have a history of organized dissent within political parties. As Wearing points out, the British system has a long history of policy groupings within the Liberal, Conservative, and Labour parties that have served to steer each party in new directions (Wearing, 1988). The possibility of shifting party policies through the actions of a policy grouping or dissenting faction opens up opportunities for interest groups to influence party directions. However, Canadian parties have been intolerant of this type of dissent. Organized dissent within the PC Party in the 1980s led to the breakup of the party and the founding of the Bloc Québécois.

Parliamentary Committees

Most public legislation is introduced in the House of Commons and is scrutinized by the House and by the Senate through three readings and the committee stage. For group influence, the most important stage in the passage of legislation is the committee. Except for the Public Accounts Committee, which is chaired by an MP from the official opposition, legislative committees are chaired by and dominated by MPs from the governing party who are expected to do the will of the government. Nonetheless, committees do hear from groups and individuals who wish to be heard on the principle or details of the legislation. Legislative committees are a key component of Parliament because they provide the only structured and systematic forum for groups to appear before Parliament to give their views to MPs. As such, they provide the potential for groups to influence the evolution of legislation. At the committee stage, amendments to legislation are considered and voted upon; therefore, groups who wish to influence legislation may find an opening there.

The most successful interventions in parliamentary committees are likely to come from groups who are defined as legitimate stakeholders in the policy field under consideration. If the bill affects farming, then farmers' organizations will have a great deal of legitimacy in speaking on agricultural issues. If the bill concerns banking, then the banks and banking associations will be considered legitimate stakeholders. These groups are particularly likely to have influence over technical matters such as how to improve the legislation so that it will meet the objectives set out by the government. Of course, many times the groups may not agree with the overall goal or principle of the bill; again, groups that are viewed as legitimate stakeholders will be more powerful in disagreeing with the government through legislative committees than groups who are not defined as having a "stake," an "interest," or expertise in the issue at hand. Thus, one of the most important stages of policy development concerns the definition of the issue and of the affected stakeholder groups. To take an example, women's organizations may not be defined as legitimate stakeholders on the issue of North American free trade. Such an issue may be defined in such a way that "expert" advice is privileged. So economists, who are viewed as experts on the economic implications of trade changes, may have more influence than activists from the women's movement. Similarly, groups representing Canadian business may be viewed as more knowledgeable than feminists about trade issues because the business community is clearly viewed as having an interest in and knowledge of trade rules. Bringing gender into an analysis of trade challenges the view that trade is gender-neutral and implies that men and women's work is differently affected by the move to free trade (Macdonald, 2003). For example, women may be overwhelmingly concentrated in industries that will decline under free trade (such as textiles), or women may tend to dominate the temporary and part-time jobs that may be creating a more flexible work force. In order to make these arguments, women's organizations will have to overcome the barriers to being taken seriously on an issue that, in conventional terms, does not appear to have anything to do with women or with women's interests.

The parliamentary committee system tends to favour entrenched groups who are already seen as legitimate actors in their policy fields.

The committee system itself divides legislation up and categorizes it using conventional standards such as social, legal, external affairs, and so forth. Each committee deals with a different area of legislation. The committee structure to some extent parallels the caucus and cabinet structures and, in this way, tends to reinforce the dominant definitions of policy and entrench past understandings of policy. Women's issues may be defined as belonging to the social affairs, rather than to the economic affairs committee. At the same time, the parliamentary committee system provides invaluable information about the views of various groups in Canadian society. The committee reports are a veritable compendium of the views of groups who have spoken to Parliament.

Groups may successfully exploit parliamentary committees, especially if they are able to use them to draw attention to their issue in the media. At times, parliamentary committees have held hearings on the GST and medical marijuana and even traveled across Canada to hear different views. After the 1985 McGrath Report on parliamentary reform, the role of committees in the House of Commons was strengthened in an attempt to give individual MPs more say. Increasingly, the parliamentary committees are seen as important to individual MPs and to the government. As Docherty comments, "The increasing demand among Canadians for consultation has forced governments to use parliamentary committees as sounding boards of public sentiment. While still limited in their effectiveness, the increasing role of committees is a clear signal that the government believes committees play an important and legitimate role in public-policy formation" (Docherty, 1997: 257).

The Nature of Political Parties: Mass versus Cadre

The tendency of the parliamentary system of disciplined parties to shut interest group and social movement organizations out of the legislature is reinforced in the Canadian political system by the nature of the historically dominant parties, the Liberals and the PCs. Maurice Duverger (1967) divided political parties into two main types: mass parties and cadre parties. This distinction is still useful in explaining the nature of Canadian political parties and their relationship to outside group and social movement influences.

Duverger argued that the traditional political parties in European countries, particularly France and the UK, emerged from the informal political clubs that drove democratization and political discussion from the French Revolution through the nineteenth century. Political parties began as informal grouping of like-minded individuals, with no structure outside of legislatures. These informal political groups gave rise to liberal and conservative parties, which, as they developed in the era of mass democracy in the twentieth century, shared many common features. According to Duverger, such parties were dominated by a "cadre" of professional politicians who sat in the legislature. The party in Parliament or the party in the legislature dominated the party organization outside of the legislature. Party organization outside the legislature was an afterthought in the cadre party and was grafted onto the preexisting model of the political party as a political club of MPs or legislators. In the cadre model, the party organization remained relatively weak; the party was leader-dominated and did not have a formal program or official set of principles to which it officially adhered. While such parties may have supported certain values such as free markets or a religious identity, these values were presented as the "common sense" of their day, rather than as programs for change. Many conservative parties did not believe in sweeping social change and, in fact, had organized in opposition to such reform and radical currents. They were often skeptical of the party program or plans for sweeping social change as forms of social engineering.

In contrast to the cadre party, Duverger pointed to a new form of party organization that was pioneered on the left by socialists and social democrats: the mass party. Mass parties challenged the dominance of cadre parties as the political system democratized and new voters were enfranchised. They organized large numbers of these new voters through party branches and party clubs and built economic resources to contest elections through creating the concept of the party membership, which could be bought for a small fee. Social democratic parties built alliances with trade unions— another form of mass organization—and received donations from union members. They challenged the dominant values of liberal capitalism with party programs that ranged from short-range demands such as the 40-hour work week through to the transformation of the capitalist economic system. Unlike the cadre party, which was dominated by the leader and by the sitting members of the legislature, the mass party began its life without any members of the legislature and was constituted by the party outside of the legislature, with formal democratic rules for the election of the leader and the development and approval of the party program.

The mass party had a different concept of political leadership and constituency organization than the cadre party. Whereas, in the cadre party, the idea was that voters would choose a representative whose judgement they trusted, the mass party pioneered the idea that elected members would stand for the party's enunciated and published program and principles. The party was expected to win seats and then implement the party program. In contrast, in the cadre party, the leaders were elected to govern as they saw fit. In the early period of democracy in which the franchise was restricted to (large) property owners, the cadre party relied on a network of notables who could command the deference of electors during election campaigns. In an era in which the franchise was expanded to include all white males and, by the 1920s, all white voters, the mass party relied on its large organization of clubs and branches. The mass party chose its leader through democratic election by members, while the cadre party chose its leader in the proverbial smoky backroom.

From Duverger to the Brokerage Model

The historical distinction between the mass and the cadre party still tells us much about the historical origins of Canadian political parties, even though, in the North American context, the two types of parties evolved somewhat differently than the European model suggested by Duverger.

The cadre parties of Canada—the Liberals and Conservatives—indeed evolved from informal groupings of like-minded individuals in the legislature, along the lines suggested by the cadre model. Informal parties emerged in the colonial assemblies and were particularly important to the evolution of the parties in the post-Confederation period. The four major cadre parties of the period were Reformers or Grits in Canada West, led by George Brown; the Conservatives in Canada West, led by John A. Macdonald; the *Rouges* or Liberals of Quebec, led by A. A. Dorian; and the *Bleus* or Conservatives of Quebec, led by Georges-Étienne Cartier. These were classic cadre parties for the period, as described in Duverger's model (Moore, 1998). They were informally organized and dominated by their leaders, with no formal organization outside of the legislature. Politically, their plans and programs were pragmatic and concerned with the development and growth of the colony as part of the British Empire. These parties diverged from Duverger's model by adding a consociational element into the mix; that is, the parties—for instance, the Conservatives of Ontario and Quebec—were organized along the lines of religion and language as well as region. The future Liberals were even more handicapped; not only were the two groups of liberal politicians divided by religion and language, they were also divided by the active mobilization of anti-Catholic and anti-French sentiment by the leaders on the anglophone side.

The Conservative party pioneered a Canadian model of the cadre party, the brokerage party. As Brodie and Jenson have pointed out in their classic work on Canadian political parties, the dominant parties in Canada have deliberately chosen strategies that emphasize a definition of politics in which national, regional, and linguistic divisions are highlighted at the expense of other issues (Brodie and Jenson, 1988). In the traditional European political party model, parties are arrayed from left to right in the spectrum, depending on their views on the questions of collectivism, state intervention, and religion and ranging from traditional conservatives on the right through liberals in the centre to social democrats and socialists on the left. In some cases, such left-right cleavages have been cross-cut by urban/rural, religious, cultural, and linguistic differences as well. In the brokerage party model, the parties seek to reconcile national, regional, and linguistic cleavages within their parties. The search for consensus across social differences has made Canadian parties flexible and consensus-oriented, a model that some analysts have labeled the "brokerage model" (Brodie and Jenson, 1988). Brokerage refers to the attempts of the dominant parties (the Liberals and PCs) to broker or bring together different ethnically, linguistically, or regionally defined sections of the country. Hence, the brokerage model rests on the mobilization of linguistic, national, and religious cleavages (historically, between French and English) while, at the same time, the successful brokerage party presents itself as the "solution" to the "problem" of disunity posed by the multiple identities of language, region, nation, and religions.

The early Liberal Party, for example, had its roots in the Grits or Reformers of Ontario and the *Rouges* of Quebec. The *Rouges* were liberal and moderately anti-clerical nationalists while the Reformers were anti-French and anti-Catholic. Although both parties shared typically nineteenth-century liberal and anti-clerical values, they had problems uniting into a cohesive party as the anti-French sentiment of the Reformers or Grits created an insuperable obstacle to unity. After Confederation, the Liberals learned the lessons of Sir John A. Macdonald's successful Conservative Party and, especially under the leadership of Sir Wilfrid Laurier, sought to broker English-French divisions, creating consensus and compromise rather than emphasizing the conflicts between the two groups. In the 1896 election, Laurier successfully built a coalition between his Quebec base and the emerging voters of Western Canada, creating the beginning of the most long-standing and enduring brokerage party in Canadian politics.

Cadre parties are well equipped to become brokerage parties because of their lack of a systematic party program and principles and of democratic organizational structure. These features greatly increase the latitude for political leaders to craft compromises and to build alliances among themselves. In the cadre model, the leader of the party can command the support and loyalty of his troops, thus facilitating bargaining, negotiation, and compromise behind the scenes. By the same token, these features exclude interest group leaders and social movement or NGO leaders who do not have access at the highest levels or who do not have organizational forms that are able to project influence and provide elite leaders. Intersectional organization focusing on reconciling the interests of the official language groups or the major regions in Canadian politics creates an exclusionary political dynamic for social movements and groups that are based on other identities and interests.

In contrast to the cadre party, mass parties have provided for the mobilization of other groups and identities in Canadian political history, but, in turn, they have also encountered obstacles. According to Duverger, the mass party is characterized by extraparliamentary organization, usually organized through trade unions or socialist groups who are able to mobilize newly enfranchised working-class or peasant voters into the political system. This type of party is based on individual branches and clubs or links to trade union organizations, in which individuals pay membership fees. The party has a democratic form of internal organization in which leaders are elected and the program of the party is democratically determined. Unlike cadre parties, which are associated with conservative or liberal values, the mass party form was pioneered by socialists and social democrats and, in the European party, took the form of the Social Democratic or Labour Parties of the UK and Western Europe.

In Canada, the first party of this type was the Progressive Party, which, in turn, gave birth to the CCF and Social Credit parties. Over the late nineteenth and early twentieth centuries, farmers increasingly joined organizations that resemble the modern-day social movement organization or interest group, such as the Canadian Federation of Agriculture; in the classic fashion of group mobilization, these organizations began to agitate for changes in government policies in a number of areas affecting farmers. Yet, time and time again, farmers came up against the power of the brokerage model and found that they could not make their voices heard in Parliament through the party system. Therefore, they decided the solution was to establish their own political party: the Progressive Party. In its origins, then, the Canadian Progressive Party was similar to the British Labour Party, which was founded in the same period to represent the interests of the trade union movement in politics when trade unionists found the door to political influence shut in the wake of anti-trade union decisions from UK courts. In both cases, a socioeconomic group found itself shut out of the system and attempted to get in by establishing a political party to directly express its interests.

The Progressives were a party of left populism, rather than socialism or social democracy, and, as representatives of the interests of farmers, also mobilized the regional resentments of the West against the brokerage parties—the Liberals and Conservatives—who were perceived as representing the interests of Central Canada. Thus, the Progressives reflected and expressed the multifaceted social movement politics of the farmers' movements of Western Canada in the late nineteenth and early twentieth centuries. As we have seen, the mobilization of farmers in the American Midwest and the Canadian prairie provinces gave birth to a social movement that generated demands for political and social change as well as solidifying a new sense of political identity for farmers as participants in politics.

The rise and fall of the Progressive Party in Canadian politics teaches enduring lessons about how power is organized, whose interests are organized into Canadian politics, and whose interests are organized out. The party represented the interests of farmers in classic mass party fashion as suggested by the Duverger model. Like the socialist mass parties of Europe, the Progressive Party organized in order to bring new voters into the political system; in the case of the Progressive Party, these were the European settlers in Western Canada who were establishing new communities. Similarly, the Progressives based their organization on local branches and individual membership. Further, although the Progressive Party was not a socialist party, like the mass parties of the European model, it had a set of principles and a developed program of substantive policy change and political institutional reform. Not only did the Progressives object to policies of the federal government which militated against farmers, they also objected to the party and electoral system which, they argued, worked to keep farmers out of the political system. Borrowing in part from the populist movements of the American Midwest in this period, the Progressives argued that Canadian political institutions needed to be reformed in order to decrease the influence of party discipline on the behaviour of MPs. In this way, the Progressives introduced yet another principle of political leadership into the mix; in addition to the idea that party leaders should act on their own best political judgement (the cadre/brokerage model) or that party leaders should act based on the principles and detailed program of their party (the mass or social democratic party model), the Progressives introduced the idea that the MP should represent the interests of his or her constituents. Further, if the MP failed to represent these interests, he or she should be recalled by voters in the constituency. The Progressives also argued for the use of the referendum and the initiative, all institutional features found in the American separation of powers system, especially in some of the state constitutions. These suggestions for political reform were meant to provide institutional solutions to the problem of the exclusion of farmers' interests from federal politics and the party system. Contemporary debates over the reform of party discipline in the House, proposals to give more power to individual MPs, and proposals for reform of the electoral system all recall the Progressives' drive to circumvent the barriers to the participation of excluded groups in the political system.

Those who inherited the mantle of the Progressives were the CCF (later the NDP) and the Social Credit parties (except for a small group of Progressives who joined the Conservative Party of Canada to form the now disbanded Progressive Conservative Party). As a socialist party, the CCF resembled the mass parties of Europe in some ways; however, it differed in that it was mainly based on electoral and organizational support from farmers. Trade unions in Canada were relatively weak and divided during the Depression years when the CCF was founded; therefore, they were not in a position to support the CCF, and the dominant trade union confederation, the Trades and Labour Congress, devoted itself to bread-and-butter unionism, rather than supporting the new party. Like the Progressives, the CCF was not only a party of Western protest but also, during its early years in the late 1930s and1940s, had strong support in Ontario. The right-wing populism of Social Credit succeeded in winning the provincial election in Alberta in 1935, inaugurating a long period of Social Credit dominance of

Alberta politics. As an agrarian revolt and as a social movement, Social Credit died off in Alberta after the party took power; once in office, it became a conventional conservative party. However, the legacy of right-wing populism created by the Social Credit movement formed a strong regional legacy in Alberta politics that was later picked up in the 1980s by the Reform Party (Finkel, 1989; Harrison, 1995).

In the face of the threat posed by the emergence of mass parties, the leaders of the cadre parties could not continue to hide out in the smoky backrooms of party politics. The mass party was the harbinger of the new democratic era in which the franchise was extended to all adults, and the mass media began to play a critical role in election campaigns. The pressure of the mass electorate and the rise of the mass media as key components of election campaigns caused the cadre party to adopt some of the forms of organization of the mass party. For example, the Liberal and Conservative parties began to elect their leaders and develop and debate party programs in party conventions. New political parties, such as the Parti Québécois (PQ) at the provincial level and the Reform and Canadian Alliance Parties at the federal level, pioneered hybrid forms of party organization. The PQ, for example, shared many of the features of the social democratic party at its inception, including a highly democratic internal organization, debates over principles and program, a strong extraparliamentary organization, and democratically elected leader. Like the Progressive Party model, the PQ was founded as a social movement organization; in fact, it was formed through the union of several smaller sovereigntist parties that had grown out of the nationalist movement in Quebec in the 1960s. As a political party, it retained close ties to both new and old social movements in Quebec, including the labour movement and the women's movement. Further, the party put forth a program that reflected classic social democratic principles, at least relative to the origins of the modern sovereigntist movement in the period of the 1960s and 1970s. However, the party eschewed any direct connection with the trade union movement, instead basing party financing entirely on individual member donations. Not only did the PQ follow this model in the organization of its own party, it also enacted one of the most far-reaching reforms of election spending in Canada, banning both corporate and trade union donations to Quebec political parties and election campaigns.

On the other side of the political spectrum and the other side of the country, the Reform Party, founded in Alberta in 1987, was the inheritor of many of the populist ideas of the Progressives as transmitted through the Social Credit Party. Just as the Progressive Party was influenced by the populism of the farmers' movements of the American Midwest in the nineteenth century, so too politics in Alberta and British Columbia in the 1980s was influenced by the right-wing evangelical movement that became an important political actor in the US with the rise of the Moral Majority during the Reagan era (Laycock, 2001). The Reform Party and its successor party, the Canadian Alliance, were strongly opposed to "special interest" politics, especially as represented by progressive groups such as unions or by groups that threatened evangelical values such as the lesbian and gay rights movement. The Reform and Canadian Alliance parties, like their forerunner parties, the Progressives and Social Credit, had a strong extraparliamentary organization, were democratically organized, elected their leaders, and maintained a strong programmatic commitment to principles and platform.

However, mass parties like the NDP and, in a different form, the Reform and Canadian Alliance parties had difficulty in breaking through to a dominant position in the Canadian party system at the federal level. Even as the old cadre parties—Liberals and PCs—adopted some mass party features in response to the modern era of media-based politics, they continued to demonstrate the ongoing viability and, indeed, necessity of brokerage politics in forging majority governments at the federal level. While more polarized politics might exist at the provincial level—in British Columbia with right-left conflict over economic development and Aboriginal issues, and in Quebec over the national question—at the federal level, the mass parties that organized around a programmatic appeal based on principles and substantive policy stances were doomed to marginalization and defeat.

Hence, the evolution of political parties in Canada has deviated substantially from the path sketched out in Duverger's classic study of parties. Although the traditional cadre parties adopted some of the features of the mass party, the dominance of a consociational brokerage style in the Liberal and PC parties prevented the programmatic mass parties from dominating Canadian political life. This development was critically important for the political mobilization of non-territorial interests and identities in Canadian politics. Social movements, especially the farmers' movement of the interwar period, were successful in founding their own political parties and breaking into the system. This success was based in part on the territorial concentration of farmers in the West which, in turn, was based on a specific farming economy. Yet, farmers' parties were ultimately co-opted by the dominant brokerage parties. Further, in the postwar period, farmers' interests and identities were transformed with the transition to large-scale agribusiness and the decline of the rural population.

Other groups were not even as successful as the farmers. The labour movement was not able to establish a mass party; labour's support for the CCF was weak, one of the factors that undermined the chances of the new social democratic party from the start. Although certain types of trade unions and certain forms of labourism were regionally concentrated—for example, the anarcho-syndicalism of workers in the mining and forestry industries in British Columbia or the bread-and-butter Gomperism of the southern Ontario craft unions—the labour movement on the whole provides a prime example of a non-territorial interest in Canadian politics. Unlike other countries where farmer-worker alliances were successful (Esping-Andersen, 1985), the relative fragmentation of the labour movement undermined the chances of a successful alliance with farmers in the establishment of the CCF.

The inability of the mass social movements of the modern era—the labour movement and the farmers' movement—to institutionalize their interests in the party system cemented the hold of the cadre/brokerage model on the Canadian party system. As Brodie and Jenson (1988) argued, the brokerage system is based on the accommodation of national (Quebec-English Canada), linguistic (English-French), and regional (West, Central Canada) interests in the party system. The elite accommodation system, as it was called by sociologist Robert Presthus (1973), mobilizes certain issues into politics and mobilizes other issues off the political agenda. In Canada, national, linguistic, and regional political issues take centre stage. Brodie and Jenson's analysis emphasizes that economic and class issues are marginalized in the brokerage system or converted into territorial, regional, or national grievances. Other non-territorial interests, such as gender and race, are also marginalized (Dobrowolsky, 2000b) in a party system that places a premium on the accommodation and management of regional, national, and linguistic cleavages.

The New Canadian Party System

The 1993 election signaled a crisis for the brokerage party system. In the wake of the failure of the constitutional negotiations and the rejection of the Charlottetown Accord, the system of elite accommodation was widely seen to be in crisis. The populist rejection of the Accord and of the whole system of elite accommodation and executive federalism led to demands for greater citizen participation in the political process. A decision-making process that privileged "eleven white men" (one for each of the provincial and federal governments) in constitutional negotiations was condemned from all sides as excluding women, Aboriginal people, and the mythical ordinary Canadian championed by populists in the newly established Reform party (Russell, 1992). As we will see, this populism has been largely channeled against government in the service of neoliberal and pro-market policies.

In the 1993 election, two sets of regional interests that had formed the core coalition for the PC party broke away and formed new regional parties: the Reform Party (later the Canadian Alliance) and the Bloc Québécois (the Bloc). In a recent survey of the Canadian party system, Carty, Cross, and Young (2000) emphasize the extent to which the Canadian party system has regionalized in the wake of the realigning election of 1993, with Quebec as a contest between the Bloc and the Liberals, the Maritimes as a traditional Liberal-Conservative contest, and Alberta and British Columbia as a contest between Liberals, PCs, and Alliance.

Carty, Cross, and Young see the new parties as more ideological than the older brokerage parties and depict recent elections as ones in which there has been more divergence in party positions, in part as a response to voter demands for specific policy positions. Yet, the breakup of the parties further reinforce the Brodie and Jenson analysis of the party system as essentially based on regional, national, and linguistic divisions. As Carty, Cross, and Young themselves point out, the new parties presented themselves as the representatives of regional and national interests. While the Reform Party clearly embraced neoliberal precepts such as lower taxes and smaller government, it also claimed these ideas reflected the regional economic interests of Western Canada. When the Reform Party recalled the injustice of Trudeau-era policies designed to nationalize the Western Canadian oil industry (e.g., the establishment of Petro Canada), it cast Western Canadian regional interests in the oil industry in terms that reinforced the power of American-based multinationals in the Alberta oil patch.

The downfall of the PC party may be seen as the failure of one of the two main brokerage parties of Canadian politics, but not as the end of the brokerage system itself. The 1993 election simply paved the way for the Liberals to be seen as the dominant and unopposed brokerage party. In fact, the quintessential brokerage party—the Liberals—has proven to be quite well suited for the neoliberal era. Unlike the programmatic mass parties in other countries that converted to third-way policies through a wrenching process of political and ideological adjustment (e.g., the British Labour Party), the Liberal party's empty politics of accommodation was perfectly suited to the new era of market-driven individualism. The very lack of a fixed set of programmatic commitments, principles, and values made it possible for the Liberals to move to the right and to embrace many neoliberal policies put forth by Reform. It remains to be seen whether the newly minted Conservative Party of Canada (a merger of the Canadian Alliance and the PCs) will be able to establish its place as the alternative brokerage party to the Liberals. In part, this will depend on the party's ability to broker between social conservatives and social liberals as well as its ability to reach out to Quebecers. In either case, the breakup of the Mulroney coalition in the post-1993 era accelerated the neoliberal shift within the Liberal party.

The post-1993 party system is also affected by developments that are reshaping party politics across different countries in the neoliberal era. Carty, Cross, and Young's analysis of Canada emphasizes the ways in which the heightened regionalization of the party system—the fact that different campaigns are held in different parts of the country—means that the electorate is increasingly fragmented and that targeted election campaigning using new polling and communication technologies has become the order of the day. As they put it: "The parties are increasingly able to rely on sophisticated new communication strategies to, first, identify and, then, target those voters crucial to their electoral success. With little national political dialogue, and an effective absence of some parties from the campaign in each region, elections have lost their capacity to engender a national political debate" (Carty, Cross, and Young, 2000: 8). These Canadian developments are occurring in the context of a heightened mediatization of politics. As the global media become more concentrated while providing more channels (through cable and the Internet), the production of culture and symbols has become more and more central to the economy. The cost of access to media has risen, forcing parties to find new sources of financing (Castells, 1997). The influence of the media has grown at the expense of traditional party organization on the ground, as campaigns are increasingly planned and run by media consultants and professional pollsters.

What are the effects of this restructuring of the party system for group and social movement politics? The growth of targeted messages and the use of professional marketing techniques makes politics look more like another form of consumption and political parties more like corporations seeking market share by using standard advertising techniques. The fragmentation of political debate means that groups and social movements must also be adept at the use of media and at framing messages as media sound bytes rather than the substantive and in-depth analysis of issues. This disadvantages groups whose views are far from the mainstream and those who wish to question the deeply embedded structure of social, economic, and political power (e.g., capitalism, patriarchy, racialized inequalities). As Keck and Sikkink have argued of transnational advocacy networks, political mobilization is easier when there is an identifiable chain of blame and responsibility and more difficult when advocacy networks try to draw attention to complex structural problems (Keck and Sikkink, 1998).

This resurgence of brokerage politics in the 1990s has resurrected the barriers to the mobilization of non-territorial interests in the political system and reinforced the centrality of regional accommodation. While the establishment of mass parties—the Progressives, the CCF, Social Credit, the NDP, the PQ, the Bloc, and Reform/Canadian Alliance—demonstrate the ways in which social movements based on societal organizations— farmers and workers' organizations, the women's movement, nationalist movements—can form parties, the same history demonstrates that such parties will not win power at the federal level.

However, even if mass parties have tended to lose in Canadian electoral history, this does not mean that they have not had an effect on Canadian politics. On the contrary, establishing a political party and establishing a toehold in the electoral system is an important means by which new ideas may be introduced into the system. In the 1940s, the King Liberals are thought to have moved left in response to the growing electoral clout of the CCF during the war years, while in the early 1990s, the Liberal party in opposition (as well as many governments at the provincial level) were converted to the war on deficits in part by the growth of the Reform Party, with its neoliberal economic platform. The circumstances in which a group or social movement will be successful in founding a political party that will have influence on other parties and in shaping the public perception of policy issues, however, are quite specific. It is not an easy task to convert societal support for a movement or sympathy for its beliefs into electoral support. In recent years, the failure of the Green Party to win any electoral seat, despite the widespread interest in and sympathy for the environmental movement, is an example. To understand the circumstances in which political parties may be vehicles for social movement activism in the contemporary context, we must look beyond the political parties and the party system to the political institutional rules that govern the electoral system in which the parties compete. These rules make it difficult for new parties to break into the system unless they have a regional toehold. Therefore, in addition to the fusion of executive and legislative authority in the political system, we must also examine the rules of the electoral system and how these rules influence the ways in which organized interests and social movements can enter into the system.

Electoral System

Features of the electoral system and voting behaviour, as well as the nature of the political parties themselves, exacerbate legislative-executive fusion and undermine the independent role of the MP as policy-maker. The first-past-the-post electoral system produces parliamentary majorities for the dominant party—recently the Liberals—even when the party fails to win a majority of the popular vote. The system exaggerates the regional strengths of parties by assigning them 100 per cent of the representation in a constituency, even when they may have only won 30 per cent of the vote. If a party is the most popular alternative in a particular region, even if it is not favoured by the majority of voters, it is certain to elect MPs. If a party's support is spread thinly across regions, the party will elect fewer members.

A classic case occurred in the 1993 election, which saw the dismantling of the PC electoral coalition of Brian Mulroney; the entry of one new party, the Bloc; and a surge in support for the recently founded Reform Party. In the 1997 election, the Reform Party received 19.4 per cent of the vote and 19.9 per cent of the seats, while the PC party received 18.8 per cent of the vote and 6.6 per cent of the seats. Recently, a number of commentators have called for the reform of Canada's electoral system and the adoption of a proportional representation (PR) system. According to advocates, a PR system would be more democratic because it would permit minorities' points of view within the electoral system to be heard (Milner, 1999). In a PR system, seats would be allocated in rough proportion to the percentage of the popular vote gained by each party. Minority points of view—Liberal voters in Western Canada or NDP voters in Quebec—would be represented in this system. Small parties such as the Greens would have a reasonable chance of electing MPs to Parliament. Because one party would be unlikely to have a majority, the winning party would have to accommodate diverse points of view by building coalitions with other parties in order to form a government. PR has been suggested at various points in Canadian history; however, conventional wisdom holds that it is unlikely to be adopted because the largest political parties, the very parties that would have to spearhead such a reform, are the beneficiaries of the current system and are unlikely to change it. Despite skepticism regarding the reform of the electoral system, several provinces are exploring new options for electoral rules. Calls for PR highlight the nature of the first-past-the-post system as one that benefits regionally concentrated dominant parties by exaggerating their strengths. The current electoral system, then, reinforces the representation of territorially, rather than sectorally or non-territorially, organized interests and identities in Canadian politics. A reformed electoral system, currently under consideration in British Columbia and other provinces, has the potential to open up the system to non-territorial interests and would likely see a strengthening of parties such as the Greens, whose strengths cut across regions.

Party and Election Financing

One of the most important ways in which groups and organizations try to influence policy outcomes is through supporting political parties, candidates for election, and even candidates for the party leadership within specific parties. Such contributions may be a means to ensuring access to party leaders and, along with this, comes the danger that public policies may be influenced by financial contributions. Corporations have been major donors to Canadian political parties. Lobbying firms may contribute to campaigns in the hope of ensuring access for their clients, which may in turn include corporations and interest groups. NGOs and social movements may give money in the hope of ensuring that their issues are heard during the campaign. Cadre/brokerage parties such as the Liberals and PCs have long been strongly supported by the business community (Stanbury, 1991), while mass parties such as the NDP have been financially supported by trade unions (Archer, 1990). New parties such as the Canadian Alliance and the Bloc have fallen midway between the cadre and mass party models in terms of issues like financing. Individual contributions have played an important role in the Canadian Alliance party, in keeping with the party's emphasis on untrammeled individualism. Interest group and social movement organizations may also contribute to furthering the cause of a party or candidate through third-party spending in election campaigns.

Important controversies have arisen over the financing of political parties. In the 1995 referendum on Quebec sovereignty, sovereignty supporters accused non-Quebecers of spending money in the campaign in violation of Quebec's referendum spending laws. In the 1988 free trade election, millions were spent by coalitions for and against the deal, although much more was spent by the Canadian Alliance for Trade and Job Opportunities, the pro-free trade business coalition. Social movement organizations have sometimes tried to infiltrate parties in order to target MPs or to change party policies on specific issues. For example, evangelicals targeted NDP MP Svend Robinson for defeat because of his stance on abortion; during the 1980s, evangelical activists often took out memberships in the Liberal Party in order to influence party policy on abortion. The National Citizen's Coalition (NCC), a right-wing advocacy group, has consistently called for the right to spend money during elections and has challenged Canada's election spending limits three times before the Supreme Court of Canada, most recently losing out in a close decision (Freeman, 2004). The NCC has argued that limits on third-party spending during election campaigns is a violation of freedom of expression. In its view, groups of citizens should have the right to advocate on any issue during an election campaign and spending on behalf of such advocacy should not be limited. The tricky aspect of the NCC's argument concerns the line between the regulation of spending in support of a specific candidate or party versus regulation of spending in support of a specific political position. On some issues, it might be difficult to see who would benefit from advocacy unless the advocacy group provided a specific report card on government performance and a comparison of parties' positions on the issues. On other issues, though, advocacy would clearly benefit one party or another. For example, advocacy for lower taxes or against the gun registry would clearly benefit the Conservative Party, which has strong positions on these issues, positions that are consistent with those advocated by the NCC when Stephen Harper was its leader. In the most recent challenge to the electoral law, the Supreme Court ruled that limits on third-party advertising during election campaigns were constitutional. The court decided that, although limits on third-party spending violate the free expression provisions of the Charter, these limits are justified under the "reasonable limits" clause of the Charter (section 1). The court argued that "[p]romoting electoral fairness by ensuring the equality of each citizen in elections, preventing the voices of the wealthy from drowning out those of others, and preserving confidence in the electoral system, are pressing and substantial objectives in a liberal democracy" (see *Harper v. Canada*, 2004: 2). Thus, the NCC's argument was decisively rejected by the court.

Death of Parties?

A number of changes in recent years have affected parties in parliamentary systems. Many systems have been characterized by declines in voter turnout, partisan identification, and party membership (Katz, 2001). While some parties have taken measures to give members more power, many remain leader-dominated and influenced by the professional political class. Analysts have offered several new models to describe the emerging types of parties in Canada and elsewhere. For example, the cartel model assumes that parties are increasingly dependent on the state for campaign funds. As the mass party declines, parties must seek new sources of funding, and state funding through election financing laws offers one possibility (see McIvor, 1996). Parties will collude in setting the rules governing party finance in order to restrict the benefits of state funding. However, McIvor points out that some of the features of the cartel model broke down in the Canadian case upon the demise of the old PC party and the founding of the Reform Party and the Bloc. Another model of party organization that attempts to depict parties in the contemporary context is the franchise model (Carty, 2004). Carty characterizes some of the changes in contemporary Canadian political parties using this model, which is drawn from the business world. Carty describes the key features of the franchise as follows:

> Typically, a central organization recognizable by its common brand, determines the product line and sets standards for its production and labeling, designs and manages marketing and advertising strategy, and provides management help and training as well as arranging for the supplies needed by local outlets. For their part, individual franchises exist to deliver

the product to a particular market. To do so they invest local resources, both capital and personnel, in building an organization focused on the needs and resources of the community they serve, and are preoccupied with delivering the product to their target market. (Carty, 2004: 10)

Carty argues that contemporary parties fit this franchise model of organization in that party leaders brand the party and develop the advertising and marketing messages for election campaigns. As he puts it, the party leadership delivers the "basic product line", while the local party organization is the home base for party members and mobilizes supporters during the campaign (Carty, 2004: 11). This tendency of parties to operate like franchises is reinforced when the party leadership overrides local decisions about who will run to impose candidates who are more to the liking of head office.

In response to the picture of the depopulated political party that acts as a more or less empty shell for branding by the professional political class at the centre, some analysts have argued that citizens are deserting political parties for other forms of collective action, such as interest group and social movement organizing. Social movements in particular have attracted attention. As voter turnout has plummeted in Canada, with barely one-quarter of young people 18-24 voting in the 2000 election (Pammett and Leduc, 2003), many young people have mobilized in the environmental movement and the anti-globalization movement, among others. The contrast between the low youth turnout in the 2000 election and the strong youth-fuelled protests against globalization at the Quebec City Summit of the Americas in 2001 was particularly striking. However, the idea that youth have turned to social movement politics in place of participation in conventional political parties has not been demonstrated in empirical research on youth political participation.

Changes in party organization—the strengthening of the leaders combined with the empowerment of individual party members—has served to accelerate the commodification of political parties. Carty's franchise model perfectly captures the idea that, in the neoliberal era, political participation has become a form of political consumerism. As such, increasing numbers of young voters are rejecting the products on offer. As Pammett and Leduc's study of youth voter turnout states, "voting rates will likely continue to decline in Canada." Young non-voters do not grow up to become voters; each generation of Canadians has voted at a lower rate than the previous one, according to Pammett and Leduc's analysis. After exploring a broad range of possible reasons for declining turnout, they conclude that lack of party competition is a major factor in the generational decline in voting (Pammett and Leduc, 2003: 73-74). Placing these results in the context of the broader shift to neoliberalism, it is perhaps not surprising that young people do not vote when they have been raised on a steady diet of political discourse that identifies governments as the problem and markets as the solution. If governments do not provide programs that shield the individual from some of the effects of the market economy and if the responsible citizen is to be the master of his fate, then voting is an act without meaning. Indeed, even Pammett and Leduc are driven to the conclusion that voters perceive the act of voting as "meaningless" (2003: 73).

Conclusions

The deck is stacked against interest group and social movement influence through the legislature in the Canadian political system. The institutional features of the Canadian Westminster system make it highly unlikely that MPs will influence public policy; therefore, lobbying MPs is unlikely to pay off for interest groups and social movements except under exceptional circumstances of internal party division or on the rare occasion of a free vote or through committee debates. The bias against non-territorially based collective political action extends to the party system, where the cadre/brokerage style has placed a premium on regional, national, and linguistic politics at the expense of other interests and identities. Social movements and interest groups have exercised influence through political parties by founding their own parties, in the case of workers and farmers, and, less successfully, by organizing within political parties to secure changes in the party's stance. The business community has long cultivated strong ties to party elites in both of the main brokerage parties.

The trend to neoliberalism has affected the organization of political parties. For-profit political professionals dominate political organizing at the centre. The move toward inner party democracy means that party leaders must manage their message for both the voters and for their own members. The need for complex and skilled political management at the top and the necessity of competing through media campaigns has enhanced the position of the for-profit political class. The commodification of political parties and the electoral process has proceeded apace in the neoliberal era, and this process of commodification has tended to undermine the influence of other groups and movements, unless these are able to buy media access themselves.

While Parliament and parties are not the most fruitful sites for interest group and social movement influence in the Canadian political system, institutionalized relationships of mutual influence between organized interests and the state bureaucracy have often proven to be venues of influence for group and social movement organizations. In the next chapter, we explore the impact of group and social movement influence in the policy community.

FIVE

Arenas of Influence:
Bureaucracy and Policy Communities

As we saw in the last chapter, the fusion of executive and legislative authority in Canada's Westminster-style system means that Parliament and political parties are not necessarily the most effective venue for civil society actors to influence the state. Exploiting election campaigns and seeking influence through political parties may be useful for certain ends, such as drawing public attention to an issue, and these avenues of influence may be successful when an issue is embroiled in a caucus revolt or a free vote in Parliament. However, on a day-to-day basis, the dominance of the governing party in Parliament and the operation of tightly controlled party discipline means that most government initiatives will be passed by Parliament and are largely a "done deal" by the time they arrive in the House of Commons. Many important policy decisions are made without the passage of legislation, through decisions of the cabinet, legally encoded as orders-in-council, or result from "delegated legislation" in which the government has delegated decision-making authority to agencies or departments of government. Short of direct access to the prime minister and the prime minister's office or to top-ranked cabinet ministers with political influence, the best route of access for groups seeking to influence public policy is through the permanent apparatus of the state: the bureaucracy.

Civil servants in line departments and central agencies of the federal government play a critical role in policy development. Group actors, especially those with resources and policy expertise, have long-standing institutionalized relationships with bureaucratic power-holders, called policy communities. The first part of this chapter provides a brief over-view of the institutional practices and norms that govern the political and policy role of the bureaucracy. The second part provides a description of the concept of the policy community and the factors that shape policy communities in action. The subsequent sections of the chapter explore the impact of neoliberalism on the development of policy communities over the last 15 years, exploring the centralization of power, the rise of professional lobbyists, the shift to new public management in the civil service, and the changing policies towards advocacy groups and professional lobbying.

Politics and Administration

The bureaucracy's role in policy choice and policy development is governed by a complex set of formal and informal rules and practices. In the Westminster constitutional system, the government is responsible to Parliament and stands or falls in the House of Commons as one. The principle of collective ministerial responsibility states that members of the government (i.e., cabinet ministers) must not publicly disagree with the government or express policy differences in public because this would lead to confusion over the government's positions and policies. If cabinet ministers express conflicting positions about government policies, it would be difficult for the public or the House of Commons to hold the government accountable for policy choices and their consequences because some members of the government could evade responsibility by claiming to have disagreed with the government's policy direction. Therefore, the idea that the government stands or falls together means that the individual cabinet minister must toe the line in public, whatever his or her private views. Furthermore, as an individual, the cabinet minister is responsible for the conduct of the affairs of her department, must answer to Parliament, and must rectify problems or resign her position. These two constitutional conventions of collective and individual ministerial responsibility govern the relationship between cabinet ministers and civil servants in theory (Sutherland, 1991).

The growth of government in the twentieth century and the transition to large-scale bureaucracy in the state, as elsewhere, entailed the development of a distinction between politics and administration, which, to some extent, conformed to the broad conceptual outlines of ministerial responsibility. The job of the bureaucracy was to develop policy choices and to furnish the technical advice needed to understand these choices and their consequences. The job of the cabinet minister was to exercise the power of choice among the competing policy alternatives. The bureaucrat would then carry out and implement the policy choices made by the politician. The job of the politician was "politics," and the job of the bureaucrat was "administration." In this way, the responsibility of the minister and of the government was preserved. The members of the government were individually and collectively responsible for government policy, and civil servants could not be blamed or held responsible for decisions made by their political masters.

The academic fields of public administration and public policy analysis, which arose at the turn of the twentieth century, reinforced the distinction between "politics" and "administration" by emphasizing the importance of technical methods and rationality in defining public policy problems and devising their solutions. American and British developments were influential in Canadian thinking about public administration as a practice and as an academic field, even though, as we shall see, some of the ideas and preoccupations of American public policy analysis were better suited to public policy-making in the context of American political institutions than to Canada's Westminster-based political system.

The hope for rational and expert solutions to public policy problems was politically expressed in the US during the Progressive Era and in the UK by socialists and social scientists, such as those involved in the influential Fabian Society. In the US during the Progressive Era, there was a strong movement against elite dominance of the political system, and this movement became defined as a movement for "the people" against the "special interests" which dominated in Washington. This long-standing theme in American politics became the battle cry of the Progressive movement, which was closely tied to the rise of academic public administration. The movement emphasized the importance of the application of expert technical knowledge to public policy problems. The job of the public policy expert was to assess the nature of the problem, systematically gather information about it and likely solutions, and then choose the most effective solution to the problem. In an era in which many public policy decisions were shaped by an openly corrupt party-based patronage system for public service appointment (even more so than in Canada during the same era), the Progressives' (and others') emphasis on technical knowledge marked a radical change and provided an ideological justification for the development of a merit-based civil service.

By the postwar period, a number of critics of rational decision-making had pointed out that public policy-making did not always follow a "rational" pattern, even when decisions were left to the experts. A number of influential critiques of the rational decision-making model suggested either that rationality was not followed in practice or that it was a cover for the political interests of the bureaucracy as a self-interested institution. These critiques, along with recent political developments, have brought the traditional distinction between "politics" and "administration" into question.

Organizational theories have suggested that bureaucracies are structurally incapable of following the precepts of rational decision-making. From Charles Lindblom's famous article on incremental decision-making (1995 [1959]) through discussions of the "garbage can" model (March and Olsen, 1989), organizational theory suggests that large-scale bureaucracies do not operate wholly according to norms of rationality. Lindblom argued that rationality was too expensive for bureaucratic decision-makers and that, for this reason, it was rejected in practice in favour of incremental decision-making. Rather than devising large-scale plans for public policy based on comprehensive information gathering and expert assessment, Lindblom argued that bureaucrats made a series of smaller decisions, which he labeled "incrementalism." Incrementalism was based on the cognitive limits of decision-makers, who were unable to process the large amounts of information required in the "rational" model of decision-making. Further, incrementalism was based on the idea that, rather than setting out comprehensive goals, decision-makers often clarified goals through a series of limited decisions.

Similarly, in an early analysis of the model of rational decision-making, Herbert Simon, like Lindblom, argued that bureaucratic decision-makers do not follow the rational model but, instead, engage in the process of what he termed "satisficing," namely, decision-makers will choose the first available option that gets the job done, even if it is not the best option in terms of cost/benefit analysis (Simon, 1989). Not only do decision-makers suffer from cognitive limits, but there is also time and expense involved in collecting information. Lindblom and Simon both base their analyses on the assumption that "time is money," meaning that they factor in the fact that fathering information and conducting the cost/benefit analysis of carious policy options is time-consuming and that, in practice, decision-makers have limited time at their disposal.

Public choice theory views organizations as negotiated bargains between collections of self-maximizing and self-interested individuals. Through such negotiations, bureaucracies seek to empire-build and to extend their own influence, rather than to implement rational or good public policy. In this way, public choice theory sees the individual as acting based on rationality but suggests that the rational self-interest of the individual may not necessarily create public policy choices that are efficient or that are in the best interests of the public or, indeed, of any group beyond the bureaucratic insiders. Therefore, even from within the disciplines of public administration and organizational theory, strong challenges have been posed to the rational model of decision-making and to the separation of politics from the decision-making processes.

Some of the political science theories we canvassed in Chapter 1 also bring the politics/administration divide into question. Pluralists, neopluralists, and historical institutionalists question the separation of politics and administration. Pluralists and neopluralists point to the ways in which group politics shapes public policy and explore the relationship between organized groups and the bureaucracy. Pluralists tend to view the state as the relatively passive object of group struggle and influence, while neopluralists see the bureaucracy as an actor in its own right, one which may develop various types of institutionalized relationships with organized interests. Neopluralists have been at the forefront of the development of the concept of the policy community and the policy network as institutionalized relationships between organized interests and the state bureaucracy. Historical institutionalists also examine state bureaucracies as independent political actors in their own right, exploring the ways in which the state capacity shapes policies as well as the ways in which previous policy legacies and institutional developments influence policy debates and group preferences and demands. Rational choice theory suggests that empire-building by government departments and the struggle for power between central agencies and line departments are examples of politics within the civil service, as institutions seek to defend their own interests, and entrepreneurial bureaucratic leaders extend their spheres of influence (Niskanen, 1994). Taken together, all of these political science theories suggest that seemingly technical choices have political implications. The existing capacity of the state may steer the bureaucracy in certain directions when evaluating policy choices, and the bureaucracy may defend its organizational interests in developing policy advice. The choices presented to politicians by bureaucrats may exclude other policy alternatives that are forced off the agenda before they are brought to the attention of the political decision-makers.

Policy Communities and Policy Networks

In the Canadian literature on group politics, a number of different concepts have been used to write about regularized linkages between the bureaucracy and organized groups. These include policy community, policy network, subgovernment, partnership, consultation, and civil engagement (Pal, 2001). The concepts of partnership, consultation, and civic engagement are regularly used by the government itself to emphasize its commitment to engaging with civil society organizations.

In the scholarly analysis of public policy, the concepts of the policy community and the policy network are the most useful. These originated in the neopluralist approach to understanding the relationship between group actors and the state. While the original pluralists focused on the ways in which groups brought pressure to bear on the state and tended to treat government as the passive object of group struggle, neopluralists emphasize the potentially active role of the state in shaping the policy agenda through its relationship with organized interests. These ideas were first developed in the American literature, which focused on the subgovernment of the public policy system in which "iron triangles" of political influence between legislators, bureaucrats, and interest groups formed an important fulcrum for the formation of public policy (Ripley, 1988). The term was applied in particular to the relationship between influential congressional committees and regulatory agencies, implying that regulatory agencies could be captured by special interests and congressional committees, who would form an alliance or "iron triangle" in favour of higher spending and program expansion, thus making it difficult to stop the passage of legislation in favour of their interests. In principle, this might seem similar to pluralist analysis because it views the state as reflecting the interests of social groups, but, in effect, there are important differences. In the "iron triangle" literature, the regulatory agency is viewed as having interests of its own, critically, an interest in program expansion and higher spending in its own area. Further, the support of the agency, along with the support of key legislators, is seen as critical to the passage of programs favouring interest groups. Each of the three sides of the triangle is defined as having interests of its own, which play into the policy process: the "iron triangle" is an alliance of self-interested political actors. Although this model has been superseded in the American literature, the concept moved the discussion forward by identifying the interests of politicians and bureaucrats as components of the policy process distinct from the agendas of group actors.

The concepts of the policy community and the policy network developed as refinements of the "iron triangle"; they refer to the patterns of regularized relationships between the bureaucracy, legislators, and organized interest groups. The two concepts have been distinguished in a number of ways in the public policy literature. Some use the terms to distinguish the static (community) from the dynamic (network) relationships between the political actors, while others use the term to distinguish "insiders" (network) from "outsiders" (community) (Coleman and Skogstad, 1990). Here, I will follow the distinction between the static and dynamic dimensions, while discussing insiders and outsiders more fully in the following section.

Policy communities describe the network of stakeholders who may be involved in a given policy issue. While American discussions of these terms follow from the "iron triangle" concept by including legislators as the third leg in the set of regularized relationships of influence between bureaucrats and interest groups, in the British, Australian, and Canadian literatures, legislators are not included as policy insiders because of their lack of independence under most political circumstances and the concentration of power in the hands of the prime minister. Hence, the triangle is not relevant in most circumstances to the policy community in Canada; here, the traditional picture of the policy community refers to a dyad relationship between a regulatory agency and the most important interest groups in the sector or between a lead line department and interest groups. Some examples are shown in Table 5.1.

The idea of the policy community posits that public policy is made in this dyad between organized relationships and bureaucrats in each policy area. Paul Pross's (1992) discussion of the policy community in Canada makes it clear that most policies are decided by bureaucrats and interest group actors in defense of what they carve out as common interests in their policy area. These policy decisions are then communicated upward to the political level where they are recommended to the minister and cabinet. Pross argues that much public policy is made in the nexus between groups and the bureaucracy and never reaches the level of controversy within the cabinet or draws the attention of the top-level decision makers in the Privy Council Office (PCO) and Prime Minister's Office (PMO) except as part of larger policy envelopes. In fact, as Pross emphasizes, most policy relationships between organized interest groups and bureaucrats are disrupted

Table 5.1: Policy Community: Simple Dyad

Line Department (Section) or Lead Agency	Organized Interests
Labour	Canadian Labour Congress Canadian Autoworkers, Canadian Union of Public Employees (CUPE), Public Service Alliance of Canada (PSAC)
Health and Welfare Canada	Canadian Medical Association Canadian Public Health Association Canadian Hospital Association
Indian and Northern Affairs	Assembly of First Nations Congress of Aboriginal Peoples Native Women's Association of Canada Métis National Council
Finance	Canadian Council of Chief Executives

Source: Adapted from Pross (1992).

by political interference from above. Open controversies in caucus and cabinet, media coverage of policy issues, or open dissent and protest from groups against government policies are signs that the policy community has broken down. While this might be taken to mean that policy communities are undemocratic, in that they work most effectively when they are shielded from public debate and public view, they are not sinister conspiracies. Public policy is highly specialized, detailed, and complex, especially in certain areas, and policy communities provide a vehicle for managing this complexity, while involving the most knowledgeable and interested sectors of society in the process of policy deliberation (Pross, 1992).

This is the simple picture of the policy community. Additional layers must be added onto the dyad in order to capture the full complexity of contemporary policy communities and networks. This is done by adding complexity to both sides of the dyad and by multiplying the number of actors involved in the policy community as shown in Table 5.2.

In this depiction, the policy community is expanded beyond the lead agency to include the central policy-making agencies of the federal government such as the PCO or Treasury Board. Other governments

Table 5.2: Policy Community: Multiple Actors

Governments	Groups	Attentive Public
Central agencies	Federal/pan-Canadian interest organizations with major stake in policy area	Academics, journalists, think tanks
Lead departments	Interest organizations with secondary stake	
Provincial governments	Provincial or regional interest organizations	
Foreign governments	Urban groups	

Source: Adapted from Pross (1992: 100).

are also included. As we will explore in detail, intergovernmentalism cuts across policy communities and brings provincial actors into federal policy-making. For interest organizations, we can distinguish between pan-Canadian groups and groups that are operating at the provincial, regional, or urban level. Furthermore, Pross adds the concept of the "attentive public," academics and journalists who watch policy areas closely. As Pross puts it, the job of the attentive public is to "maintain a perpetual policy-review process" (1992: 99). As he states, "[It] intercedes into the policy community an element of diversity inhibited at the sub-governmental level by the need to maintain consensus" (1992: 99).

Table 5.3 gives an example of multiple actors in a single policy community, focusing on groups and government, adapted from Pross's example of agriculture. It shows the complexity of governmental and nongovernmental actors in the policy community in an area such as food production. The same could be said of policy communities in other areas.

The number of actors—governmental and non-governmental—at work in the policy community does not tell us much about who influences whom in the policy network. In order to understand the typical patterns of influence in policy communities, typologies of policy networks have been developed (Coleman and Skogstad, 1990; Coleman, 1988). These typologies refer to the number of organizations at work in a specific societal sector, the number of actors on the governmental side of the equation, and

Table 5.3: Policy Community: Farm and Food Policy

Governments	Groups
Privy Council Office, Treasury Board	Canadian Federation of Agriculture
Agriculture Canada	National Farmers' Union
Agriculture Canada Regulatory Agencies	Dairy Farmers of Canada
National and Provincial Market Boards	Commodity Groups
Canadian Wheat Board	Consumers Association of Canada
Canadian Dairy Commission	Wheat pools
Transport Canada	
Provincial Government Departments of Agriculture	
US government	
European Union (EU), other governments	
World Trade Organization (WTO)	

Source: Adapted from Pross (1992).

the relationships of influence between governments and groups. If there are many organizations seeking to represent a specific group in society, such as business or labour, then the policy community is referred to as pluralist; if there is one peak association representing the sector relatively monopolistically, then the sector is said to be organized in a corporatist manner. If the organizations and associations within the sector are relatively centralized in organization, they are defined as corporatist; if they have a decentralized organizational form, they are referred to as pluralist. When interest organizations are centralized, they can speak more credibly on behalf of their members. When they represent all or most of their sector, similarly, they simplify the process of political communication by ensuring that the sector speaks with one voice. When the associational system is highly pluralist, many organizations may compete to represent a particular sector. Even if associations are not directly competing, they complicate the picture for governments by multiplying the number of players in the policy community (Coleman, 1988). With regard to influence, these typologies depict situations in which the government department or agency is captured or successfully pressured by its clientele groups, cases in which the government dominates the groups in the sector, and cases in which the two sides work together in a partnership built on a balance of power between the two sides (Coleman and Skogstad, 1990).

The policy community works best for groups that meet several criteria. They must be relatively well organized and institutionalized, have a regular membership, a secure financial base, and policy expertise in order to inter-act with government. The group's claim to represent a certain constituency is important to the influence it can exercise. Some groups may represent a large number of members and may thus claim to speak for a certain social group. For example, at one time, the National Action Committee on the Status of Women (NAC) had 500 member groups (Vickers, Rankin, and Appelle, 1993). Other organizations, such as the Canadian Council of Chief Executives or the Canadian Bankers' Association, may have a few large and influential members (corporations and banks, respectively). Furthermore, the group must have relatively narrow policy goals that can fit within the ambit of existing government policies. Groups whose goals are too broad or which are at odds with the stated principles and direction of government policy will be unlikely to obtain a foothold in the policy community. To participate in the policy community, groups must have a certain degree of knowledge about government and its workings as well as specialized knowledge about the particular policy area.

The bureaucracy has many reasons for seeking to bring organized groups into the policy process. For government, it may be cheaper to obtain information— about the views of group members or information about policy options and implementation—from groups than to seek it out directly. For example, if government wants to know what farmers think about the implications of the WTO Agreement on Agriculture, one of the fastest and cheapest ways to find out is to ask farmers' groups. Groups also have information about the effects of existing policies and about the feasi-bility of policy alternatives, based on their own experience and expertise (Pross, 1992). Aside from information, the bureaucracy may also be seek-ing the legitimacy that groups can provide for government policies. While the views of opposition parties in Parliament may receive some media play in coverage of the government's policies or legislative initiatives, opposition parties are expected to oppose the government of the day, and the public may discount their views to a certain extent. In contrast, the opinions of groups that do not appear to be associated with the governing party may appear to be more legitimate in the public eye. The annual release of the federal budget is a good example of the ways in which the media seeks out groups to approve or disapprove of the government's course of action. Predictably, budget reaction starts with the views of the opposition parties and then moves on to reaction from business and labour, as well as from farmers, consumers, small business, and anti-poverty groups. In this way, governments gain legitimacy from group support as well as information about the views of group members, about policy effects and policy options, and about the role of groups in policy implementation and enforcement.

Pross's classic depiction of the policy community emphasized that much public policy is actually made in the nexus between formal group organization and the public service. On many routine matters, the pattern of institutionalized interaction between groups and the bureaucracy churns out low-level policies and regulations that are rubber-stamped by higher levels of government and for which, ultimately, elected politicians are responsible. In his work on interest groups in Canadian politics, Pross argued that when groups resort to using the media, this is a sign that the policy community has broken down. For Pross, regularized and institutionalized relationships of influence between groups and the state are part of the policy process; in his view, then, such relationships are a legitimate and useful aspect of public policy-making, rather than an underhanded relationship of illegitimate influence.

The structure of government in part determines the role and organization of policy communities. In Canada, a relatively decentralized federal system means that organized interests must often participate at both levels of government and may themselves develop a decentralized organization with strong regional blocs that may inhibit concerted action. The government may directly encourage the formation of organized interests to represent particular sectors by providing them with core or occasional funding. Government policies may shape the nature of the policy community by providing incentives for alliances among groups or by privileging some types of groups at the expense of others. Because of these differences, policy communities vary greatly across policy areas. Some contain one dominant group that represents most of the interests in the sector. Others are highly pluralist, with a large number of competing groups. In some, the state is able to play the lead role, while in others, the state itself is fragmented, and particular departments and agencies may depend on the groups themselves for information and policy expertise. Intergovernmentalism is one of the most important political-institutional influences on the policy communities and policy networks.

Intergovernmentalism and Organized Interests

Intergovernmentalism or executive federalism refers to the ongoing and institutionalized relationships between the federal government and the provinces, involving negotiation and agreement between political and bureaucratic elites (Smiley, 1976). Over the 1990s, such institutionalized relationships increasingly occurred without the federal government, that is, provincial leaders held meetings to discuss their common problems in areas such as health care funding. In 2003, the premiers established a steering committee and ongoing secretariat for interprovincial meetings, called the Council of the Federation. Intergovernmentalism or interprovincialism commonly entails summits or meetings of government leaders. While such meetings are often important symbolically, they also involve bureaucrats in one government with their colleagues in other governments to discuss the development and administration of policy. Because intergovernmentalism requires the representation of one government to another, it is centred in the executive or leadership of each government, whether federal or provincial. Thus, much of the ongoing process of policy negotiation takes place either through government leaders or through the process of negotiation in the bureaucracy.

Executive federalism developed as a means to permit the construction of the Keynesian welfare state. The federal division of powers had been written for a nineteenth-century agricultural society with a small-scale state, while the transition to an urban industrial economy and the crisis of the Depression years required large-scale state intervention (Simeon and Robinson, 1990). Much of the jurisdiction for modern social policy lay with the provinces, while the federal government had the fiscal resources to fund social programs. This fiscal imbalance between the jurisdiction and responsibilities of the provinces in social policy and their relative lack of fiscal capacity was solved during the construction of the Keynesian welfare state from the 1940s to the 1960s through the development and institutionalization of intergovernmental negotiation and bargaining.

In some cases, constitutional amendments were used to give the federal government some leverage in the policy area. For example, on contributory old age pensions, a constitutional amendment transferred the responsibility and jurisdiction from provincial jurisdiction to joint federal-provincial jurisdiction with provincial paramountcy, allowing the federal government to lead negotiations for the establishment and administration of the Canada Pension Plan. However, in most cases, the provinces were naturally reluctant to surrender their jurisdiction to the federal government. Therefore, the federal government entered into negotiation with the provinces over the transfer of funds to permit the provinces to establish, develop, and maintain social programs in areas such as health care and education.

The intergovernmental system is yet another feature of Canadian political institutions that reinforces territorially based political identities. Richard Simeon's classic work (1972) on executive federalism highlights this important dimension of the intergovernmental system. Simeon focuses his attention on the behaviour of the political and bureaucratic elites in the decision-making process and explores the sources of their power and effectiveness in intergovernmental negotiation. In exploring how executive federalism works and the policy outcomes produced by the system, he highlights the weight of political institutions in shaping the processes through which decisions are made. As such, he argues that intergovernmentalism shapes policy outcomes by foreclosing certain paths of policy choice and by determining the players who will have access to the table.

One of Simeon's most important insights concerns the way in which interest groups, as he calls them, are able to access the decision-making process of executive federalism. Essentially, he provides an alternative to the "multiple crack" hypothesis presented in studies of American federalism and interest group behaviour. The multiple crack hypothesis suggests that groups will have greater access and political influence in federal systems if they can step up to bat at two levels of government, rather than one; that is, if groups fail to exercise influence at one level of government, they may try at another level and even play the two levels of government off against each other in pursuit of their policy goals (Schultz, 1977; Kwavnick, 1975; Bucovetsky 1975). In contrast, Simeon points out that executive federalism privileges government elites in the negotiating process and that groups are simply barred from participation. Therefore, their interests must be represented by governments themselves. In his case studies of executive federalism, Simeon argues that provincial governments did not consistently champion the interests of business, for example, and that the provinces varied greatly in the extent to which they consulted interest groups at all in formulating their positions. Moreover, as he makes clear, interest group points of view could be easily sacrificed by governments in pursuit of other goals (Simeon, 1972). Thus, for him, intergovernmentalism, then, tends to exclude non-territorial interests.

In part because of the elite-driven nature of the process, intergovernmentalism and executive federalism came under attack during the 1990s in the wake of the failed constitutional negotiations surrounding the Meech Lake and Charlottetown Accords. Group and movement experience with the intergovernmental process mirrored the arguments made by Simeon about the ways in which nongovernmental interests were excluded such negotiations. The women's movement and First Nations were vocal critics of the process that led to the negotiation of the Meech Lake Accord, and, in part because of these criticisms, Aboriginal political organizations were invited to the negotiating table for the Charlottetown round. The criticisms of the elite model, which came to be labeled as "eleven white men" negotiating behind closed doors, focused on the exclusion of other identities, interests, and groups from the process. When the Charlottetown Accord was concluded, many other groups, including women's organizations, some Aboriginal groups (such as the Native Women's Association, representing non-status Aboriginal women), and ethnocultural organizations, criticized the Accord and the process by which it was reached.

These themes were taken up in work that specifically explored the evolution of the constitutional debates. The most important of these analyses came from long-time constitutional observer Alan Cairns, who, in a series of writings, analyzed how the process of constitutional negotiation privileged the position of governments, rather than the role of individuals or non-governmental groups in the policy process. Cairns contrasted the logic of the 1982 constitutional amendment, which, especially with the Charter, had reinforced a sense of Canadians as rights-bearing citizens against the logic of intergovernmentalism that consistently gave governmental actors the upper hand in decision-making on constitutional issues (Cairns, 1992).

Hence, intergovernmentalism reinforces the politics of territorially and regionally based identities such as Western alienation and Quebec nationalism. These issues are mobilized into the intergovernmental process while the politics of gender, class, and race are organized out. Nationalisms that are not territorially concentrated or institutionalized through governmental status (such as most Aboriginal nationalisms) are institutionally excluded by intergovernmentalism. Groups and movements that represent other identities and interests and that raise other types of political issues, such as environmental issues, are systematically marginalized through the politics of territory, reinforced by intergovernmentalism. In the intergovernmental system, public policy issues are redefined in terms of federal-provincial wrangling, rather than understood and discussed as issues of corporate power or the public/private divide. In this way, the strong role played by intergovernmentalism *vis-à-vis* non-governmental interests in the Canadian political system has facilitated the transition to neoliberalism and the sapping of the role of politicized mobilization and advocacy in Canadian politics.

Policy Networks in Action

Exploring the evolution of policy issues and the pattern of decision-making over time within a single policy area is a good way to evaluate the structure of policy communities and the influence of policy networks. In this section, I explore climate change policy as a case study of a policy community in action.

Climate change policy is an excellent case study of the current complexities of the policy environment. First, it demonstrates that the concept of the policy community has been developed for the domestic context and that it must be expanded to encapsulate what Robert Putnam (1988) called the "two-level game" of domestic and international policy-making. Canada is part of the international community and a signatory to the Kyoto Accord on climate change. At the international level, the two-level game suggests that the Canadian government might seek to influence other governments and international organizations and/or that it would itself be the object of international pressure and influence (Putnam, 1988). In fact, Canada has followed a policy of seeking to minimize the commitment to climate change in order to reduce the monetary cost of cutting emissions, while, at the same time, it has been pressured by other governments to stick to Kyoto, even after the Accord was abandoned by President George W. Bush in 2001 (VanNijnatten and MacDonald, 2003).

Many governmental and nongovernmental actors have been involved in the evolution of Canadian climate change policy, including environmental organizations and coalitions in both Canada and the US. Business interests have organized across the border around the climate change issue as well.

Transnationality adds another level of complexity into the policy community, which not only operates across the two levels of the domestic and international "game" as Putnam conceives of it, but also spans the divide between domestic and international policy issues and political mobilization, a divide exacerbated by globalization (Putnam, 1988; see also Bernstein, 2003).

Environment Canada and Natural Resources Canada are the main federal departments involved in environmental policy-making; such policies inevitably overlap with other issues and with provincial jurisdiction over natural resources. In order to coordinate policies between federal and provincial levels of government, intergovernmental mechanisms in this area have been built up over the last 30 years. These include the Canadian Council of Ministers of the Environment and, since 1993, the National Air Issues Steering Committee. Because of the overlap between environmental and energy policy-making on the climate change and clean air issues, new forms of intergovernmentalism have developed, such as the Joint Meeting of Ministers of Environment and Energy and the National Climate Change Secretariat (VanNijnatten and MacDonald, 2003).

At the provincial level, business interests play an important role in pressuring governments because of the threat of loss of revenue from the lucrative fossil fuel industries in Western Canada and the threat of higher energy costs for manufacturers in Ontario. The Quebec government has supported Kyoto because of the possibilities for expansion of hydroelectric sales as fossil fuel usage is decreased (VanNijnatten and MacDonald, 2003). At the federal level, business interests have also been well organized through the main organization of Canadian business—the Canadian Council of Chief executives (formerly BCNI), as well as through Canadian Manufacturers and Exporters and the Canadian Chamber of Commerce. As in the free trade campaigns of the 1980s and 1990s, these organizations sought to influence elite and expert opinion by releasing opinion papers and studies on climate change. Then, they moved on to popular venues by buying large-scale advertising on television and newspapers against the Kyoto Accord. As VanNijnatten and MacDonald comment, "[t]he attempt by business to influence national policy was the most vigorous seen since the 1988 Canada-United States free trade debate" (2003: 81).

This policy arena has also been shaped by the diffusion of policy from the European Union (EU). The EU provides hefty incentives for the development of wind and solar technology. Multinationals have been influenced by the need for legitimacy in public opinion, which, through the anti-globalization protests and various anti-corporate campaigns on issues such as child and sweated labour, have demonstrated that corporations, like governments, must pay attention to legitimacy and to public opinion in their dealings. Therefore, some of the big oil companies have undertaken initiatives on renewable energy and have even joined environmental NGOs to from the Clean Air Renewable Energy Coalition. This coalition is made up of corporations including BP and Shell as well as respected environmental groups such as the Pembina Institute, Friends of the Earth, and Pollution Probe. Specifically, it has sought government policies that would provide incentives for renewable energy, such as those provided in the EU (VanNijnatten and MacDonald, 2003).

Thus, the policy community in this area is composed of two line departments and a plethora of groups from both the business community and environmental NGOs (McKenzie, 2002). Each of the sets of group actors is quite complex. On the business side, influence is exercised through umbrella business groups such as the Canadian Council of Chief Executives, through sectoral business groups, and through individual corporations, especially those in the oil industry. On the environmental side, there are a plethora of organized groups, ranging from small activist networks through to larger and better financed NGOs such as the Pembina Institute. Within the federal government itself, in addition to the two line departments there are wide-ranging mechanisms for coordinating climate change policy and for integrating environmental thinking across the policy process. In addition, there are extensive intergovernmental mechanisms for policy negotiation between federal and provincial governments (Juillet, 1998). At the provincial level, the structure of group influence, especially from the business community, is replicated again.

Provincial governments tend to reflect the economic interests of the business community in their region, for example, Quebec in hydro development and Alberta in the oil and gas industry. For both business and environmental groups, there are multiple opportunities for political influence at the provincial and federal levels, although the provincial level is likely to be less open to environmental NGOs because of the privileged position of the business community *vis-à-vis* provincial governments. Both the business community and environmental NGOs operate transnationally, which means that they may act as agents for the diffusion of policy ideas and influence from other contexts and participate in international debates on climate change. While, domestically, intergovernmentalism tends to shut out environmental NGOs and to privilege those with elite access to decision-makers, both the business community and environmental NGOs have staged media events and public relations campaigns to sway public opinion. While business has relied on simply buying media access through marketing and advertising, environmental groups in Canada have a long history of successfully orchestrating direct actions and media events in order to capture public attention (Dale, 1996). Media and public attention are of central importance in the environmental area because, when public attention is focused on environmental issues, governments reap the credit from undertaking new environmental initiatives. As Kathryn Harrison points out, "[w]hen public attention to the environment subsides, however, both orders of government are inclined to avoid blame from regulated industries, and thus to relax their environmental ambitions" (2003: 314).

An Unequal Playing Field

The policy community is not an equal playing field. The theoretical perspectives from the first chapter of this book help us to understand the nature of the inequality in policy communities and policy networks in the Canadian context. Three main factors that structure policy communities are: 1) political, economic, and social inequality; 2) the organizational and ideological requirements for groups and social movement organizations to participate in the policy community; and 3) the impact of the underlying political-institutional structure on the policy community.

With regard to the first, relationships of political influence in policy networks are shaped by the forces of social, economic, and political inequality in Canadian society. In order to participate in the policy network, groups must be well organized and reasonably well resourced. In most cases, interest organizations in the policy community are institutionalized and have stable financing and membership. Groups that participate in the policy network are professionalized; that is, they have full-time and salaried staffs that work at representing the interests of the association to government, and that are able to develop long-term relationships with key policy-makers. Further, the staffs of such professionalized interest organizations develop substantial policy expertise over time and are able to deploy this expertise in policy debates and discussions.

Many sectors of Canadian society that might wish to represent their views to the state through regularized participation in the networks of influence in the policy community are simply excluded from doing so because they lack the organizational and financial resources and the expertise to deal with government bureaucrats. Poor and homeless people in Canadian society, for example, are not organized into professionalized associations that directly represent their interest in equitable housing and social policies to the governments responsible for these policies. Unemployed or underemployed Canadians do not have an association that represents their interest in economic and labour market policies that would bring about full employment. In contrast, a broad range of business associations and taxpayers' groups have kept up sustained pressure on governments and, indirectly, on the public (through media campaigns) to bring down the deficit, cut spending, implement restrictive fiscal and monetary policies, and retrench social programs.

Second, aside from inequalities in participation caused by systemic economic, social, and political inequality, the organizational and ideological culture of certain groups and sectors may be at odds with the organizational and ideological culture of government. Subcultural communities may have strong local groups that are oriented toward service provision to their communities and yet which lack organization at the pan-Canadian level, where participation in the policy community and policy networks takes place in terms of federal policies. Social movements are based on informal activist networks as well as formal social movement organizations (SMOs). In some social movement sectors, there may be a relatively large number of SMOs, some of which may join in formal or informal coalitions. For example, in the environmental sector, it has been estimated that there are hundreds of environmental SMOs in Canada alone (McKenzie, 2002). As we have seen, the environment is the quintessential cross-border issue; some environmental activism is transnational and global in scope. Social movements will typically constitute a pluralist sector in the sense of the Coleman typology, in the sense not only of having a larger number of formal organizations but also of resting on important informal activist networks with the potential to undercut or challenge the position of formal interest organizations. Questions of representation are much more important in social movement organizing than in other forms of interest organization in part because of the participatory and democratic culture of many grass roots movements.

Organizationally, social movement networks and organizations may face substantial challenges in dealing with governments because of their participatory and democratic structure. If a movement is composed of many smaller groups that have come together in a coalition, tensions inevitably arise between the principle of democratic participation and the principle of credible leadership. If leaders of SMOs must consult a large number of groups or members before taking positions or making commitments, then participation in the policy community will be very difficult. States seeks to make society "legible" in James Scott's phrase (Scott, 1998). In doing so, they prefer to have one group, set of groups, or leaders in each area, leaders and groups that are authorized to speak on behalf of the clientele they claim to represent. SMO leaders cannot always provide such credible commitments, simply because such styles of leadership run counter to the democratic and participatory culture of their organizations.

Even when social movement networks produce stable and professional organizations such as Greenpeace or NAC, there may be systematic tensions between the functioning of such organizations and the technocratic culture of the bureaucracy. Networks of social movement activism around issues such as anti-globalization, deep ecology, or radical feminism may be dedicated to thoroughgoing social, economic, and political change. Activists in networks of this type are less likely to find ideological common ground with government bureaucrats who participate in and reinforce the very structures of political and economic power to which these groups are opposed.

These ideological differences between movements and states have been characterized in a number of different ways. For example, Claus Offe, working in the European context, describes differences between movements such as peace and human rights movements as a distinction between divisible and indivisible goals, emphasizing that social movements may have goals that are not easily divisible and, hence, not easily negotiable. Offe implies that it is easier to negotiate over the division of the material pie than over questions of fundamental human rights, peace, or environmental protection (Offe, 1985). In the Canadian context, Neil Nevitte (1996), drawing on post-materialist literature, emphasizes that social movements may have "post-materialist" goals, centred on the growing salience of a political culture based on quality-of-life values over material interests. In these ways, policy communities demand an ideological conformity that excludes certain types of movements and groups.

Just as social movement activists face the dilemma of whether or not to participate in mainstream party politics, so too social movements face the dilemma of co-optation when choosing to participate in policy communities. In the Canadian context, this issue has been most extensively canvassed for the case of the women's movement (Findlay, 1987). The dangers of participation are perceived to be that the women's movement will be co-opted, conservatized, and deradicalized by engagement with the state (McKeen and Porter, 2003). Yet, by not participating, the women's movement might lose opportunities for political and policy influence.

The issue of state funding for certain SMOs compounds this dilemma. As we will see in more detail below, during the 1970s-1990s, the federal Secretary of State program funded groups such as official language minorities, Aboriginal organizations, and women's movement organizations (Pal, 1993). This funding came under attack from the right during the 1980s. By the Chrétien period, the program had been greatly reduced. Funding for women's organizations was cut substantially. Thus, one of the dilemmas of participation is dependence on government funding and the ways in which this may undercut the viability of women's organizing. The fact that NAC went defunct following the cuts in federal funding to the organization seems to validate this fear.

Another debate about participation revolves around the question of the creation of special agencies that institutionalize the interests of social movements as part of the state bureaucracy. On the one hand, the creation of such agencies enables SMOs to obtain institutionalized recognition (Eisenstein, 1996). However, while these forms of recognition may provide some legitimacy for the state, these agencies may not accomplish much in terms of concrete policy outcomes. As such, they may divert SMOs from other types of organizing and other forms of political mobilization (Adamson, Briskin, and McPhail, 1989); as we will see in the chapter on courts, the same arguments are made regarding social movement involvement in litigation. These strategies of participation are thought to divert the movement from more radical strategies and tactics.

In sum, it is more difficult for SMOs to participate in the policy community because of social, economic, and political inequalities in Canadian society, inequalities that structure the establishment of groups and that allocate more resources—financial, organizational, and expertise—to some groups over others. In addition, groups that undertake political mobilization based on broad goals of social change—typically, social movement networks and organizations—face specific barriers to participation in policy networks. These forms of organizing directly clash with the technocratic, hierarchical, and bureaucratic culture of public administration, and this clash produces dilemmas of co-optation and participation that do not arise for interest organizations whose ideological and organizational style matches that of the state bureaucracy.

So far, we have explored the impact of social, economic, and political inequality on the formation and functioning of policy networks as well as the clash of organizational and political cultures between SMOs and governments. A third critically important factor in shaping policy networks is the structure of the political institutions that frame the functioning of policy communities. Recent changes in the functioning of Canadian political institutions have had important effects for the functioning of policy networks. The Canadian model of the policy community and the policy network fundamentally rests on bilateral relationships between the bureaucracy and the organized group. In the US, this bilateral relationship becomes a triangle, as the legislative branch plays a much more active role in the formation of policy than in the Westminster system. The policy community and the policy network in the Canadian context rest on the constitutional convention of ministerial responsibility, both individual ministerial responsibility, in which the individual minister is responsible to the House of Commons for the conduct of his or her department, and the doctrine of collective ministerial responsibility by which the government stands or falls in the legislature as one. This provides the basic institutional substructure of the policy network; in the model, it is assumed that decisions made in the policy network are passed up the chain for approval from cabinet and are codified as regulation, order-in-council, or legislation.

Yet, the traditional model of public administration, based on a purposive separation of politics and administration, is in decline. The constitutional conventions of ministerial responsibility no longer seem to bind political actors, and, as ministerial responsibility is undermined, the traditional policy community also declines. Policy communities and policy networks rest on the assumptions that line departments are an important source of policy advice and policy implementation and that there is a political minister "at the top" whose presence provides a mechanism of democratic accountability. As the role of ministers declines, so too the traditional policy community has been displaced to some extent by the rise of centralized power in the hands of the PMO and the PCO. This shift means that fewer organized groups will be able to influence public policy through the policy community. While the traditional policy communities and policy networks were an unequal playing field, as has been detailed here, at least they provided some means for organized societal interests to influence policy outcomes. In the world of increasingly concentrated political power, the playing field for organized group influence has been narrowed. There is an elective affinity between these shifts and the functional requirements of neoliberal government policy and neoliberal ideology. Neoliberalism valorizes individuals and commodifies political relationships. As political institutional changes shut down the traditional avenues for collective influence, what remains is an elite-driven system in which access to the political leadership is increasingly commodified and in which collective actors and collective identities are delegitimated.

New Public Management and Citizen Engagement

In the neoliberal context of the 1980s and 1990s, a number of countries took a turn toward a new style of public sector organization called "new public management." Its principles were intended to enable state bureaucracies to become leaner and more efficient in the context of cutbacks to government programs, deregulation, and privatization. New public management was based on the values and practices of the private sector, such as profitability and market-based solutions. Kernaghan, Marson, and Borins (2000) distinguish three important aspects of new public management: 1) practices concerned with reducing the role of the state, such as privatization and contracting out; 2) practices concerned with restructuring government itself, such as the idea of making government "post-bureaucratic"; and 3) practices concerned with improving management within the public sector, such as consultation and empowerment (2000: 24). The application of these principles and practices to the functioning of state bureaucracies has important implications for the contemporary evolution of policy communities and for the relationship between organized interests, SMOs, and the state.

Most analyses of the federal public service tend to agree that the new public management has not been applied very thoroughly in the Canadian case. Although the *PS 2000* report on public sector renewal, published in 1990, recommended new public management reforms, these subsequently stalled. Unlike other countries such as Britain, New Zealand, and Australia, the federal bureaucracy has not been fundamentally restructured (Kernaghan, Marson, and Borins, 2000). Saint-Martin's comparative analysis of the role of management consultants and the state demonstrates the differences in the legacies of previous policies, the organization of management consultants, and the institutional access for such consultants to the state. He finds that principles of democratic accountability for tapping these private-sector principles are not well developed in Canada (Saint-Martin, 2000). Neoliberal principles of new public management have had important effects with regard to norms governing the bureaucracy's relationship with civil society actors.

One of the key aspects of new public management is the idea of engaging and consulting citizens. According to the federal government, consultation is "an interactive and iterative process that seriously elicits and considers the ideas of citizens and encourages their involvement in decision-making in the tasks of vision-setting, policy developments, issues resolution and in the design and delivery of government programs" (cited in Kernaghan, Marson, and Borins (2000): 179). Civic engagement refers to a pattern of consultation or the institutionalization of consultative exercises as a way of doing things in a particular policy area. While a consultation could be a one-off exercise (and, indeed, the federal government has held many of these "consultative exercises" across a broad range of policy areas), the idea of citizen engagement in public policy refers to the idea of institutionalized participation in policy-making by individual citizens. In their description of the concept of citizen engagement, Abele *et al.* (1998) emphasize the participation of the individual citizen as the first criteria: "[citizen engagement] involves the participation of citizens as individuals" even though groups and "intermediary organizations" may be involved in the process (Abele *et al.* 1998: 10). The concepts of civic engagement and consultation demonstrate the trend in public administration in Canada away from recognizing collective actors as valid and legitimate representatives of societal interests and identities. In keeping with neoliberal values, the individual is considered to be supreme in the process of citizen engagement, at the expense of collective interests. In this way, the values of neoliberalism become institutionalized as government practices, even in policy areas that may be ostensibly concerned with collective provision, such as social policy and the welfare state, and even when the policy goals and directions do not explicitly aim toward such neoliberal goals as marketization or privatization.

While descriptions of citizen engagement emphasize the iterative nature of the process of consultation, the obligation of each side to provide information and to be accountable for decisions, and the exchange of "deliberation, reflection and learning" (Abele *et al.* 1998: 3), real-world examples of citizen engagement often look suspiciously like pollster-run focus groups whose intention is to feel out public opinion on particular policy issues and to steer public opinion toward the government's preferred outcome. As Savoie puts it, "policy proposals no longer bubble up from line departments. Even when they do, they need to be 'wrapped around' a consultative process of some sort to gain legitimacy" (Savoie, 2003: 129).

Susan Phillips' (2001a) examination of the way in which citizen engagement has worked in the Social Union Framework Agreement (SUFA) between most of the provinces and the federal government demonstrates the limits of the concept. Phillips discerns a shift away from traditional intergovernmentalism, which, as we have seen, tends to systematically marginalize civil society actors, towards what she calls instrumental federalism (Phillips, 2001a: 3). Inspired by the neoliberal philosophy of new public management, instrumental federalism refers to a new form of intergovernmentalism which embodies three principles: 1) "doing what works for Canadians" in the words of the federal government (cited in Phillips, 2001a: 3), meaning that the government should be less concerned with jurisdictional issues and more concerned with the pragmatic delivery of services to citizens; 2) measures to involve citizens in the policy process; and 3) accountability through auditing, outcomes-based reporting, and public transparency (Phillips 2001a).

This form of intergovernmentalism is very different from other concepts of Canadian federalism. It is not concerned with questions of centralization or decentralization or the issue of which level of government has more power. Rather, instrumental federalism is focused on delivering the goods to citizens, reinforcing both the conception of the citizen as a consumer and client of government. The idea that government policies, programs, and spending should pragmatically serve the client in ways that can be audited, controlled, and measured is central to instrumental federalism. The alert citizen—like the alert customer—will ensure efficiency by holding both levels of government accountable. The client/consumer/citizen turns into a mechanism, designed to ensure the accountability of governments with regard to government spending and service delivery.

Health care spending, a perennial battleground in intergovernmental relations, is a classic case for auditing by the active consumer citizen. If the federal government transfers funds to the provinces for health care, the alert client/consumer/citizen, out to protect his or her interests as a taxpayer and client of the medicare system, must be given the tools to audit the government's performance. If provincial governments buy lawn mowers instead of MRI machines with federal funds, the citizen's engagement in the policy process and public scrutiny of spending decisions will eventually punish the government. Provincial government that appear to waste money will be subjected to a public opinion backlash. For the federal government, relying on the mechanism of public opinion is much less confrontational than simply enforcing the conditions of the *Canada Health Act* by trying to withhold transfers to the provinces. Instead of withholding funds—an increasingly ineffective device as the federal share of health care spending declines—the federal government can rely on public accountability to force provincial compliance. Like the savvy consumer who punishes inefficient companies in the marketplace, savvy citizens will keep governments in line.

Hence, citizen engagement can be read as yet another neoliberal governmental practice. Instrumental federalism is based on a fundamentally neoliberal view of society in which citizens are stripped of political identities or social and economic interests and reconceptualized as clients and consumers of government services. In this way, collective action, interest group politics, advocacy, and social movement organizing are delegitimated, and the focus is shifted back to the seemingly neutral ground of the individual citizen. Collective political action is transformed into focus group and watchdog activities in which the individual citizen gives his opinion of how well he has been served by a government service. While instrumental federalism may purport to involve citizens in policy-making, in a telling comment, Phillips writes: "perhaps even more essential than actually fixing policy problems is being seen to do so, in part by involving citizens in the policy process" (Phillips, 2001a: 3).

From Policy Communities to Professional Lobbying

In a series of important books, Donald Savoie has detailed the extent to which, over the last ten years, professional lobbying, pollsters, and media consultants have become more important than ever in the policy process at the expense of the traditional public service (Savoie, 1999; Savoie, 2003; see also Simpson, 2001). As Savoie has documented, a number of features of the contemporary Canadian political environment make it very difficult to maintain either the clear-cut distinction between politics and administration or the traditional constitutional convention of ministerial responsibility. The political responsibility of ministers has become problematic in Westminster systems. The heightened power of the media in scrutinizing certain bureaucratic decisions and behaviour, the increasing assertiveness of legislatures in wishing to directly audit the bureaucracy, and the centralization of political power in the office of the prime minister and his or her advisors have all undercut the collective role of the cabinet. In Canada, these factors are compounded by one-party dominance in the political system, which has led to unparalleled political power in the hands of prime ministers. Challenges to prime ministerial authority have come from the restless backbenches of the Liberal Party and succession struggles in the cabinet. These have led to repeated situations in which, in complete violation of constitutional convention and democratic accountability, one cabinet minister has criticized the policies of another, as a function of jockeying for position among various party factions. This has occurred on issues such as drug pricing, medical marijuana, and same-sex marriage. The long-time presence in the cabinet of the prime minister's main leadership rival also led to a situation in which the press repeatedly questioned his loyalty to government policies. Increasingly, the cabinet itself is becoming a formality, a rubber stamp for prime ministerial power.

Furthermore, there have also been cases in which Parliament has sought to directly question members of the bureaucracy, asking them to be accountable for their own decisions, rather than asking the minister to answer for his or her department. A famous case of this occurred in the Al-Mashat Affair (Sutherland, 1991), when the former Iraqi ambassador to the US was given refugee status in Canada after an unusually short waiting period; a second was the 2004 sponsorship scandal, which saw public servants grilled before parliamentary committees and profiled in the media. The Auditor General (AG) has also put forth the idea that Parliament may expect to hear directly from civil servants and has increasingly taken over the auditing function of Parliament itself. The growth of the audit culture fits in with the precepts of neoliberalism; as the AG excoriates government waste, she contributes to the constitution of the dominant neoliberal ideology in which government is the problem and the private sector is the implicit solution. Her work reinforces the idea that the government is corrupt and thus, by implication, should probably not be trusted with functions such as health care. After all, if the government cannot account for its advertising contracts, how will it account for MRI machines?

The role of government patronage in the political process is also in flux. The offloading of government responsibilities through neoliberal policies of privatization and deregulation has created a large number of new patronage positions in quasi-public boards and agencies. This has vastly increased the scope for the governing political party to reward its friends. The centralization of power in PMO and the primacy of political advisors and consultants has vastly increased the role of political professionals at the top levels of government at the expense of the traditional role of the cabinet. According to Savoie, the decline of the cabinet's role as decision-maker is precipitous; it has become little more than a focus group for the prime minister to float his ideas. Similarly, Savoie's analysis indicates that think tanks have displaced the traditional public service as a source of policy advice. Along with these developments, there has been an explosion of professional lobbying in Ottawa. Professional lobbyists sell consultation, research, and other services. Corporations and well-resourced interest organizations increasingly buy their services when seeking to influence public policy debates and outcomes. Lobbying registration legislation was first put into place in 1989. In response to allegations that it did not go far enough to stem the influence of lobbyists, it was amended again in 1995 and 2001. The legislation requires those who sell professional lobbying services to register with the government through an on-line registration system, which is accessible to the public. However, many feel that this legislation does not go far enough and that politicians and bureaucrats should be forced to disclose the identities of those who contact them seeking to influence policy decisions (Small, 2004). Further, the current law does not entail the regulation of lobbyists. This means that lobbying firms have been able to secure government contracts for themselves while lobbying on behalf of paying clients. The lobbyist code of conduct does not provide for sanctions or meaningful regulation. Although lobbyists are forced to register under the *Lobbyists' Registration Act* and may choose to consult the federal ethics counselor, there is general agreement that these measures have not prevented very close relationships between professional lobbying firms and the top levels of government.

These developments have led to the decline both of constitutional conventions of individual and collective ministerial responsibility and of traditional policy community and policy networks, which are centred on the role of the minister and the line department in the development of policy. Although policy networks and policy communities are still functioning below the radar, Savoie's analysis suggests that the influence of policy-making in the line departments has been displaced by the rise of the professional political class of pollsters, consultants, and lobbyists. Savoie also suggests that the role of the public service, line departments, and the cabinet in policy-making has been fundamentally altered by the institutionalized involvement of interest organizations in the consultative process. Nevertheless, the decline in influence of the public service, line departments, and cabinet due to the reliance on professional lobbyists and consultants has resulted in a lessening of group influence in traditional policy networks and policy communities. Savoie may be right to point to the role of outside groups as increasingly important in policy-making. However, he is referring to groups that are able to access the elite political level of government (PMO and the prime minister), to groups that hire lobbyists, or to "partnership" and consultation exercises designed to legitimate government policy. In sum, the decline of the role of public service in policy-making means less influence for the groups that have participated in traditional policy networks.

In turn, these developments are linked to the shift to neoliberalism. The displacement of the notion of public service and its replacement by a class of professionals who operate for profit and with close ties to political parties demonstrates the commodification of the very process of public policy-making. Increasingly, policies are viewed as commodities that are bought, sold, and packaged for public consumption, thus prioritizing the role of advertising and public relations in the policy-making process. The government's relationship with civil society organizations, then, is less based on mutual influence than on the government's need to package its policies in ways that will be acceptable to the public and that will assure the reelection of the government. In areas such as child care, health care, and Aboriginal issues, the government has packaged policies such as "audits" and "report cards" that are focused on empty accounting policies that convey an impression of action, rather than on substantive policies that deliver programs to Canadians. While governments have always been concerned about reelection, the growing power of the for-profit lobbyists, consultants, and pollsters as a new form of political class that mediates between society and the state has served to commodify the very process of gaining access to political leaders and exercising influence on them. In the past, no matter how close the relationship between an interest organization and a line department in the policy network or policy community, this relationship was not mediated by private sector lobbyists and consultants.

The growth of the professional for-profit political class is also related to other aspects of the neoliberal transition—the relative decline of the authority of the domestic state and the growing power of the media. Manuel Castells (1997) suggests that the latter is central to globalization as the production and manipulation of symbols and images has become a critically important economic activity. At the same time, politics has become a much more expensive business for politicians because of the media influence on politics. The symbolic manipulation of politics is becoming its content. According to Castells, the very high cost of media campaigns attracts corruption in the financing of political parties and elections, a phenomenon that has led to controversies over election financing and political scandals in Europe, Asia, and North America. The impact of the manipulation of images is crucial to neoliberal policies and practices.

From Advocacy to Charity

Federal government policies toward advocacy groups have also changed substantially over the course of the 1990s. These changes signify a shift from politics that recognized the importance of advocacy, especially advocacy on behalf of disadvantaged groups, towards a policy that conceptualizes nongovernmental actors as "voluntary sector" organizations or charities, that is, as organizations that deliver services to citizens and provide an arena for volunteer work (Jenson and Phillips, 1996). From the 1970s to the early 1990s, federal policy-makers recognized that group and movement organizing was an unequal playing field and levelled it by providing funding to some groups. In contrast, the policies of the 1990s have been shaped by neoliberal values that emphasize the role of voluntary sector organizations or charities in taking up the delivery of services that were once the job of government and assisting such organizations in developing the capacity to do so.

The government's early policies on funding civil society organizations stemmed from the state-building imperatives of an ethnically and linguistically diverse settler society. The federal state had long undertaken programs to build a sense of national identity and citizenship and to ensure the integration of immigrants into Canadian society (Pal, 1993).

These efforts accelerated with the shift to formal Canadian citizenship, with the *Citizenship Act* of 1946. During this early period, the government was primarily interested in state-building, social stability, and the racialized assimilation of immigrants into the dominant English-Canadian culture. These programs, which were quite marginal during most of the postwar period, gained new importance in the early 1970s, as the Liberal government of Pierre Trudeau developed policies to defuse the rise of Quebec nationalism. Citizenship policies were concentrated in the Secretary of State and were designed to provide funding to develop stable organizations for groups in Canadian society that were deemed to lack resources. One of the most important areas was that of official language minorities, especially, francophones outside Quebec. This reflects the Trudeau government's policies toward bilingualism and multiculturalism, flowing from the Royal Commission on the issue. Following the passage of the *Official Languages Act* and, eventually, the constitutional entrenchment of minority language education rights, the Trudeau government found it necessary for francophones outside Quebec to have the organizational resources to defend their interests and to ensure the enforcement of these new policies (Pal, 1993). Hence, the Secretary of State began funding official language minority groups. Eventually, the program was expanded to include Aboriginal organizations, women's organizations, and ethnocultural groups.

Over the decade of the 1980s, these policies came under attack from the growing neoconservative movement within the governing Progressive Conservative government and, after 1987, from the Reform Party. Right-wing populists attacked the federal government for "funding its enemies." Anti-feminist groups such as REAL (Realistic, Equal, Active, for Life) Women of Canada questioned the funding of feminist women's organizations (Dubinsky, 1985). Critics of multiculturalism argued that the Secretary of State funding programs subsidized tokenism and folklore (Bissoondath 2002). Populist attacks on "special interests" took on a right-wing bias during this period; as we have seen in previous chapters, Western populism during the first part of the twentieth century often targeted special interests such as business elites. In the 1980s, special interests were depicted as obtaining special privileges from the state or as representing all-powerful forces, despite the fact that most of the groups named were minorities (Aboriginal people, ethnic minorities, gays and lesbians) and/or historically marginalized (women) (Harrison, 1995). While the Secretary of State programs had recognized the need to level the playing field of civil society organization, albeit in the service of the federal government's definition of citizenship, these groups were redefined as "special" or "privileged" because of their government funding in the populist logic of the new right during the 1980s and 1990s.

These attacks on government funding of interest organizations through the Secretary of State program formed part of a larger discursive shift during this period that systematically attacked any form of collective identity or interests beyond those of the business community, which, as always, were identified as the interests of all Canadians. Increasingly, public discourse and policy discussions no longer recognized groups in any positive way, but only included the individual, the family, and the community. The idea that Canadians might freely associate in organizations in recognition of their diverse identities or interests was discredited.

When the Liberals were elected in 1993, they faced a new neoliberal landscape in which some of their usual civil society allies had been discredited. Seeking to distance themselves from the hard-right, pro-market forces in the Reform (later Canadian Alliance) Party and from experiments such as the "common sense revolution" of Ontario's PC government led by Mike Harris, the Liberals turned to the idea of the knowledge economy to provide the discursive and ideological means of appearing to counterbalance market forces. The Liberal governments of Jean Chrétien were reluctant to challenge business power and, indeed, quickly accepted NAFTA, embraced hemispheric free trade, and undertook restrictive fiscal and monetary policies that looked little different from the previous PC governments. However, the Liberal embrace of the newly popular doctrine of social capital gave the government a way to differentiate itself from the Reform Party and to depict the hard-right neoconservative movement as "extreme." The Liberals took up the idea of "social capital," that is, the importance of informal networks of social trust, communication, community, and collective action. Yet, the "social" was defined in terms that left the commodified individualism of neoliberalism undisturbed (Brodie, 1997).

The Liberal government's emphasis on the knowledge economy and social capital as a policy template entailed a new set of federal government policies on advocacy organizations. Clearly, its direct funding of organizations such as the NAC could not continue in the new environment. As Susan Phillips (2001b) has pointed out, until 1997 the Chrétien Liberal government followed in the footsteps of the previous Mulroney PC government in cutting back on state support for advocacy organizations and in discursively undercutting the legitimacy of nonprofit organizations in the policy process. However, the new economic and social analyses of the knowledge economy suggested that strong and well-educated communities would build the social trust that was essential to intellectual creativity and economic growth in the emerging post-industrial era. Social organizations and associations were an important component of social capital. SMOs, interest groups, and advocacy organizations were now understood to be part of the "voluntary sector." Principally, the term voluntary sector refers to nonprofit or charitable organizations, a much more politically neutral concept than "social movement organization," "advocacy organization," or "interest group". The voluntary sector policies depoliticize collective action by redefining it as charity rather than as advocacy. Thus, this shift reinforced neoliberal policies and practices by discursively recasting civil society as a terrain of competitiveness for the knowledge economy and as a site for the development of social capital. Collective actors were called charities, rather than advocacy groups. Citizens were defined as volunteers, rather than as activists or political participants.

These tendencies can be seen at work in the Liberal government's new policies toward civil society organizations, assembled under the rubric of the Voluntary Sector Initiative (VSI), founded after its reelection in 1997 (Brock, 2002). According to Phillips (2001b), policy-makers realized that the federal government increasingly needed voluntary sector partners to deliver services and programs. At the same time, the government treated voluntary sector partnerships as a means to strengthen citizen engagement and rebuild social trust in an era of political alienation (Phillips, 2001b). Moreover, the sector itself had reorganized during the late 1990s, through the Voluntary Sector Roundtable (VSR), an informal network of voluntary sector leaders, who lobbied the federal government for recognition. The VSI was a framework policy that reasserted the importance of the voluntary sector and committed the government to building a new relationship with it, spanning a range of policies such as building policy capacity, devising new regulations for charitable activities, and establishing partnerships between the voluntary sector and the government. The various aspects of these new policies were to be designed with the active participation of the sector through a series of "joint tables" or consultations between government and sector organizations (Phillips, 2001b).

VSI policies continue both to define the role of civil society organizations as partners in neoliberal downloading and offloading of service delivery and to recast political participation and political activism as depoliticized volunteer work. The government has established "best practices" for funding and governance of voluntary sector organizations; essentially, these reflect neoliberal values on auditing and transparency. Clearly, "best practices" privilege well-resourced and well-organized groups at the expense of smaller grass roots organizations. Furthermore, the federal government has also established policies to develop the "policy capacity" of voluntary sector organizations, suggesting that ensuring their participation in the policy-making process is a matter of developing the technical capacity to discuss "policy." Again, this technocratic language devalues conflict and contestation and suggests that disagreements can be hammered out through a technical process of policy discussion. Finally, the federal government has ensured that "charities" will be prevented from participating in advocacy and politics, even as they are asked to deliver more of what were once government services. Despite the politicization of the tax laws governing charitable organizations and recommendations that the law should be revised to permit political activity by registered charities, tax laws have remained among the most restrictive compared to the regulation of political activities by charities in the US or the UK (Drache, 1998).

Conclusion

The changes outlined in this chapter indicate that relationships between organized interests, SMOs, and the state have been fundamentally restructured in the neoliberal era. Most of the changes described here have been well documented and, in some cases, such as the Al-Mashat Affair or the sponsorship scandal, were the subject of fierce public debate. Debates on the decline of social and political trust are a reflection of the very tenets of neoliberalism. Neoliberal philosophy is based on a mistrust of the state, a valorization of the individual, and a suspicion of groups. The changes outlined in this chapter, when read together, demonstrate the ways in which the bureaucracy and policy communities have been reshaped to fit the dominant neoliberal template. In the next chapter, we will explore the relationship between group and movement organizing and another set of Canada's centrally important political institutions: the courts.

SIX

Arenas of Influence: Courts

Over the course of the 1970s and 1980s, the courts have become an increasingly important venue in Canadian politics for interest group and social movement activity. In the years since the enactment of the Charter of Rights and Freedoms (the Charter), we have seen a wholesale change in the extent to which groups use the courts. As a model of collective action, the recourse to litigation suggests an organizational and mobilizing structure that favours the legal expert, the formally organized and well-resourced group, and the individual litigant in whose name the case is taken forward. As we will see below, certain types of groups tend to use litigation as one weapon in their arsenal, while others concentrate on litigation at the expense of other strategies. There are also marked differences in the extent to which groups are successful before the courts.

In the first section of this chapter, I will discuss the ways in which groups used the courts before the Charter as well as some of the debates that have arisen over judicial activism. I will then go on to discuss the extent to which the Charter expanded the range of political opportunity available to collective actors and the ways in which groups have used the courts to achieve their political goals. As scholars such as Ran Hirschl (2004) have suggested, empowering the judiciary within the political system is a process that reflects the interests of both political elites, who seek to insulate certain questions from the political process, and judicial elites, who seek to enhance the legitimacy of courts as political institutions. Hirschl also points out that empowering courts strengthens business elites, who "view the constitutionalization of rights, especially property, mobility and occupational rights, as means of placing boundaries on government action and promoting a free-market, business-friendly agenda" (Hirschl, 2004: 12). As scholars of critical legal studies have long recognized, the legal system is built on procedures and rules that privilege the individual and undermine considerations of structural social, economic, and political power (Glasbeek, 1989). Despite the fact that many groups have tried to leverage the courts for symbolic recognition or public policy advantage, engagement with law is a problematic and ambiguous project for disadvantaged groups.

The power of law may be deployed by the state to police and regulate dissent. Such efforts have a long history in Canada. To the repression of the North West Rebellion, the break-up of the Winnipeg General Strike, and the detention of Japanese Canadians during World War II, police powers have been used to regulate dissent and enforce the dominant definition of security (see Sheldrick, 2004).

The Changing Structure of Legal Opportunity

Legal opportunity may be provided by the written and unwritten constitution, by the expressed attitudes of judges toward "cause lawyering," or by rules on standing to bring cases or third-party intervention. Prior to the 1982 Constitution, legal opportunities were limited for interest groups and social movements. Legal opportunity has been transformed in the Charter era, not only by changes in the written constitution itself, but also by the seemingly changed attitudes of Canadian judges toward their role and the changes in the rules that have facilitated access to courts for collective actors. Further, the Charter itself is only one aspect—albeit an important one—of the changes wrought to the structure of legal opportunity by the 1982 Constitution. Section 35 of *Constitution Act 1982*, a section that is outside of the Charter itself but part of the constitutional amendment, provides a relatively expansive recognition of Aboriginal rights, which some scholars have used to claim that Canada has entered a postcolonial era (Henderson, 1994).

The limitations of legal opportunity for group actors prior to the Charter were located first and foremost in the Canadian constitution. Unlike the US with its entrenched Bill of Rights, the Canadian constitution did not contain a bill of rights as a separate statement of justifiable and enforceable citizen rights against the state. It did include rights guarantees of a certain type, however. Aside from the implicit protections of a democratic political system "similar in principle to that of the United Kingdom," section 93 of the *British North America (BNA) Act* (1867) stipulated protections for Catholic separate schools in Ontario, Protestant and Catholic schools in Quebec, and a general right of appeal to the federal government for any Protestant or Catholic minorities whose education rights were infringed by a provincial government. Section 133 provided for the use of English or French in the legislatures of Canada and Quebec as well as in federal and Quebec courts. Other constitutional legislation also provided protections for religious and linguistic rights, notably the legislation which admitted Manitoba to Confederation. The *Manitoba Act* provided for the use of English and French in the government of Manitoba, including court proceedings, and provided for public funding of Catholic schools. In addition, the federal division of powers in the *BNA Act* often provided grounds for group litigation. Groups could roll back or alter objectionable legislation by arguing that it was beyond the jurisdiction of whichever level of government had passed it. These constitutional opportunities provided legal openings for collective actors to use the courts.

With regard to the attitudes of courts and the rules governing group access to them, there is no doubt that they were more restrictive in the pre-Charter period. The Charter itself did not change the rules on standing; these were changed by the Supreme Court of Canada in the early Charter era. Prior to the Charter, standing to bring a case was determined by the nature of the dispute, and only the parties to the dispute had standing to bring the case. This restricted access to the courts to cases in which there was a concrete dispute at issue. In contrast, in the post-Charter era, standing has been broadened to permit citizens with an interest in a constitutional issue to bring a case. The best example of expanded standing is the case of Joe Borowski, who challenged Canada's abortion laws under the Charter in 1989. Borowski was not a party to any dispute concerning abortion. Clearly, he was not going to have an abortion himself. He was not a prospective father. Rather, he was an evangelical Christian who believed that life began at conception and wished to establish a constitutional right to life for the fetus.

Similarly, third-party intervention has grown substantially in the wake of the Charter. Third-party intervention occurs when an outside individual or group (usually a group) makes a presentation to the court about the legal and constitutional issues of the case. The presentation is justified by the fact that the information provided may be useful to the court much in the same way that an expert witness supposedly provides factual background for legal decision-making. It may also be justified because the "third party" or "outside" intervener is deemed to have a stake in the case. For example, in the Borowski case, a number of stakeholders in the abortion issue claimed an interest in speaking to the court on the constitutionality of Canada's abortion laws. These included pro-choice feminist organizations as well as a broad range of religious groups. The result was a relatively thorough airing before the court of the constitutional issues surrounding abortion. In contrast, in the pre-Charter era, this type of third-party intervention was not permitted as often. Even if third-party intervention had been permitted or encouraged, few groups or individuals would have had the resources to appear before the Judicial Committee of the Privy Council (JCPC) in London, Canada's highest court of appeal until 1949.

The attitudes of judges is another important variable in providing access to courts for group actors. In the post-Charter era, judges, especially on the Supreme Court, seem to be relatively favourable to the idea that representatives of social interests should have the opportunity to speak to the court. This has been confirmed by empirical studies of judicial decision-making, which surveyed judges on this and other questions (Greene *et al.*, 1998).

Another aspect of legal opportunity is state funding for litigation. The costs of litigation create a tremendous burden for disadvantaged social groups and decrease the possibility that they will be able to access the courts, whatever their legal rights on paper or the favourable attitude of judges toward their cause. Government funding of litigation costs for disadvantaged groups increases the probability that they will be able to vigorously pursue the defense and expansion of their constitutional rights through the courts. In the Keynesian era, litigation funding was provided as part of the Trudeau government's support for official language minority groups in order to build political support for the bilingualism policy after the passage of the *Official Languages Act* in 1969. The Act provided, among other things, for education rights where numbers warranted. Such rights would have been meaningless unless there were official language minority group organizations that were ready and able to defend their rights before the courts. The government deliberately strengthened these groups through litigation funding. Eventually, under the Court Challenges Program, this funding was expanded to include other groups as well.

Within the less promising structure of legal opportunity for group activity prior to the Charter, collective actors nonetheless used the courts to achieve policy goals and symbolic victories. However, before the Charter, Canadians tended to think of themselves as a less litigious society than the US. The recourse to a constitutional bill of rights and the political strategy of using the courts to push public policy issues seemed a quintessentially American phenomenon. The study of Canadian courts was a relatively neglected corner of political science, as Peter Russell noted in his 1983 review of the literature on the eve of the great change brought about by the Charter (Russell, 1983). Of the pre-Charter era, Gregory Hein has noted, "few organizations entered the courtroom to affect public policy" (Hein, 2000: 8). Yet, even before the Charter, there had been some important cases in which collective actors—including business, francophones outside of Quebec, Aboriginal people, women, and racialized minorities—had sought to use courts to achieve social and political change. The fact that this litigation was undertaken demonstrates that the idea of defending group interests before the courts was not something that was created by the enactment of the Charter; instead, it is rooted in Canadian history. Because of the lack of an entrenched bill of rights, such arguments were often couched in other constitutional terms such as federalism.

Litigation in Action Pre-Charter: Manitoba Francophones

Francophones outside Quebec were among the first to pursue litigation in defense of language rights in education and government. Specifically, they petitioned for Catholic separate schools in which French was the language of instruction, as well as the right to use French in legislatures and courts. In 1890, the government of Manitoba passed legislation that cut off funding to Catholic schools and denied the use of French in Manitoba's courts and legislature. Francophones—a majority in Manitoba in 1870 but a minority by 1890—pursued various means to put pressure on the provincial government to change its policies on language rights. An appeal was made to the federal government to disallow the Manitoba legislation, but the federal government declined to do so. Several legal challenges were mounted, one of which ended up in the JCPC. These strategies were not successful. Franco-Manitoban leaders returned to the politicians, petitioning the federal cabinet on the schools' question. The federal government referred the question to the Supreme Court, hoping for a ruling that would remove the federal duty to remedy the appeal. The Supreme Court let the federal government off the hook, but, again, appeal to the JCPC by the francophone leaders found that the federal Parliament clearly had a remedial responsibility. The cabinet itself heard the issue and decided to ask the Manitoba government to reconsider its position. Two requests from the federal government to Manitoba were turned down. The federal government then introduced the contested remedial legislation that would restore public funding to Catholic schools. However, the 1896 election intervened. The Laurier government famously compromised with the Manitoba government. Manitoba agreed to permit limited religious instruction in the schools and education in "other" languages where numbers warranted. The net result of this compromise was the end of French schools in Manitoba for a century.

As Kent Roach (1993) has argued, this incident demonstrates important points about the use of litigation as a political strategy by interest organizations. First, Manitoba francophones appealed to politicians and to courts in their struggle to reverse the decision of the Manitoba government. That is, their strategies were not limited to litigation. Rather, litigation was undertaken after appeals to both levels of government had failed. As a minority in Manitoba, francophones were not able to influence the Manitoba government, given the political dynamics of the period. So, they appealed to the federal government, demonstrating the "multiple crack" available to groups in federal systems. If groups are not able to influence one level of government, they may appeal to another, assuming that both levels of government are willing and able to exercise jurisdiction over the public policy issue at hand (Thorburn, 1985).

The case of language rights shows the difference between formal constitutional jurisdiction and the political will to exercise jurisdiction. Clearly, the *BNA Act* contained a remedial clause on the rights of separate schools, and this clause obviously applied to the case of Manitoba Catholic schools. Further, the federal government possessed the power to disallow provincial legislation, a power that, as Garth Stevenson (1993) has argued, was explicitly designed to permit the federal government to strike down provincial laws that were *ultra vires* provincial authority. Stevenson makes a convincing case that the power of disallowance was intended to enforce the federal division of powers because of doubts about the political efficacy and wisdom of placing this power in the hands of courts. Despite the fact that disallowance was repeatedly used in the nineteenth century, the federal government refused to use it on the Manitoba schools legislation. Therefore, contrary to the view that it was the Charter that created the legal opportunity for litigation, the case of the Manitoba francophones shows that there was plenty of opportunity for certain groups prior to the Charter.

Further, both the courts and the federal government attempted to evade political responsibility for the rights of Manitoba francophones by passing the hot potato of minority rights back and forth between them, each attempting to shift the burden of blame onto the other. Courts in this case were as sensitive as governments to the political dynamics of English-French and Catholic-Protestant relations that made the case of Manitoba's minority particularly sticky. The case of language rights in Manitoba struck at the heart of the Canadian enterprise as an English-French partnership and as a colonial enterprise against Aboriginal peoples of the West. At the time of the political debates over Manitoba language rights from 1890-1900, the hanging in 1885 of Louis Riel, leader of the rebellion against Euro-Canadian colonialism in the West, was an event of the recent political past. The conflict between Protestant and Catholic, anglophone and francophone, that had been stirred by the events in the Red River colony greatly increased the political costs for the federal government and the courts themselves in remedying the clear constitutional injustice done to Manitoba francophones. Thus, this case provides an example of the fact that courts may be sensitive to public opinion in the protection of minority rights and, therefore, may overlook constitutional protections in the pursuit of a course of action that will protect their own legitimacy. Manitoba francophones received negative decisions from the Supreme Court and mixed results from the JCPC (one positive, one negative). From the federal government, they received one positive piece of legislation, which was allowed to die on the order paper when the 1896 election was called, and one compromise from Laurier. Even when the legal and political opportunities are plentiful and constitutional protections are strong and clearly stated in the written constitution, litigation may fail to protect minorities, if majority opinion is strongly opposed. Courts, like other political institutions, are not immune from considering their own organizational interests and their own political legitimacy (Dahl, 1957).

Another important dimension of this litigation is the extent to which the Manitoba Schools Question sparked the creation and reinforcement of political identity among Manitoba francophones, as well as among francophones in other areas of Canada. The suppression of French language rights in Manitoba schools was bitterly recalled by the francophone minority across Canada long after Laurier's famous compromise. Similar events in other provinces, notably Ontario, helped to solidify the political identity of the francophone minority. These events became part of the history of the group, a basis for the symbolic construction of minority identity, and helped to constitute the francophone minority as a political actor in Canadian politics. Further, events such as the Manitoba Schools Question sparked outrage in Quebec and demonstrated the gulf between anglophone and francophone understandings of justice and fairness. The court rulings were recalled by all sides during the 1970s, when a new generation undertook the same struggle for public education in French in anglophone provinces. A new round of litigation from the 1970s to the 1990s continued to meet recalcitrance from the Manitoba government and resulted in it being placed under court-mandated supervision with regard to French language rights. René Lévesque recalled the situation of franco-Manitobans during the debates over the passage of Quebec's Bill 101, legislation which made French the official language of Quebec. Lévesque stated that education rights for English-Canadians educated in other Canadian provinces would be recognized by the government of Quebec when the other provinces recognized the rights of their francophone minorities. He offered a reciprocal recognition of language rights between Quebec and the other provinces. Claims for minority rights protections through the courts, then, helped to transform latent minority groups into collective actors.

Litigation in Action Pre-Charter: Women's Rights and the Persons Case

Another domain in which litigation was used to achieve the goals of a social group was the Persons Case, which concerned the eligibility of women to appointment in the Senate. The case was so named because of the fact that it concerned the definition of the word "person" in section 24 of the *BNA Act*, which governed Senate appointments. The case originated in Alberta, which had been one of the first provinces to enfranchise women in 1916. That year, the government of Alberta appointed Emily Murphy as a police magistrate in Edmonton. Murphy was aware of the limitations of section 24 and began to organize to ensure that women could sit in the Senate. The Women's Institutes of Canada and the National Council of Women, part of the network of women's suffrage organizations described in Chapter 2, became the venue for a petition from women from eight provinces who requested that the prime minister appoint a woman to the Senate (Cleverdon, 1975). Women's organizations in Central Canada rallied behind the idea of giving the Senate appointment to Judge Murphy. Although a vacancy arose for Alberta during the 1920s, the governments of the period (both Conservative and Liberal) did not want to tackle the question. They suggested various ideas such as amending the *BNA Act* or undertaking a constitutional reference on the issue, but, in practice, none of them took up the question.

The manner in which the issue was finally forced onto the agenda demonstrates once again that the structure of legal opportunity is quite malleable when faced with a determined challenger. An obscure section of the *Supreme Court Act* permitted any five citizens to ask the cabinet to seek a ruling from the Supreme Court on any question of interpretation of the *BNA Act*. It provided that the government could also choose to pay the costs associated with the question, which the Justice Department under the King government agreed to do. In his typical meandering style of leadership, McKenzie King did not take up the issue on his own initiative, but when Judge Murphy and four others petitioned the court, the government decided to defray their costs (Cleverdon, 1975).

The other women who petitioned in the Persons Case with Judge Murphy all had political experience, either as legislators or in the women's suffrage movement. They included the well-known Nellie McClung, first elected to the Alberta legislature in 1921. The government of Alberta, Judge Murphy's home province, was the only one to support the five women, while the federal government and the Quebec provincial government lined up against them in the Supreme Court reference.

Although the King government had stated its willingness to amend the *BNA Act* to include women as legal persons under section 24, the Quebec government opposed any such amendment, thus presenting a serious obstacle for the federal government. When the Supreme Court ruled against the "five" and when it became clear that the federal government would not amend the *BNA Act*, the "five" appealed to the JCPC. Ironically, by this time, under pressure from the nascent Quebec labour and women's movements, the Liberal Quebec government of Taschereau had been induced to drop its opposition to the court case (although supporting a constitutional amendment would likely have been politically difficult). The case went forward, and, in 1929, the JCPC ruled that women were entitled to sit in the Senate (Cleverdon, 1975). Although this seemed to be a major victory for the early feminist movement, the Persons Case, however, marked the end of the first cycle of protest for women's equality. Women remained underrepresented in Canadian legislatures, and another cycle of social movement protest in women's organizing would not occur for another 30 years. The Persons Case reflected the interests of elite, white, anglophone women who were able to access courts during this period. Nonetheless, it was a potent symbol of the struggle for women's political equality in Canada during the second wave of feminism in the 1960s and beyond.

Litigation in Action Pre-Charter: Business in the JCPC

Another important example of the use of litigation by organized groups prior to World War II was the use of the courts to defend the interests of the business community against state intervention during the Depression. A series of cases were brought to the JCPC that contested the federal government's capacity and competence to deal with the Depression as an economic emergency and to pass legislation along the lines of the American New Deal, such as those proposed by the Conservative government of R.B. Bennett in 1935. As J.R. Mallory wrote in his classic *Social Credit and the Federal Power in Canada* (1954), business interests pressured provincial governments to bring cases contesting federal jurisdiction in areas such as social welfare, unemployment insurance, and agricultural marketing boards with the purpose of forestalling state intervention in the economy.

There are several important points to note about such business intervention. First, during this period neither corporations nor business interest organizations undertook much constitutional litigation on their own. This pattern forms a contrast to the post-Charter period in which individual corporations have often used the courts to advance their public policy goals, as will be discussed in detail below. In the early history of Canada, business power was exercised through the interaction of business/government elites and through the structural power of business over provincial governments. In Alberta, for example, the agricultural economy of the pre-World War II period meant that the government was understandably sensitive to agricultural interests, while in Ontario and Quebec, provincial governments championed the interests of manufacturers and primary resource industries (Thorburn, 1985). Rather than undertaking litigation directly, business often worked through provincial governments, using the argument that interventionist policies were a violation of provincial jurisdictions. These arguments were also made in the US during the same period in the form of a constitutional defense of states' rights against Roosevelt's New Deal policies.

Second, during the prewar period, business benefited from the use of the litigation strategy because the courts were strongly sympathetic to the point of view of business on the question of state intervention. A number of reasons have been cited for this pro-business attitude. The judiciary was strongly dominated by upper-class white men who, by education, socialization, and training, were unlikely to support policies that cut against the interests of the business community (Mallory, 1954). Further, the political atmosphere of the 1930s was rife with debates over the proper place of the state in economy and society. As Simeon and Robinson (1990) have suggested, there was strong opposition to the Bennett New Deal in Quebec, and public opinion in English-speaking Canada was deeply divided over the question of state intervention. Therefore, it was difficult for courts to step out in front of a divided public during a politically explosive period. In this sense, encouraging provincial governments to undertake federalism litigation was a strategy that was successful for the business community during this period.

Litigation in Action Pre-Charter:
Aboriginal People and the Courts

Perhaps the most striking use of litigation by collective actors prior to the Charter is provided by the case of Aboriginal peoples. Since the late 1940s, Aboriginal peoples in Canada have expressed a strong preference to the federal government for a land claims policy similar to that available to Aboriginal peoples in the US. In many parts of Canada, Aboriginal peoples were displaced from their ancestral lands by European settlement (Dickason, 2002; Miller, 2000). Even where treaties were signed, treaty peoples had been dispossessed by developments ranging from the expanding urban population, the exploitation of natural resources in northern Canada, hydro developments, pollution, and local municipal encroachment on native lands for various purposes such as, in the infamous case of Oka, the expansion of a golf course. Further, many parts of Canada were not covered by treaty, and Aboriginal land claims in those areas had never been dealt with. Such was the case in much of Quebec and British Columbia, as well as northern Canada. Despite the calls for policy change, the federal government has been reluctant to put into place a land claims policy.

Aboriginal peoples faced substantial barriers to the pursuit of litigation or, indeed, to any form of collective action. Cultural dislocation, economic devastation, and national and linguistic diversities made coordinated collective action difficult. These barriers were exacerbated by a legal system that imposed an Indian status on some Aboriginal peoples, placing their economic and political affairs under the tutelage of the federal Department of Indian Affairs. The department's relationship with Aboriginal peoples was deeply colonial and, for much of its history, frankly assimilationist. One aspect of these colonial policies was that Aboriginal peoples were legally prohibited from certain types of organizing. Until 1951, it was illegal to receive funds for the pursuit of an Aboriginal land claim. Obviously, outright legal barriers of this kind made it impossible for Aboriginal peoples to raise money for land claims or to pay lawyers to represent them in court (Miller, 2000).

During the 1960s, a wave of social movement organizing across North America galvanized such groups such as American Indian Movement (AIM) in the US and Canada to espouse an indigenist politics that challenged the colonial treatment of Aboriginal peoples in the Americas. A new generation of Aboriginal leadership arose to challenge federal policies. In Canada, there was a substantial mobilization of Aboriginal organizations in federal politics at the end of the decade, especially as a response to the Trudeau government's White Paper on Aboriginal Affairs, which proposed the dissolution of the treaties and an end to any specific legal status for First Nations. In 1973, Supreme Court's *Calder* decision set new limits on federal policies on Aboriginal land claims. This decision was a result of a long-standing contestation by the Nisga'a people of British Columbia over their land claim, a claim they had asserted continuously since first contact with Europeans in the nineteenth century. In 1887, Nisga'a chiefs had demanded recognition of their claims from the provincial government, followed by similar demands to the British government in 1913. Modern litigation began in 1968 and resulted in the case known as *Calder*, named after the Nisga'a leader of the time, Frank Calder. The Nisga'a litigation went through two levels of courts in British Columbia before reaching the Supreme Court in 1973.

This landmark case demonstrates that it is possible to lose in court but to win in terms of changing policy conceptions. The Nisga'a claim was turned down; however, the Supreme Court recognized that Aboriginal title existed in Canadian law by virtue of the Royal Proclamation of 1759 and in English common law. Similar legal issues had arisen in the case of *St. Catherine's Milling* in 1888. In that case, the court had ruled that while Aboriginal title existed in English common law and by virtue of the Royal Proclamation, such title granted only personal and use rights and did not entitle the Aboriginal side to any compensation for loss of territory. *Calder* signified an important change in the interpretation of the existing legal base in Canadian law for Aboriginal title. Although the Supreme Court rejected the Nisga'a claim to land title on a technicality, three of the seven justices argued that the burden of proof was on the federal government to show that Aboriginal title had been extinguished, a decision that had far-reaching implications for federal land claims policy. While the Trudeau government had earlier claimed that those First Nations without treaties would not have their land claims recognized by the federal government, the *Calder* decision made it clear that the federal government would be forced to deal with Aboriginal claims.

Until *Calder*, the federal government had refused to recognize non-treaty claims based on the general principle of Aboriginal title; in the wake of *Calder*, it established the contemporary land claims process. This policy change has not prevented litigation on Aboriginal issues. In fact, over the years since *Calder*, there has been an explosion of litigation in this area, and this increase can be traced to the changing structure of legal opportunity that includes section 35 of the 1982 constitution. The structure of legal opportunity also includes the changed attitudes of some courts toward Aboriginal legal rights as indicated in *Calder*; the rise of the Aboriginal movement, which has changed the political atmosphere as well as the resources available to Aboriginal litigants; and the litigation funding made available to some First Nations as part of the federal land claims policy. The ruling in *Calder* that forced the federal government's hand in land claims policy occurred before the 1982 constitutional amendment. Therefore, it is clear that collective actors have sought to achieve their policy goals—sometimes successfully—well prior to 1982.

After the 1982 Constitution

The 1982 constitutional amendment ushered in a new era for group politics and the courts in Canada. It not only entrenched the Charter, it also contained a new section (35) that provided the most sweeping recognition of Aboriginal rights and Aboriginal title to date. Both the Charter and the new section on Aboriginal rights were to have far-reaching effects on the role of courts in relation to the evolution of public policy. Although, as we have seen, litigation occurred before the Charter, it has exerted an important influence on the political mobilization of organized interests and social movements in Canada. The enactment of the Charter was the culmination of a long development of human rights consciousness in Canadian politics. Its impact has been shaped by the role of the Supreme Court as a political and legal institution, as it chose to take up the Charter and to use it proactively to shape a new human rights regime for Canada. In the process, the Supreme Court has opened up new opportunities for groups and movements to exercise influence through legal mobilization on public policy and on Canadian political culture. In order to understand how this occurred, it is essential to probe the historical background of the development of human rights in Canada.

The Charter is often depicted as Trudeau's brainchild, a constitutional device intended to defuse Quebec nationalism and regional alienation and to strengthen the attachment of Canadians to the federal government. However, the idea of a constitutionally entrenched bill of rights was part of the international growth of human rights consciousness during the postwar period. In Canada there was substantial organizing by ethnic and racial minorities in the 1950s and 1960s in favour of stronger human rights protections in Canadian law and practice (Howe, 1991; Howe, 1993). This resulted in measures such as the Ontario government's ban on employment discrimination against women; the establishment of provincial and federal human rights commissions, beginning in Ontario in 1961; the passage of provincial and federal human rights codes, beginning in Ontario in 1962; and the Diefenbaker PC government's project of a bill of rights for Canadians, passed in 1960 (Axworthy, 2002). The direct link between the events of World War II and the rise of interest in human rights was the internment of Japanese Canadians. The Diefenbaker Bill of Rights was not constitutionally entrenched; it was a piece of ordinary federal legislation and could be repealed or amended by Parliament. Like the Charter, it contained a notwithstanding clause that would allow the legislature to override its provisions. Unlike the Charter, it only applied to the federal government, not to the provinces. In part because of these limitations, the Bill of Rights was not taken very seriously by the Supreme Court and was not interpreted expansively.

When the Charter was entrenched, opinion was divided among court-watchers as to its likely impact. One school of thought suggested that the Supreme Court would follow the practice established in the adjudication of the Diefenbaker Bill of Rights and interpret Charter rights very narrowly. Another urged the court to seize the opportunity and take an expansive view of human rights (Russell, 1983). Over the years following the Charter's enactment and, particularly following the coming into force of the equality rights clause in 1985, it became clear that the court had exploited the opportunity provided by the Charter to expand its role in the Canadian political system. Changes in public opinion on human rights (Nevitte, 1993; Nevitte, 1996) and the development of a multicultural public discourse helped to make the Charter popular with Canadians. The Supreme Court changed its rules and practices, increasingly opening up legal standing and opportunities for third-party intervention in Charter cases. The Supreme Court justices were well aware of the criticisms that had been made of the adjudication of the Bill of Rights and sensitive to the definitions of rights issues that were provided by third-party interveners. Overall, the Supreme Court's expansive interpretations of the Charter have greatly strengthened its impact as a political institution and have made the legal arena more attractive for group mobilization.

Data on third-party intervention in the Supreme Court shows the extent to which litigation has become an important political strategy for interest organizations and social movements (Koch, 1990; Levine, 1993). In an important study of group politics and litigation, Hein finds that 30 per cent of cases before the Federal Court of Canada and the Supreme Court included organizations as parties or interveners (Hein, 2000: 8). Overall, Hein's study finds that corporations and professionals are more likely to use the courts by a very wide margin. Third-party intervention has been important in Supreme Court adjudication on Aboriginal and Charter cases, as the court has recognized that it is important to hear from interested parties to legal disputes and often draws on interventions in giving reasons for its decisions.

Yet, it is difficult to make convincing claims for the influence of groups. Even when the court may side with a particular intervener, there are many other factors that affect judicial decision-making, including the impact of public and legal opinion, the prior attitudes and background of judges, and institutional considerations such as the defense of the political and legal legitimacy of the court. While "special interests" are sometimes depicted as reflecting the minority, in fact, third-party interveners may act as a conduit for the influence of public opinion by reflecting the majority view on some issues.

The Debate on Judicial Activism

The impact of the Charter on Canadian politics and the growing status and power of the Supreme Court as a political institution has sparked backlash from both right and left against the court's power. Alan Cairns (1992) has explored the ways in which new citizen and social movement identities have been mobilized into the Canadian constitutional debate. Beyond the impact of the Charter on the group politics of the constitutional debate, however, there is a broader question about how it may have influenced social movements and group politics generally, a debate that has generated an explicitly normative literature. As Richard Sigurdson (1993) has pointed out, the negative effects of the Charter for group politics have been decried by both left- and right wing-critics.

Among right-wing Charter critics, Knopff and Morton (1992) claim that the Charter has placed some types of political questions in the realm of law and thus in the jurisdiction of the judiciary, resulting in the legalization of political disputes and the politicization of law. They defend the idea that it is possible to separate law from politics; in their view, law focuses on concrete and specific disputes and need not influence public policy or, indeed, even set precedents for similar legal conflicts. They explicitly introduce normative elements into the empirical question of the Charter's impact, arguing that placing political disputes into the hands of appointed judges may not be the best way to improve the Canadian political system. Specifically, for Knopff and Morton, the Charter has opened up a new and nefarious avenue for organized interests seeking to influence the state. In general, in their view, this influence has privileged "special interests" at the expense of the majority rule. Accordingly, the Charter does not create the citizens' constitution (Cairns, 1991)—it creates a constitution of special interests. Knopff and Morton show how "special interests," including women and prisoners, have used the Charter to circumvent the democratic political process by claiming Charter rights before the courts. The language of "special interests," of course, resonates from the right-wing populist attacks of the Reform Party.

The idea that law and politics can be separated recurs in the work of other critics of the Charter from the right. For example, in Christopher Manfredi's survey of Charter politics, he asserts that litigation was "a process for resolving indivisible conflicts between private interests" while politics was "the search for that compromise among private interests that best coincided with the public good" (Manfredi, 1993: 213). The legal seduction of politics in the wake of the Charter has led to the view that "politics is a process whereby private groups capture public resources to promote their own interest" (Manfredi, 1993: 213). The effect of this for interest groups is that they can avoid politics, that is, the necessity of engaging in the traditional processes of electoralism and lobbying, which require compromise and moderation rather than the extremism and zero sum clashes that are produced by litigation.

Ironically, the same claims about the negative effects of the Charter for group politics are made by Charter critics on the left. Michael Mandel (1994) has criticized the Charter as a conservatizing force that demobilizes movements seeking societal transformation. In seeking judicial solutions to political problems, social movements devote resources and political energy to litigation that could otherwise have been used for grass roots organizing and for mobilization through the democratic political process (lobbying and party politics). Furthermore, Mandel counts the win/loss ratio of progressive groups before the courts in a completely different way than Knopff and Morton. While Knopff and Morton see the "special interests" (Mandel's progressive groups) as dominating Charter litigation and political discourse and significantly influencing the course of public policy on issues such as abortion, Mandel cautions that courts are not a venue for progressive social change. In his view, the law itself inherently reflects the dominant values of capitalist society, which will undermine the possibility of progressive equality-seeking. Judges themselves are drawn from the conservative upper reaches of Canadian society and are unlikely to interpret the law in ways that are favourable to progressive causes. Similarly, W.A. Bogart (1994), drawing on US evidence, argues that litigation has not resulted in substantive legal and policy victories for progressive groups but instead, as Mandel claims, has deflected groups from other political strategies. Although Mandel and Bogart might not agree that law and politics can be clearly separated, they clearly see litigation as a particular form of politics that can have damaging consequences for progressive groups.

However, changes in law must not be simply interpreted as "victories" or "defeats" for given policies and for the interests of groups without any broader consideration of how such victories and defeats shape the politics of the movements themselves and how the construction of identities and interests by movement actors shapes the litigation. Victories and defeats before the courts are treated as questions of Charter interpretation instead of as reflections of the social and political struggles of social movements or other group actors. The courts are seen as key decision-makers rather than as one element in an institutional mix that is connected to other social and political developments. The interests of litigants and their group allies before the courts are assumed, rather than problematized. The effect of rights-claiming on the mobilization of collective actors cannot be evaluated by discussing court decisions; the collective actors themselves must be examined.

The Empirical Study of Group Politics and the Charter

Turning from the normative analysis of judicial politics to empirical studies of organized interests and the courts, we find a number of factors that influence the propensity for groups to undertake litigation as a political strategy. According to the political disadvantage theory, organizations have a tendency to undertake litigation when they are likely to lose in other political arenas. Typically, this argument has been applied in the US where minority groups who have lost out in the political arena have turned to the courts for redress (Cortner, 1968; but see Epstein, 1985; and Olson, 1990). The best example is that of African Americans in the southern states who, under Jim Crow laws, were barred from voting. As they could not vote and hence suffered "political disadvantage," they turned to the courts and undertook civil rights litigation, beginning in the late 1940s. Other cases of political disadvantage may not be so extreme. For example, in the EU context, Alter and Vargas found that minority groups and groups without policy influence were also more likely to litigate than other groups, as the political advantage theory suggests (Alter and Vargas, 2000).

Hein's (2000) systematic empirical study of group politics and Charter litigation points to a number of other crucial factors that have shaped the propensity for organizations to litigate in Canada. First, Hein emphasizes the common law rules that shape the Canadian legal system. Common law practices limit the types of issues that can be brought before courts, the rules on who can bring a dispute to court (the question of legal standard), and the types of evidence that can be offered. Traditionally, as Hein describes it, "[j]udges wanted to sift through intrinsic evidence to settle discrete legal questions raised by two parties engaged in live controversy... Citizens who organized to address public problems were usually sent away" (2000: 9). Second, unsurprisingly, Hein finds that groups and organizations with legal advantages are more likely to litigate. By this, he means that groups that have a good legal case under existing laws, such as groups whose rights are explicitly protected by section 15 of the Charter, will be more likely to litigate than those whose rights are not so explicitly protected. Another example is provided by environmental groups. According to Hein, these groups will be less likely to litigate because environmental regulations are often written expressly to defuse litigation by failing to specify the causes of action or the duties that must be performed. Third, Hein points to the fact that groups with stable characteristics and political opportunities will be more likely to litigate. By "stable characteristics," he refers to stable funding, legal resources, "collective identities energized by rights and normative visions that demand judicial activism" (2000: 4).

Comparative work on legal mobilization supports Hein's view on the importance of collective identities and normative visions of political and legal change as central to the litigation process. Studies of the use of courts in the US have argued that the deployment of legal strategies, especially those centred on rights-claiming, is particularly important for traditionally marginalized groups. In the US, Scheingold (1974) argued that the "myth of rights" is a powerful legitimating force in claims-making for organized interests and social movement organizations. Alan Hunt (1990), drawing on Scheingold's work, argues that litigation by social movement actors must be understood as a tactic "to be deployed within a much broader conception of an essentially political, rather than legal strategy" (1990: 317). In this view, rights discourse and equality-seeking are deployed by social movements in order to legitimate their claims both to their own constituency and to the wider society of which they are a part. The main goal of litigation and equality-seeking discourse is to build the movements themselves rather than to achieve substantive legal or policy change. From this perspective, the success of equality-seeking social movements must be measured not in win/loss ratios before the courts but in the success of the movement in the broader process of social and political mobilization. Consequently, the influence of the Charter on social movements must be evaluated not only in the context of the types of rights claims that are brought before courts but also in terms of the role that such rights claims play in the politics of social movement organizing and mobilizing.

These possibilities have been examined in the American literature on social movements and litigation, particularly in the case of the civil rights movement. Stuart Scheingold (1989), summarizing this literature, argues that court victories were not decisive to the success of the civil rights movement and that the failure of legal victories to translate into political change led the movement to other avenues of political mobilization. At the same time, however, the civil rights case demonstrates that rights claims can play a key role in "*activating* a quiescent citizenry and *organizing* groups into effective political units" because "… rights carry with them connotations of entitlement, a declaration of rights tends to politicize needs by changing the way people think about their discontents" (1974: 131; emphasis in the original). Rights claims, in Scheingold's view, are political resources and must be considered as part of multifaceted political struggles. The "myth of rights," as he terms it, is the view that courts and court decisions actually bring about social and political change when, in fact, it is the political mobilization around rights claims that has the capacity to effect social change. Even where favourable court decisions are obtained, the implementation and effect of these decisions is shaped by societal power relationships (Rosenberg, 1991). Recent scholarship on the origins of the New Deal suggests that the impact of courts on legal mobilization may be traced back to executive action. In this analysis, Kevin McMahon (2004) traces the impact of Roosevelt's choices for American Supreme Court judges as well as the establishment of a new civil rights section in the Department of Justice as key factors shaping the litigation process. His analysis demonstrates how the National Association for the Advancement of Colored People (NAACP) worked with the Roosevelt justice department in developing test cases for civil rights litigation. This is an excellent example of the complexities of the interaction between political institutions (the executive, the bureaucracy, and the judicial branch) and between political institutions (courts and bureaucracy) and organized groups, in this case, social movement organizations (see also Cardinal, 2001).

Litigation in Action Post-Charter: Lesbian and Gay Rights

In 2004, Canada is in the forefront of lesbian and gay rights in the world. Only the Netherlands equals Canada's human rights protections for lesbian and gay citizens. This public policy outcome is the result of a long process of legalized mobilization by the lesbian and gay movement. Its evolution provides a particularly striking example of the role played by organized interests and social movement organizations in the process of litigation and policy change as well as the impact of engagement with the law and rights-claiming on social movement politics (Rayside, 2001). In 1982, the movement was weak and fragmented. After a decade of locally based lesbian and gay organizing, little had been gained in terms of human rights protections (Warner, 2002). Over the 20-year period following the Charter's enactment, Charter-based litigation generated lesbian and gay organizing in preexisting organizations such as trade unions and led to the creation of new advocacy groups and legal networks. Judicial empowerment sparked lesbian and gay organizing around the project of Charter litigation. In turn, lesbian and gay litigation and organizing helped to transform attitudes towards lesbian and gay citizens in Canadian society and to persuade courts to grant lesbian and gay rights claims. Prior to the Charter, lesbian and gay citizens were hardly recognized in human rights law; by the late 1990s, they enjoyed better human rights protection than lesbian and gay people almost anywhere else in the world.

The gay liberation movement in Canada, as elsewhere, drew on the template of civil rights organizing, developed in the US. The movement sought to use the courts to politicize gay identity and to mobilize a new social movement. During the 1970s, several human rights cases were pursued around very straightforward human rights issues, such as employment discrimination. At the time of the Charter's enactment, lesbian and gay citizens were absent from public debates, and, unlike groups such as Aboriginal people, the women's movement, and ethnic minorities, they did not mobilize in favour of Charter rights. Lesbian and gay organizations were very weak during this period; they were beginning to deal with the onset of the AIDS crisis; and, with the exception of Quebec's amendment of its human rights code to include sexual orientation as a prohibited ground of discrimination, they had been unsuccessful in attempts to secure human rights protections (Warner, 2002).

After the enactment of the Charter, though, lesbian and gay organizing began to take root around section 15, the equality rights section. In 1985, the Mulroney PC government appointed a parliamentary committee to consider the implications of the new equality rights provisions. Its hearings drew a large number of submissions from local lesbian and gay groups and galvanized a number of lawyers and trade union activists to form an Ottawa-based group to keep up the pressure on the federal government with regard to lesbian and gay equality rights. The Equality Writes Ad Hoc Committee was formed to conduct a letter-writing campaign, to network with other human rights groups, and to lobby MPs and the Mulroney government on its response to the parliamentary committee report. In response to the committee deliberations, the federal government suggested that it would interpret section 15 of the Charter as including sexual orientation and stated that it would take "whatever means are necessary" to ensure that sexual orientation was a prohibited ground for discrimination in federal jurisdictions (Hiebert, 2002; Smith, 1999). In reality, this promise would not be fulfilled for over ten years and, even then, only in response to Charter decisions favoring lesbian and gay litigants. Nevertheless, at the time, the government's positive response was attributed to the Equality Writes campaign and to the broad range of lesbian and gay groups that had appeared before the parliamentary committee. In the wake of these small successes, the Equality Writes Ad-Hoc Committee transformed itself into Egale with 35 members at its first meeting in May 1986 (Smith, 1999). In this way, the through the process of the parliamentary committee hearings, the implementation of the Charter sparked the establishment of a pan-Canadian lesbian and gay advocacy group and marked the formal beginnings of Charter-centred political activism by gay and lesbian groups.

There were important differences between the gay and lesbian organizations of the 1970s, which explicitly sought to use litigation to politicize lesbians and gays and to build a lesbian and gay social movement, and Egale, which sought equality rights as ends in themselves. While the early gay and lesbian groups were rooted in part in the youth counterculture of the period, Egale was based on the emerging middle-class communities of visible lesbians and gays who potentially stood to benefit from the recognition of lesbian and gay relationships in law. Its leadership, especially in its early period, was provided mainly, although not exclusively, by white male professionals, especially lawyers and trade unionists from Ottawa's powerful public sector unions (Smith, 1999).

Hence, the enactment of the Charter not only sparked the creation of new organizations but the creation of legally focused organizations. After many fits and starts, Egale was able to stabilize itself as an organization by the mid-1990s. Recalling Hein's argument, we can see that Egale developed a stable base of resources, mainly provided through individual member donations, contributions to legal research by the Court Challenges Program, and the *pro bono* work of sympathetic lawyers. In addition, it was animated by a strong normative vision and given comfort by the decisions of lower courts through cases such as *Haig and Birch* that made it clear that sexual orientation would be included by the courts as within the ambit of section

15 of the Charter (equality rights) as a ground of discrimination. Egale has been able to increase its interventions, and its arguments on rights issues have been picked up in Supreme Court decisions (Smith 2002). The policy result has been that governments, federally and provincially, have substantially altered anti-discrimination and relationship recognition policies.

At the same time, the legal mobilization of the lesbian and gay movement has been disconnected from broader goals of social change. During the 1970s, gay liberation and lesbian feminist organizing were part of the counterculture of the period. Many gay and lesbian activists had links with socialist and working-class movements as well as the women's movement. The nature of lesbian and gay organizing has changed fundamentally from a focus on grass roots mobilization, consciousness-raising, cultural activities, and local service provision to a pan-Canadian network of legal activism in which equality is the main goal. Relationship recognition and the same-sex marriage campaign are issues that entail the inclusion of same-sex couples in the existing system of increasingly privatized social provision. As Boyd and Young have recently pointed out, "the positive element of symbolic recognition of same-sex relationships is too often accompanied by a negative element of exacerbated economic disadvantage" (Boyd and Young, 2003; see also Young 1994). In this sense, Charter-based rights-claiming reinforces neoliberal values of privatization, individualism, and consumerism.

Litigation in Action Post-Charter: LEAF and Feminist Litigation

Like the lesbian and gay movement, the women's movement has undertaken substantial litigation based on section 15 of the Charter, although in a much different political context. The second wave of feminist activism in Canada began in the 1960s and functioned as a precursor to the emergence of lesbian and gay organizing in the 1970s. Many lesbians were active in the women's movement and prioritized the pursuit of equality in terms of gender. By politicizing gender and undermining traditional sex roles second-wave feminism provoked a broader and deeper questioning of sexuality and paved the way for the lesbian and gay movement. The women's movement was much larger than the lesbian and gay movement, however, and had much more in the way of political, economic, and organizational resources. It built on a broad range of women's organizations that had been solidified during the long period of movement quiescence between the first and second waves of feminism. Organizations such as the National Council of Women, which organized mainly middle-class white women, or Voice of Women, which brought together women in the CCF/NDP and the peace movement, have no parallel in lesbian and gay organizing. When second-wave feminism emerged during the 1960s, the ongoing infrastructure helped furnish organizational and political resources to the emerging movement.

These differences in the starting points of women's and lesbian and gay activism help to explain why the women's movement was able to play a relatively larger role in the constitutional debates leading to the Charter's enactment. As we have seen, when the Trudeau government proposed the Charter in the early 1980s, the lesbian and gay movement lacked a pan-Canadian organization to pursue constitutional rights issues. The rights template of lesbian and gay activism that had been pushed through the 1970s in the pursuit of provincial and federal human rights protections had failed, as most governments were intransigent on lesbian and gay rights, even in areas such as employment discrimination. In contrast, the women's movement was positioned differently in relation to law and human rights protections. The drive for legal personhood had largely been achieved in the first wave of feminism, and some human rights protections for women had been put into place, such as, for example, the prohibition on employment discrimination. While sexual orientation was barely mentioned in a single human rights statute in Canada in 1980 (only in Quebec), discrimination based on sex was well recognized in human rights legislation and public discourse on human rights. So, by 1980, the women's movement had been much more successful than the lesbian and gay movement. This success can be attributed to the longer history of organizing in the movement, the superior resourcing of the women's movement, and the fact that the women's movement had had some successes in influencing and shaping public debates on equality over the course of the 1970s.

Thus, at the time of the announcement of a new Charter, the women's movement was able to mobilize to shape the process and to pressure the Trudeau government to strengthen the rights guarantees for women. In turn, the Trudeau government turned to groups like the women's movement to demonstrate that its proposed bill of rights was supported by Canadians. Because it needed support for its constitutional initiative, an initiative that had been the subject of long-standing and conflictual constitutional negotiations, it was willing to accommodate some of the groups that demanded changes to the proposed Charter. Through the winter of 1980-81, the government held parliamentary committee hearings on the proposed Charter, and the women's movement was able to demand a recasting of women's equality rights (Kome, 1983; Dubinsky, 1985).

The women's movement focused on two specific points about the proposed Charter: the wording of section 15 and the inclusion of a new section on women's equality (eventually included as section 28). With regard to section 15, the equality rights section, pressure from women's organizations and feminist legal experts succeeded in securing strong guarantees of women's rights, based in part on the women's movement's previous experience of litigation and observation of the litigation in the US. For example, the clause specifically included the idea of "equal protection and equal benefit" as well as the ideas of equality before and under the law. This opened up the possibility for a substantive discussion of equality, one that would not only treat people in the same way, but that would treat people differently in order to provide them with equality of results. This would preclude a decision such as that in *Bliss*, a case decided under the Canadian Bill of Rights, which had concluded that a pregnant woman had not been discriminated against because her employer had fired her for being pregnant, not because she was a woman. All employees were treated in the same way, according to the Supreme Court decision in *Bliss*; thus, there was no discrimination because all those who were pregnant were treated in the same way (Majury, 2002). The new wording of this section was intended to forestall judgements of this type by specifically mentioning the concepts of equal benefit and protection. Section 15 also included explicit protection for laws and measures, such as equity measures, that were designed to ameliorate the condition of a historically disadvantaged group and that would prevent litigation from men on grounds that equity programs were discriminatory (Kome, 1983). Thus, the Charter codified the notion that some groups in Canadian society are historically disadvantaged and thus encouraged the court to explore the broad context of a group's situation relative to other groups, an element that has proven to be crucially important in section 15 litigation.

In addition to an expansive section 15, including explicit protection for equity measures, women's organizing around the Charter also resulted in the inclusion of section 28. Section 28 states that, notwithstanding any other provision, the rights in the Charter are guaranteed equally to male and female persons. This provision was important because section 15 could be overridden by legislatures using the notwithstanding clause, section 33. This clause had been inserted into the Charter as a compromise between the federal government and the provinces. It would allow provincial legislatures (and Parliament) to opt out of certain provisions of the Charter, including section 15, equality rights. Thus, by mobilizing for section 28, the women's movement ensured that equality rights could not be overridden by legislatures.

As for the lesbian and gay movement, the enactment of the Charter sparked a wave of legal mobilization in the women's movement. Unlike it, however, the women's movement already possessed an institutionalized pan-Canadian confederation of women's groups—the NAC. For much of the period following the Charter's enactment, through the 1980s and 1990s, NAC continued to participate in constitutional, political, and social debates. It claimed an active role on issues of social policy as they affected women and put forth a gendered view of public policy that contributed in important ways to debates over free trade, government cuts, and the shift to neoliberalism (Vickers, Rankin, and Appelle, 1993; Dobrowolsky, 2000b). As NAC was undertaking this role, an independent litigation fund—the Women's Legal, Education and Action Fund (LEAF)— was established in 1985 to ensure that women's rights were protected under the new Charter. There is an obvious parallel with the creation of Egale in 1986. Both LEAF and Egale were founded for the purpose of monitoring and pursuing litigation under the Charter on behalf of their constituencies.

From the beginning, LEAF was successful in obtaining funds from the federal Court Challenges Program, which was set up by the Liberals in tandem with the Secretary of State program for the purpose of assisting disadvantaged groups with litigation. However, these funds could only be used to fund legal research. For core funding, LEAF had to tap independent sources, organized through a companion foundation, the LEAF Foundation. Like Egale, LEAF was the product of the Charter and signified a new type of mobilization for feminists in Canadian politics. For 20 years, NAC and LEAF co-existed in the women's movement; thus, legal mobilization was one of the strategies for the women's movement at the pan-Canadian level along with other forms of organizing around non-legalized public policy questions in the mainstream political arenas of party politics, elections, and constitutional negotiations. Over the long term, however, legal mobilization under the Charter has come to dominate the politics of the women's movement as it has for the lesbian and gay movement. While women's organizing is lively at the local and urban levels in Canada, the organization structures for pan-Canadian women's organizing have weakened over the neoliberal era, and, increasingly, LEAF, along with the Canadian Abortion Rights Action League (CARAL), are two of the few remaining venues at the federal level for women's organizing.

A number of important public policy issues for women's equality have been determined through litigation in which LEAF has played a role (Razack, 1991). One concerned the early interpretation of section 15 by the Supreme Court. In *Andrews*, many observers have noted LEAF's role in convincing the court to accept a broad view of substantive equality (Gotell, 2002; Manfredi, 2004). Another set of important cases concerned abortion rights. These were heard soon after the Charter's enactment in the late 1980s. Following the 1969 revisions to the Criminal Code, a woman could obtain an abortion if her mental or physical health was deemed to be in danger by a hospital-based therapeutic abortion committee (TAC). This compromise measure was strongly opposed by pro-life forces, who objected to the increased accessibility of legal abortions that were performed under these new provisions. On the other hand, the pro-choice movement objected to the limitations on a woman's right to choose that were imposed by the Criminal Code regulations. In many parts of the country, abortions were not accessible to women, even under the new provisions, because local hospitals refused to perform them. Further, the pro-choice movement objected to the regulations on women's reproductive freedom that were imposed by the TACs. When Henry Morgenthaler, a Montreal doctor, began opening free-standing clinics that offered abortions outside of the hospital setting, a series of legal challenges began that ended in the Supreme Court in 1988. The Supreme Court struck down the abortion regulations in the Criminal Code as an unconstitutional violation of women's rights to due process under section 7 of the Charter, because of the capricious functioning of the TACs. LEAF was involved in other abortion cases such as the 1989 *Daigle* case (father's rights) and the 1989 *Borowski* case (rights of the fetus). Furthermore, LEAF has intervened in cases involving a broad range of other public policy issues that have come before the courts in the Charter era, including the rape shield law and sexual assault, tax regulations on child care, the regulation of pornography, lesbian and gay rights, pay equity, and social assistance regulations ("spouse in the house") (Gotell, 2002).

The feminist litigation project has been critiqued by critical legal studies scholars. The legal arena privileges an individualized and homogenized view of stakeholders and litigants. In feminist litigation, there is a danger that "women" will be treated as a homogenous category in which differences based on class, nationality, race, language, sexual orientation, or ability may be erased. Further, engagement with the law generates a strategic and organizational logic that privileges legal expertise at the expense of the participatory culture of much of the feminist women's movement. As Lise Gotell has commented, "the costs of submitting to the foundationalist requisites of legal discourse may outweigh any gains, especially if we are committed to building a feminist politics based on participation and if we seek fuller recognition of the complexity of women's lives" (Gotell, 2002: 137). However, there is no doubt that legally mobilized feminist organizing in Canada has profoundly shaped the discussion of equality rights and has pushed the courts in the direction of a more substantive and expansive definition of equality than would have been possible otherwise.

In this sense, like lesbian and gay litigation, feminist legal mobilization has contradictory and ambiguous effects; on the one hand, the movement has contributed to changing public policy outcomes on specific issues of importance to women, such as abortion, and on shaping public discourse on equality. On the other hand, as the legal arena becomes more and more important to feminist organizing, there is a danger that lawyers and legal expertise will come to dominate the articulation of women's rights at the expense of the diverse perspectives of grass roots activists. At the outset of the Charter era, NAC was a strong and vibrant organization. After 25 years of Charter politics and neoliberal restructuring, it is dormant as an organization while LEAF survives. While NAC was a confederation of grass roots women's groups, LEAF is an elite organization, funded by individual donations and dominated by lawyers. Where the Charter has been less important symbolically and politically, such as in Quebec, grass roots women's organizing is alive and well in the *Fédération des femmes du Québec*. These results seem to suggest that the Charter is having a long-term impact on the Canadian women's movement.

Litigation in Action Post-Charter: First Nations' Litigation

This brief section cannot do justice to the complex terrain of Aboriginal litigation and its political implications, since section 35 of the Charter was enacted; the legal, historical, and theoretical issues surrounding the place of Aboriginal peoples within Canada are the subject of a rich and complex literature (e.g. Alfred, 1995, 1999; Green, 2001; Ladner, 2003; Tully, 2000), which cannot all be summarized here. This section will focus on how Aboriginal peoples have used the courts as a political strategy since 1982.

The changing role of the courts in the Canadian political system following the 1982 constitutional amendment has somewhat altered the structure of legal opportunity for First Nations as it has for the other movements explored above. Resourcing is critically important in First Nations' litigation. Further, the national status of Aboriginal peoples in Canada poses a specific set of advantages and disadvantages that are distinctive in the litigation process. As we have already seen, First Nations faced legal and political barriers to litigation on land claims under the Indian Act. Between 1927 and 1951, Aboriginal peoples could not hire a lawyer to bring a case against the government regarding abridgement of treaty or Aboriginal rights without the permission of the government itself. Further, gatherings such as potlatch and sun dance were prohibited from the 1880s through 1951. These provisions undermined the political mobilization of First Nations. Outright legal bans on organizing and litigating in pursuit of land claims and rights have no direct parallel for other groups. Similarly, the extent of social, economic, and cultural dislocation and disadvantage in First Nations' communities is not paralleled in other groups. The structure of legal opportunity is shaped not only by the advantages or disadvantages that may be accorded in the letter of the constitutional law, but also by the economic, organizational, and other political resources of groups undertaking litigation.

In First Nations' communities, the amendment of the constitution in 1982 coincided with the growing strength of Aboriginal activists and lawyers that had been pushing ahead with land claims and political organizing since the 1960s. Prior to the Charter, the *Lavell* and *Bedard* (1974) cases under the Diefenbaker Bill of Rights had sparked the organization of non-status Indians as well as Aboriginal women. In these cases, Aboriginal women challenged their loss of Indian status under the Indian Act due to their marriage to non-Aboriginal men. On land claims, the *Calder* case of 1973 had already resulted in the implementation of a federal land claims policy, a policy that had been demanded by Aboriginal people in Canada since the late 1940s. However, the relative lack of success of the federal policy machinery at settling Aboriginal claims and the ongoing problems with enforcement of treaties (for those First Nations that enjoyed treaty status) has kept Aboriginal issues in Canadian courts over the last 25 years. The entrenchment of Aboriginal rights in the Canadian constitution of 1982 through section 35 has provided a fresh legal opportunity; however, profound underlying questions of sovereignty and nationhood have not been resolved. Unlike other groups here, First Nations' engagement with law raises the question of the underlying legitimacy and legality of the Canadian state. First Nations use European-Canadian law to advance their claims, and yet, many First Nations do not accept the legality or legitimacy of this law in governing their communities. European-Canadian law privileges procedures, rules, and norms that may be anathema in some Aboriginal communities. For example, procedures on evidence may prevent Aboriginal people from presenting the oral testimony of elders.

There is no single Aboriginal organization that undertakes litigation on behalf of Aboriginal rights. Cases come from many sources: First Nations themselves, individual litigants who argue that their Aboriginal or treaty rights have been violated, and advocacy organizations. The federal government has recognized the importance of funding Aboriginal litigation through programs administered by the Department of Indian Affairs and Northern Development. Nonetheless, like the federal land claims process, this program remains deeply problematic in that funding practices constitute an additional form of regulation of First Nations' communities. As in women's litigation and lesbian and gay litigation, lawyers and legal experts play an important role in determining the way in which cases go forward and the kinds of issues that are raised. Further, lawyers may fund cases themselves by undertaking legal presentation or legal research on a *pro bono* basis.

In the post-1982 era, there have been a number of very important Aboriginal cases before the Supreme Court, including *Sparrow* and *Delgamuukw*. On the issue of land claims, the *Calder* decision had left important legal and political questions undecided with regard to Aboriginal title and sovereignty. These issues were joined through the long history of the Gitxsan and Wet'suwet'en people of British Columbia, who had sought negotiations over Aboriginal title, sovereignty, and self-government since the arrival of Europeans in the late nineteenth century. The Gitxsan and Wet'suwet'en used not only litigation but also direct action and negotiation with governments. The litigation commenced in 1987 and reached the Supreme Court in 1997. This case was important in part because of the open racism expressed in the lower court rulings in British Columbia. Consistent with the long history of the provincial government's refusal to recognize the sovereignty, rights, and title of First Nations, the government of the day argued in court that the Gitxsan and Wet'suwet'en did not have any rights to their traditional territory. The Gitxsan and Wet'suwet'en countered with extensive testimony from elders who recounted the oral history of the peoples. The first ruling in the *Delgamuukw* case, from the British Columbia Supreme Court, was noteworthy for its clear expression of the underlying racism of the colonial assertion of power. The judge stated that the way of life of the Gitxsan and Wet'suwet'en people had been "nasty, brutish and short" prior to the arrival of Europeans and that there was no right of Aboriginal title or self-government. In 1993, the British Columbia Court of Appeal overturned this ruling with regard to Aboriginal title, but not self-government. By this time, the Delgamuukw case had become a symbol of Aboriginal rights. Not only did it raise the issues of Aboriginal title, Aboriginal rights, and Aboriginal jurisdiction, it also clearly articulated the conflict between colonial and postcolonial perspectives on the relationship between Aboriginal peoples and (other) Canadians. Both the British Columbia and Canadian governments argued that the right to title had been extinguished. The Supreme Court decision stated that governments could not unilaterally set aside Aboriginal title in this manner and laid out guidelines for using oral history as evidence concerning questions of Aboriginal rights (McNeil, 2001). The decision was important in that the Supreme Court reaffirmed the recognition of Aboriginal title and the legitimacy of oral history testimony in Canadian courts, but was also problematic for First Nations because it created a hierarchy of rights in which Aboriginal title was still subject to the sovereignty of the Crown (Borrows, 1999).

Other important cases have touched on the Aboriginal right to self-government. For example, in the *Sparrow* case, a member of the Musquem band of British Columbia was charged with fishing with a net that exceeded federal regulations; he argued that such restrictions were a violation of Aboriginal rights and that such rights were protected under section 35 of the 1982 constitution, which recognized Aboriginal and treaty rights. Like the *Delgamuukw* decision, the *Sparrow* decision made it clear that section 35 does not create "a constitutionally protected space for Aboriginal governments" (McNeil, 2001: 197); however, the court overturned previous case law that had permitted Parliament to regulate on such matters, even if it meant infringing Aboriginal rights. In *Sparrow*, the court set out a test by which the infringement of such rights could be justified, one that places the recognition of Aboriginal rights at its centre.

Engagement with the legal system has been a contradictory and ambiguous enterprise for Aboriginal peoples. While the *Calder* case has shaped land claims policies in Canada, these policies have been less than effective in resolving outstanding land claims. Three important claims have been signed that have been tremendously important for the peoples concerned: the James Bay agreement, the Inuit land claim that paved the way for the creation of the new Nunavut territorial government, and the Nisga'a land claim in British Columbia. However, aside from these, very few important land claims have been settled under the federal land claims policy that resulted from *Calder* (Abele and Prince, 2003). On the issue of self-government, litigation has established some new constitutional and legal beachheads for Aboriginal peoples in cases such as *Delgamuukw* and *Sparrow*. However, as we have seen, Aboriginal litigation continues to run up against the assertion of Crown sovereignty, which provides an opening for federal and provincial governments to infringe Aboriginal rights (Borrows, 1999). It remains to be seen if litigation on Aboriginal land claims and self-government can bring about the decolonization of the relationship between Aboriginal people and (other) Canadians. Given the failure of constitutional negotiation, litigation may provide one of the few routes to improvement of the relationship between Aboriginal and other Canadians.

Neoliberalism and Litigation

The enactment of the Charter and the empowerment of courts as political institutions in the Canadian political system in the wake of the 1982 constitutional amendment have reinforced the shift to neoliberalism in Canadian politics. Empowered courts pose no obstacle to neoliberal restructuring. Although the explicit protection of property rights was not included in the Charter, the courts have not opposed business power. Hein's (2000) study of interest group litigation and the Charter shows that corporations are by far the most likely to take cases to court. Private law cases are more numerous than public law cases in Canadian courts, even in the post-Charter era. Further, corporations have been adept at using the Charter's provisions to further their own interests. Charter rights have been claimed in defense of tobacco advertising and advertising aimed at children. Corporations have been accorded the rights of (corporate) persons under the Canadian Charter, following Anglo-American legal practice that defines companies as people deserving of rights protections. Hence, despite the rise of legal mobilization by social movements, the era of the Charter has seen the continuing power of business in the courts.

This view is reinforced by Judy Fudge's (2001) recent study of Charter decision-making. Fudge employs Nancy Fraser's distinction between movements of recognition and movements of redistribution to understand the Charter's impact. Fraser (1995) famously distinguished between social movements such as the lesbian and gay movement, whose claims concerned recognition, and movements such as labour whose claims concerned redistribution. She placed the women's movement in between the two. Applying this standard to Charter litigation, Fudge argues, "the closer a rights claim is pitched to the recognition pole of the injustice spectrum, the more likely that the Supreme Court of Canada will uphold it" (2001: 341). Therefore, the lesbian and gay movement has done quite well under the Charter, especially where its cases have made no claim on the public purse. Most claims for relationship recognition involve very small public expenditure in areas such as pensions and very large gains for the state from the privatization of social provision. In contrast, the Charter has been of almost no use to the labour movement in Canada. Early on, three cases on labour law were decided by the Supreme Court (these have been dubbed "the labour trilogy"). In these 1987 decisions, the courts ruled that freedoms of assembly and freedom of speech did not include the right to bargain collectively or the right to strike. As Fudge argues, "the labour movement's attempts to use the Charter to liberate workers' freedom to strike and picket from legislative and common law restrictions have been an abysmal failure" (2001: 348-49).

Finally, transferring responsibility to courts for certain types of decision-making fits in with neoliberal political strategies of offloading. As social services are offloaded to para-public and nonprofit institutions, it is more and more difficult to hold them accountable through the traditional mechanisms of parliamentary accountability. As we have already seen, such mechanisms are in full decline in any case. In this context, as Byron Sheldrick puts it, "courts are increasingly being asked to step into this void and exert control over decisions related to the allocation of public goods" (2003: 150). Thus, decisions are transferred into an arena that is hard to access without resources and that has proven itself to be hostile to claims to redistribution. As Michael Mandel (1994) argued at the time of the Charter's enactment, to the extent that collective actors in Canadian politics increasingly see the courts as a privileged arena of political action, they will shift away from other political strategies. The legal arena is not a level playing field. Groups with resources, groups with claims that reinforce the existing structure of economic power, and groups that can present their claims in the template of rights will have a greater chance of discursive, policy, and legal success.

SEVEN

Conclusions

This book has argued that the arenas for group and social movement politics are in the process of fundamental restructuring in the neoliberal era. This process of restructuring has drawn on the legacies of collective action from Canada's past and is shaped by the political-institutional complex at the heart of the Canadian federal state. The analysis has focused on the traditional political-institutional arena of Canadian politics and explored how changes in Canadian political institutions shape the ways in which group and social movement identities and interests will be treated in the political process. Political-institutional forces such as federalism and intergovernmental relations, the role of the courts in the wake of the Charter, the decline of the legislature, the concentration of power at the centre, the relative displacement of the public service, the regionalization of the brokerage party system, and the rise of professional lobbyists have altered the terrain for group politics in Canada. In 1996, Jenson and Phillips argued that neoliberalism was recasting Canada's citizenship regime. This book has reinforced their analysis by suggesting that the relationship between collective actors and the state has undergone a profound shift. The restructuring of Canadian politics has gone beyond the level of policy change, reshaping the central institutions of the state for the neoliberal era. The core political institutions of the Canadian state are in the midst of their own restructuring process, one that will make a less democratic Canada. It will be more difficult than ever for social movements and groups that represent the diverse interests of Canadians to make their voices heard. The recasting of the core institutions of the state opens up new avenues of influence for business elites to reinforce the "privileged position of business" (Lindblom, 1977) in the capitalist market system.

In this concluding chapter, I first describe some of the implications of the analysis for the way that political scientists in Canada study group and movement politics and the ways in which groups and movements exercise influence in the political process. Then, I review the major changes that have occurred in the political-institutional landscape of Canadian politics and how these changes have affected the ways in which groups and social movements attempt to influence the actions of the state. Finally, I consider the changes described here in terms of their impact on the quality of democratic life in Canada. The changes outlined in this book are a vivid demonstration of the decline of the domestic nation-state as the site of democratic contestation and citizen participation in public life. The Canadian political system is closing down access and influence for citizens through group and social movement politics, aside from those in the most privileged groups. Access to the political system has been commodified as never before, and the unadulterated dominance of neoliberal discourse has created a new common sense of politics.

Theoretical Approaches Revisited

In Chapter 1, we surveyed a number of approaches to the study of group and movement politics in political science and sociology, including pluralism, Marxism, Canadian political economy, neopluralism, historical institutionalism, social movement theory, and rational choice theory. I have emphasized the ways in which the transition to neoliberal globalization has shaped group and social movement politics over the last quarter century. By placing the evolution of patterns of group and social movement influence within the context of the political economy, I have suggested that economic change forms an essential backdrop to the study of collective action, especially when such changes are considered over the long term. Without such a backdrop, we lack an understanding of the structural factors that are driving political institutional change and collective action in the contemporary context.

Throughout developed capitalist democracies, changes have occurred in the functioning of political institutions and in the ways that group and social movement organizations influence public policy. The decline of programmatic mass parties, the crumbling of ministerial responsibility, the process of judicial empowerment, and the commodification of access and influence are occurring in other capitalist democracies and is especially noteworthy in systems (such as in the UK), which have similar parliamentary political institutions to Canada's. In a number of countries, there has been recognition of a growing "democratic deficit" in the functioning of the traditional institutions of citizenship in the global era. In the EU, where the term "democratic deficit" was coined, this debate has been openly joined in discussions over the proposed constitution. Analysts in EU countries have long bemoaned the dominance of the European Commission at the expense of the European Parliament and looked for ways to expand democratic participation and European citizenship. The role of courts and the place of judicial activism in democratic political life, long a subject of heated debate in the US, is now questioned in other contexts in which courts are beginning to play a more powerful role. Changes in the nature of political parties and problems in election financing have occurred in contexts as different as Japan, South Korea, Germany, and the US, all of which have experienced financial scandals and questions about party fund-raising. The long-standing mass parties of the left, such as the Social Democratic Party in Germany and the Labour Party in the UK, are not immune from Canadian-style leadership struggles or party financing scandals. The place of media consultants and professional pollsters, and the growth and centralization of the prime minister's powers and role, are the subject of debate in these systems. The cross-national similarity in these experiences suggests that factors common to all democratic capitalist states have influenced the recent evolution of political institutions and the pathways of influence and access for groups and movements in political systems. The shift from the postwar Keynesian paradigm to the era of neoliberal globalization has affected all of these countries, including Canada.

There is a powerful elective affinity between neoliberal globalization and the types of political-institutional changes that have occurred cross-nationally. Neoliberalism prioritizes markets and individuals, offering everything up for sale. The commodification of politics and the increase in corporate media concentration at the global level have undermined the traditional mass party based on the development of values, beliefs, and party program and reinforced a leader-driven politics of personality. Political identities, choices, and participation in collective action are increasingly cast as consumer choices, rather than as opportunities for democratic participation. In this context, collective efforts to bring about political change run up against a serious problem of legitimacy. The widespread dominance of neoliberal political discourse and neoliberal social practices, such as commodification and consumerism, means that the deck is stacked against collective action as never before. Collective struggles are defined as illegitimate by definition. Every advocacy group putting forward its message and every group of protestors that wants to hold a demonstration must fight against media depictions of groups and movements as advocates for special interests or as troublemakers disrupting traffic. The media sends the message of a depoliticized world in which collective action is deviant and political disagreement and conflict are an aberration from everyday life, rather than a legitimate part of it. Contentious social movements and advocacy groups themselves take on some of the features of neoliberal consumerism, thus heightening the sense in which democratic political participation is a reflexive identity choice for the individual or even a consumer choice. Increasingly, political identities and political participation is for sale. Even Greenpeace takes credit cards. With a few clicks of the mouse, anyone can be an environmentalist.

For these reasons, any analysis of group and social movement politics in the contemporary context must begin with an understanding of the changes in the political economy. However, the analysis cannot end there. As outlined in Chapter 1, political economy does not offer a guide to the agency of collective actors or analysis of political institutions. It is almost entirely a structural approach. We may note that the shift from one economic paradigm to another has been accompanied by shifts in political institutions that are similar in some ways across a number of quite different contexts, but political economy does not focus on the analysis of political institutions or on the agency of collective actors such as interest groups and social movements.

To understand both institutional change and the evolution of group and social movement politics, it is necessary to turn to other approaches. In the analysis presented here, both historical institutionalism and social movement theory have been used to suggest that shifts in political institutions and group politics are linked to macrohistorical change. Urbanization, industrialization, state-building, and the rise of literacy and printing technology are preconditions for the emergence of both organized group activity and contentious social movement politics. Historical institutionalism and historical sociology draw our attention to these long-term changes that include, but are not restricted to, the political economy. Historical institutionalism in particular draws our attention to political institutional change. As we have seen at length, Canadian political institutions have changed substantially over the course of the neoliberal era, and such changes have profoundly influenced the ability of groups and social movement organizations to influence public policy. In particular, historical institutionalism suggests that institutional changes will lead to differences in the way that interest associations and social movement organizations target the state, the types of demands that such actors will make in public policy debates, and the methods and strategies they will use to influence public policy.

Further, the macrohistorical approach is particularly important in the analysis of group and social movement politics in Canada. The literature on groups and movements, especially in political science, has tended to be "presentist"; that is, it tends to exaggerate the groups and movements of the present while ignoring their historical precursors, such as the reform and temperance movements of the nineteenth century (Weir, 1993). If the approach is overly focused on the short run, then we miss out on the longer term structural changes that are in play. In this sense, recent changes in the access and influence of civil society groups to the Canadian state cannot be fixed through institutional tinkering and such reforms at the edges as proportional representation, strong election financing laws, effective ethics counselors, or a strengthened lobbyist registration regulation. While these may be salutary and useful measures, a focus on long-term historical change suggests that they are unlikely to stem the tide of political change that is de-democratizing the domestic nation-state in Canada, as elsewhere.

However, both historical institutionalism and social movement theory have important theoretical weaknesses, weaknesses that have been highlighted through the approach, used here, of focusing on a single country case study of group and social movement politics in the age of neoliberalism. While historical institutionalists believe that political institutional change is important and that such institutional changes drive group and movement politics, they are less able to explain why institutional change occurs. At least, historical institutionalists do not have a generalized theory of the sources of political institutional change. In this sense, they would do well to pay more attention to political economy, which assumes that changes in the state are linked to the economy. One of the key links is the political behaviour of business elites. Ironically, given that organized militancy by the business community has been important in driving neoliberal policy restructuring, its role is almost entirely ignored in theoretical approaches to the study of group and movement politics (aside from Marxism). While the political economy approach has focused on particular class factions such as finance capital, it does not pay much attention to the political activity and agency of business elites and business groups. Social movement theorists, who have the most to say about the agency of collective actors, ignore business because it is not considered a "social movement." Because business plays a dominant role in politics in a market economy, it does not have to engage in the process of contention, which, by definition, refers to the process of questioning dominant norms and values. Because the perspective of Canadian business has for so long constituted the received wisdom of the day, students of Canadian politics have not paid sufficient attention to the organized political activity of the business community or what I have termed here business militancy.

Business militancy has played an important role in recent public policy changes in Canada on issues such as free trade, privatization, deregulation, and welfare state retrenchment. As Abu-Laban and Gabriel have documented, neoliberal policy change has extended into the domains of employment equity, immigration, and multiculturalism where Canadian diversity is bought, traded, and sold as the "skills, talents, and ethnic backgrounds of men and women are commodified, marketed, and billed as trade-enhancing" (2002: 12). The decision to push for such changes was made by business leaders in the 1970s. Business organizations themselves have proudly documented the process of their political reorganization (e.g., Fraser Institute, 1999), which was undertaken as a deliberate strategy of the business community. At the onset of the neoliberal era, in the wake of the oil crisis of 1973, new business organizations such as the Fraser Institute and the BCNI were formed. These organizations have not only pushed for public policy change at the provincial and federal levels, they have also engaged in a systematic public campaign to undermine the political culture of social solidarity and to vaunt the culture of consumerism. The impact of this concerted business campaign to convince the public to support neoliberal values has succeeded in constructing a dominant political discourse in which a right-wing, populist, anti-tax political discourse is the norm.

In order to understand the political role of business in Canadian politics, its militancy must be defined, considered, and analyzed as a form of collective action in the same way as contentious social movements. Business leaders articulate a strong and clearly identifiable political and social identity, put forth a specific meaning frame that identifies their supporters and opponents, create formal and informal networks of political activism ranging from golf clubs to interest associations, and exploit the structure of political opportunity. Many of the tools of social movement analysis may be profitably used to understand their political behaviour. Understanding the political evolution of this dominant group over the last quarter century tells much not only of the story of the shift to neoliberal public policy, but also of the restructuring of Canadian political institutions. Canadian business has consistently pushed for every measure that has de-democratized the Canadian political system, from its opposition to election financing laws to buying and fueling the services of professional lobbying firms. By pouring money into the production of professional policy expertise in think tanks and professional consultancies, they have substantially and actively contributed to "breaking the bargain," as Savoie (2003) puts it, between ministers and politicians, displacing the Keynesian orientation of the federal public service with the credo of "greed is good."

In explaining the specific evolution of collective actors, the tools of social movement theory have much to contribute, even to the analysis of groups normally defined as "interest groups" rather than social movements. As the above example of business militancy demonstrates, the analysis of collective identity claims by organized groups is important for all types of groups. The analysis of the way in which groups frame their claims, both in mobilizing their own constituencies and in relation to state and society, are important not only to the influence that they will exert on public policy, but also, perhaps more importantly, to their discursive impact on political debate and political culture. Producer groups may appear to function in the manner of the traditional "interest group," but using social movement analysis to understand their behaviour encourages us to bring out the ways in which business and farmers' organizations make identity claims, frame the issues they bring forward, create mobilizing structures for their activism, and seek to exploit the structure of political opportunity in the political system. As movements and collective actors articulate their sense of political identity, frame their story, and mobilize to achieve their goals, they participate in the construction of the universe of political discourse by challenging the dominant norms and beliefs of the day or by reinforcing them. The agency of groups and movements plays a critical role in defining the possible in political debate.

Thus, macrohistorical change provides the necessary conditions for political institutional change and for the emergence and consolidation of new forms of collective political action. The mobilization of collective actors in politics plays an important role in constituting, reinforcing, and challenging the dominant political discourse. Collective actors, such as business groups, have directly contributed to the restructuring of political institutions, thus reducing and recasting the access of other collective actors to the state and undermining the legitimacy of collective action.

Political-Institutional Change and Group Politics

Most discussions of neoliberalism focus on policy change in the areas of trade, economic, and social policy. Instead, this book has focused on how the central institutions of the Canadian state have been restructured over the neoliberal era in ways that have reduced and transformed the ability of groups and movements rooted in civil society to access and influence the state. Simultaneously, the federal government's policies toward advocacy organizations have changed dramatically. The government has cut funding to grass roots advocacy organizing at the same time as it is offloading more responsibility to organizations in local communities to deliver services. The shift to a public discourse on civic engagement and charity depoliticizes collective action and undermines democratic participation. The result is a political system with declining voter turnout and increased citizen alienation.

The first area in which the shift to neoliberalism has clearly signaled a decline in the ability of organized groups and social movements to exercise influence on the state is in the arena of representation and electoralism: Parliament and political parties. Generally, it has always been difficult for groups and social movements to exercise influence over MPs because of the institutional features of the Canadian political system, in which the fusion of executive and legislative authority is combined with very high levels of party discipline. In such a system, the challenges for groups and movements are such that at least one analyst has called for the elimination of the term "lobbying" when it refers to interest groups lobbying legislators, arguing that such a picture is based on the American separation of powers system in which members of Congress are less subject to party discipline and hence more open to the influence of groups. The challenges facing groups and movements that wish to exercise power in the party system are reinforced by the continuing dominance of the brokerage style of party politics based on regional interests and leader-driven policy agendas. Consequently, interest group and social movement organizations based on non-territorial and non-regional interests and identities face insuperable obstacles to influence. The rules of the first-past-the-post system continue to place a premium on regional majorities that can be converted into seats, a system that systematically disenfranchises non-territorial political interests. The environmental movement is a good example of a movement that cannot break through in the first-past-the-post system. Increasingly, Canadians support the Green Party, with percentages ranging from 2 to 7 per cent across the country (Fagan, 2004). However, support for the Greens is so dispersed that it is virtually impossible for the party to win a seat in the House of Commons under current electoral rules.

At the same time, the transition to neoliberalism and the rise of post-industrial capitalism have caused stress to the traditional political parties in Canada as elsewhere. The enhanced role of media in post-industrial capitalism and the tremendous economic weight of cultural production in the new economic system has shaped the ways in which politicians and political parties do their jobs all over the world. Increasingly, politicians of all parties must conform to the logic of an increasingly concentrated corporate media system. Although there may be cases in which such corporate media openly censor the expression of certain points of view, such as the Disney corporation's threats to refuse to distribute Michael Moore's anti-war film *Fahrenheit 9/11* (*New York Times*, 2004), the impact of media rests in the nature of the technology and its role as a profitable industry that is central to post-industrial capitalism. As many media analysts have pointed out, television privileges the short sound byte at the expense of substantive policy discussion (Taras, 2001), and the increasing cost of media access has caused political parties to seek out new sources of financing. Political parties must also pay for professional media advice. The search for funds to pay for media access and advice has led many political parties into financing scandals and has caused heated debates on election financing laws. These developments greatly strengthen the position of the leader within political parties. Even well-developed mass parties, such as the British Labour Party, have been affected by these developments, so it is no surprise that Canadian cadre parties, with their long-standing brokerage practices, have become more and more leader-centred in the neoliberal era. Therefore, group and movement access to political parties and the parliamentary arena rests on access to the leader. And the prime minister is more likely to golf with buddies from the business world than with activists from Greenpeace.

At the same time as the position of the leader has been strengthened, political parties are also facing an electorate and party memberships that are more volatile than ever. Brokerage parties in Canadian politics have always had weakly identified supporters. Party members increasingly are consumers who will desert the party if it is not meeting their needs, reflecting their views, or providing value for money. Members are demanding direct democracy measures and the empowerment of the grass roots, all of which create new challenges for party leaders in managing the production of images and messages not only for the consumption of voters, but also for quasi-empowered and fickle party members.

The new challenges for party leaders have caused them to look to the new class of professional political consultants, who have become increasingly important in the neoliberal era. Media consultants, pollsters, and professional lobbyists exist to advise governments and political leaders on how to manage the media, the public, and the party; how to raise money; and how to spend money on media access. The rise of this new class represents the commodification of political access in the neoliberal age, acting as a buffer between social groups and the state. And, given the powerful position of the Canadian prime minister in the policy-making process, its role is increasingly important to public policy. The rise of this professional class does not open up the political process; rather, it closes down access as the services of this group are open only to those with the ability to pay for them.

The same shift toward shutting down public access to policy-making can be seen at work in the broad range of changes that has reshaped the federal public service over the last quarter century. Policy communities have been affected by the decline of the position of the minister in the line department, the rise of central agencies, and the enhanced role of the prime minister's office. To the extent that policy advice from the public service has been circumvented by the influence of the professional political class of media consultants, pollsters, and lobbyists, many organized interest groups that once might have expected to enjoy a close relationship with line departments have been outflanked. Because the professional political class sells its services, there are incentives in the system for groups to buy them, rather than to cultivate relationships of influence with the public service. The transition to new public management represents an attempt to commodify the work of the public service in new ways by bringing the principles and practices of the market system to bear in government decision-making. As policy communities move away from providing a system for making public policy decisions in concert with affected stakeholders toward a system in which civic engagement and consultative exercises are managed by the professional for-profit political class, access and influence for organized groups and social movement organizations also declines.

Policy communities were never a level playing field. Groups with resources, money, and organization who were willing to tailor their demands to negotiate with the state always had the best chances of cultivating institutionalized relationships of mutual influence in the manner described in the policy community literature. However, the decline of ministerial responsibility and the consequent decline of the line departments in providing policy direction and guidance, combined with the rise of the central agencies and central political advisors in the prime minister's office, means that even traditional interest groups must recast their strategies. As Savoie states, "[p]artisan advisers are now expected to work hand in glove with partisan lobbyists and pollsters to marshal arguments to challenge, if necessary, the policy positions prepared by departmental career officials" (Savoie, 2003: 129). In this context, interest groups and social movement organizations cannot expect to influence public policy through influence in the line department, as was once the case.

At the same time, government policies toward civil society have reflected the values, practices, and paradoxes of neoliberalism. As Banaszak, Beckwith, and Rucht (2003) argue, institutional restructuring for neoliberalism requires the downloading, offloading, and lateral loading of government responsibilities. This has meant a new role for groups and organizations in delivering government services, especially since the Liberal government moved away from funding advocacy organizations such as women's groups. Thus, federal policies have set up a new incentive structure for associational life, in which engaging in political advocacy is viewed as dangerous, while engaging in service provision is seen as a way to access funding and, potentially, policy influence. Federal policies reflect the anxieties of neoliberalism, as the government is concerned about cohesion, declining social trust, and citizen alienation from the political process, even as its own policies foster these results by redefining collective action as charitable or voluntary sector activity.

There is no better example of a neoliberal attempt to re-engineer civil society organizations than the federal initiative on the voluntary sector. This policy reflects the federal government's recognition that it needs civil society actors such as interest groups and social movement organizations; however, it wants such groups to play a depoliticized role in service provision and a consultative role in providing legitimacy for government policies. This type of bargain has always been central to policy communities; that is, line departments consulted with interest group and social movement organizations because of the policy expertise such groups could provide and because of the legitimacy they were able to accord to government policies. However, in the policy community, groups were understood to represent the interests of their members and to have the right to defend their interests. In the new regime of citizen engagement and the voluntary sector initiative, the individual is the privileged political actor to be consulted via polls and focus groups, the citizen is a client or consumer of government services, and the group is just another vehicle for delivering services to the apoliticized citizenry. These initiatives reflect the government's awareness of the social problems that have arisen in Canadian society as a result of neoliberal economic and social policies and the growing social and economic inequality these policies have caused. Yet, they simply reinforce declining citizen alienation and trust by defining citizens as volunteers, clients, and consumers, rather than as active participants in democratic political mobilization, with the right to their own distinctive political interests and collective identities. The initiatives to involve the public in consultative exercises and initiatives have failed to stem the growing tide of citizen alienation from the political process, citizen mistrust of politicians, and citizen disinterest in casting a ballot in federal elections.

As political institutions have shut down and delegitimated access and influence, the courts have enhanced their role in the Canadian political system. Again, this development is not unique to Canada, even though Canadian political science has usually emphasized the domestic roots of judicial empowerment in the constitutional debates of the 1970s and early 1980s. But, as comparative works such as Ran Hirschl (2004) and Charles Epp (1998) have convincingly shown, judicial empowerment is a process that has occurred in many different contexts. In Canada, the strategy of using courts to achieve public policy goals is not a new strategy; however, judicial empowerment has greatly expanded the access of collective actors to litigation and has had important public policy effects in areas such as Aboriginal rights, lesbian and gay rights, and women's rights. Empowering courts has ambiguous effects for interest group and social movement organizations. On the one hand, the constitutional changes of 1982 have not reduced the use of litigation by corporations using private law, and, according to the data provided by some analysts (e.g., Hein 2000), judicial empowerment has been very successfully exploited by corporations in public law cases as well. For First Nations, the entrenchment of section 35 recognizing Aboriginal rights has been an important symbolic and legal step; however, the very slow progress of land claims and the lack of recognition and implementation of self-government for Aboriginal peoples demonstrates that litigation has not succeeded in bringing about the types of public policy changes that would truly decolonize the relationship between Aboriginal and European Canadians.

For other groups that have used litigation, such efforts have had mixed success. As a political strategy, the use of litigation strengthens the hand of legal elites within groups and social movement organizations. While rights-claiming can be an effective and powerful resource for social movement organizations, as the example of the lesbian and gay rights movement attests, such Charter-based rights claims also reinforce individualism and assimilation to dominant social norms. Most Charter challenges have not disturbed the structures of economic inequality in Canadian society but, arguably, have reinforced them through focusing on the inclusion of previously excluded groups into existing social policy (e.g., lesbian and gay rights). When Charter and other legal cases have challenged economic and society inequality, these challenges have tended to fail before the courts. Thus, the process of judicial empowerment opens up new points of access for group and movement organizations, but at a price. They are also available to counter movements and to corporations. Most importantly, the legalization of politics fits with the precepts of neoliberalism, because the legal system reflects the inequalities of capitalism and reinforces a rights-based conception of social relations based on the individual.

New Forms of Contention

This book has conveyed a pessimistic message about the possibilities for democracy within the Canadian nation-state. However, there is widespread opposition to neoliberalism, even if it is often choked by the restructuring of Canadian political institutions described here. In part because of the decline of the domestic state as an arena of democratic politics and in part because of the declining policy capacity and sovereignty of the Canadian government, important new forms of collective action and political action are taking shape outside and beyond the state. These forms of contention are hopeful signs, although their capacity to provide the institutional underpinnings of democratic politics and the rule of law has yet to be developed.

Transnational activism is one such form of contestation that has taken on a number of different forms across a range of global and Canadian issues. Aboriginal peoples from Canada have formed alliances with indigenous peoples around the world and sought to change the policies of Canadian governments. Women's organizations, environmental groups, and trade unions have formed cross-border contacts over North American neoliberal trade policies. Lesbian and gay activists from Canada have actively participated in the building of a transnational activist network to work for lesbian and gay rights in international organizations such as the United Nation (UN) and in the many countries of the world in which lesbian and gay rights are not yet recognized. Anti-globalization protesters from Canada have traveled to events all over the world, including the People's Summits that have been held parallel to meetings of the WTO and G-8 (the summit gatherings of the leaders of the eight major industrial countries). Counter-movements, such as evangelical Christians, have also gone global, working to oppose women's rights and reproductive freedom in UN policies and targeting development aid programs in the US and other countries (Buss and Herman, 2003).

These developments also entail changes in the targets of contention and protest. International organizations, trade agreements, and corporations have taken the place of states as the targets of collective action. Campaigns such as those against child labour or sweatshops have put a face on the suffering caused by neoliberal economic policies in developing countries. These transnational activist campaigns may ignore the Canadian state completely and focus their energies entirely on international organizations or corporations. Alternatively, they may use transnational and global strategies to pressure the Canadian state, as in the case of First Nations. These groups and campaigns offer new possibilities for political engagement.

Yet, transnational activism cannot replace interest group and social movement organizing through the domestic political arena. The nation-state still provides the essential framework of democratic accountability and the rule of law. For this reason, the changes in the nature of Canadian political institutions—changes that have moved these institutions in a less democratic and accountable direction—are of central importance for the future of democratic citizenship in Canada. As voter turnout declines and Canadians disengage from the electoral arena, this book has shown that social movement and interest group politics are not an effective alternative as a form of democratic practice. With the exception of business groups that have strong ties to the dominant political elite, most interest groups and social movement organizations in Canadian politics face a set of political institutions and a dominant discourse of politics that systematically and structurally delegitimates collective political action. This fact should be of central concern to those who wish to build a democratic political future in Canada and the world.

References

Abele, Frances, and Daiva Stasiulis. 1989. "Canada as a White Settler Colony: What About Natives and Immigrants?" In Wallace Clement and Glen Williams (eds.), *The New Canadian Political Economy*. Montreal and Kingston: McGill-Queen's University Press. 240-77.

Abele, Frances, Katherine Graham, Alex Ker, Antonia Maoini, and Susan Phillips. 1998. *Talking with Canadians: Citizen Engagement and the Social Union*. Ottawa: Canadian Council on Social Development.

Abele, Frances, and Michael Prince. 2003. "Aboriginal Governance and Canadian Federalism." In François Rocher and Miriam Smith (eds.), *New Trends in Canadian Federalism*. Peterborough: Broadview Press. 135-66.

Abella, Irving M. 1973. *Nationalism, Communism and Canadian Labour: The CIO, the Communist Party and the Canadian Congress of Labour, 1935-1956*. Toronto: University of Toronto Press.

Abu-Laban, Yasmeen, and Christina Gabriel. 2002. *Selling Diversity: Immigration, Multiculturalism, Employment Equity, and Globalization*. Peterborough: Broadview Press.

Adamson, Nancy, Linda Briskin, and Margaret McPhail. 1989. *Feminist Organizing for Change: The Contemporary Women's Movement in Canada*. Don Mills: Oxford University Press.

Alford, Robert. 1963. *Party and Society: The Anglo-American Democracies*. Westport, CT: Greenwood Press.

Alfred, Gerald R. (Taiaiake). 1995. *Heeding the Voices of Our Ancestors: Mohawk Politics and the Rise of Native Nationalism*. Toronto: Oxford University Press.

Alfred, Taiaiake. 1999. *Peace, Power, Righteousness: An Indigenous Manifesto*. Toronto: Oxford University Press.

Allen, Richard. 1971. *The Social Passion: Religion and Social Reform in Canada, 1914-1928*. Toronto: University of Toronto Press.

Almond, Gabriel. 1988. "The Return to the State." *American Political Science Review* 82(3): 853-74.

Alter, Karen J., and Jeannette Vargas. 2000. "Explaining Variation in the Use of European Litigation Strategies: European Community Law and British Gender Equity Policy." *Comparative Political Studies* 33(4): 452-82.

Anderson, Benedict. 1983. *Imagined Communities: Reflections on the Origins and Spread of Nationalism*. London: Verso.

Archer, Keith. 1990. *Political Choices and Electoral Consequences: A Study of Organized Labour and the New Democratic Party*. Montreal and Kingston: McGill-Queen's University Press.

Axworthy, Thomas. 2002. *Diefenbaker's Bill of Rights* <http://www.historia. ca>.

Ayres, Jeffrey M. 1998. *Challenging Conventional Wisdom: Political Movements and Popular Contention against North American Free Trade*. Toronto: University of Toronto Press.

Ayres, Jeffrey M. 2004. "Framing Collective Action Against Neoliberalism: The Case of the 'Anti-Globalization' Movement." *Journal of World-Systems Research* 10(1): 11-34.

Babcock, Robert. 1974. *Gompers in Canada*. Toronto: University of Toronto Press.

Bacchi, Carol Lee. 1983. *Liberation Deferred? The Ideas of the English-Canadian Suffragists, 1877-1918*. Toronto: University of Toronto Press.

Bagdikian, Ben H. 1992. *The Media Monopoly*. 4th ed. Boston: Beacon Press.

Banaszak, Lee Ann, Karen Beckwith, and Dieter Rucht. 2003. "When Power Relocates: Interactive Changes in Women's Movements and States." In Lee Ann Banaszak, Karen Beckwith, and Dieter Rucht (eds.), *Women's Movements Facing the Reconfigured State*. Cambridge: Cambridge University Press. 1-29.

Bashevkin, Sylvia. 2002. *Welfare Hot Buttons: Women, Work and Social Policy Reform*. Toronto: University of Toronto Press.

Baumgartner, Frank R., and Beth L. Leech. 1998. *Basic Interests: The Importance of Groups in Politics and in Political Science*. Princeton: Princeton University Press.

Beck, Ulrich, and E. Beck-Gernsheim. 2002. *Individualization: Institutionalized Individualism and Its Social and Political Consequences*. London: Sage.

Bentley, Arthur F. 1908. *The Process of Government*. Chicago: University of Chicago Press.

Bercuson, David. 1978. *Fools and Wise Men: The Rise and Fall of One Big Union*. Toronto: McGraw-Hill Ryerson.

Bernstein, Steven. 2003. "International Institutions and the Framing of Canada's Climate Change Policy: Mitigating or Masking the Integrity Gap." In Eugene Lee and Anthony Perl (eds.), *The Integrity Gap: Canada's Environmental Policy and Institutions*. Vancouver: University of British Columbia Press. 68-104

Bissoondath, Neil. 2002. *Selling Illusions: The Cult of Multiculturalism in Canada*. 2nd ed. Toronto: Penguin.

Bliss, Michael. 1972. "'Dyspepsia of the Mind': The Canadian Businessman and His Enemies, 1880-1914." In David S. Macmillan (ed.), Canadian *Business History* Toronto: McClelland and Stewart. 175-91.

Bogart, W.A. 1994. *Courts and Country: The Limits of Litigation and the Social and Political Life of Canada*. Toronto: Oxford University Press.

Borrows, John. 1999. "Sovereignty's Alchemy: An Analysis of *Delgamuukw v. British Columbia*." *Osgoode Hall Law Journal* 37: 537–96.

Boyd, Susan, and Claire F.L. Young. 2003. "'From Same-Sex to No Sex'?: Trends Towards Recognition of (Same-Sex) Relationships in Canada." *Seattle Journal for Social Justice* 1(3): 757-93.

Brock, Kathy L. (ed). 2002. *Improving Connections between Governments and Nonprofit and Voluntary Organizations: Public Policy and the Third Sector*.

Montreal and Kingston: School of Policy Studies/McGill-Queen's University Press.

Brodie, Janine. 1997. "Meso-discourses, State Forms and the Gendering of the Liberal-Democratic Citizenship." *Citizenship Studies* 1(2): 223-41.

Brodie, Janine. 2003. "Globalization, In/Security, and the Paradoxes of the Social." In Isabella Bakker and Stephen Gill (eds.), *Power, Production and Social Reproduction: Human In/security in the Global Political Economy*. London: Palgrave Macmillan. 47-65.

Brodie, Janine, and Jane Jenson. 1988. *Crisis, Challenge and Change: Party and Class in Canada Revisited*. Ottawa: Carleton University Press.

Brodie, Janine, Shelley A.M. Gavigan, and Jane Jenson. 1992. *The Politics of Abortion*. Toronto: Oxford University Press.

Brodie, Ian. 2002. *Friends of the Court: The Privileging of Interest Group Litigants in Canada*. Syracuse: State University of New York Press.

Bucovetsky, M.W. 1975. "The Mining Industry and the Great Tax Reform Debate." In A. Paul Pross (ed.), *Pressure Group Behavior in Canadian Politics*. Toronto: McGraw-Hill Ryerson. 87-114.

Buechler, Steven M. 2000. *Social Movements in Advanced Capitalism*. New York and Oxford: Oxford University Press.

Buss, Doris, and Didi Herman. 2003. *Globalizing Family Values: The Christian Right in International Politics*. Minneapolis and London: University of Minnesota Press.

Cairns, Alan C. 1991. "Citizens (Outsiders) and Governments (Insiders) in Constitution-Making: The Case of Meech Lake." In Douglas E. Williams (ed.), *Disruptions: Constitutional Struggles from the Charter to Meech Lake*. Toronto: McClelland and Stewart. 108-38.

Cairns, Alan C. 1992. *Charter versus Federalism: The Dilemmas of Constitutional Reform*. Montreal and Kingston: McGill-Queen's University Press.

Cameron, Duncan, and Daniel Drache (eds.). 1985. *The Other Macdonald Report*. Toronto: Lorimer.

Caplan, Gerald L. 1973. *The Dilemma of Canadian Socialism*. Toronto: McClelland and Stewart.

Cardinal, Linda. 2001. "Le pouvoir exécutif et la judiciarisation de la politique au Canada. Une étude du programme de contestation judiciaire." *Politique et Société* 19: 43-64.

Carroll, William K., and Elaine Coburn. 2003. "Social Movements and Transformation." In Wallace Clement and Leah Vosko (eds.), *Changing Canada: Political Economy as Transformation*. Montreal and Kingston: McGill-Queen's University Press. 79-105.

Carty, R. Kenneth. 2004. "Parties as Franchise Systems: The Stratarchical Organizational Imperative." *Party Politics* 10(1): 5-24.

Carty, R. Kenneth, William Cross, and Lisa Young. 2000. *Rebuilding Canadian Party Politics*. Vancouver: University of British Columbia Press.

Castells, Manuel. 1997. *The Power of Identity*. Oxford: Blackwell.

CCCE (Canadian Council of Chief Executives). 2004. *About CCCE*. <http://www.ceocouncil.ca/en/about/history.php>. Accessed February 17, 2004.

Clarke, Harold, Jane Jensen, Lawrence LeDuc, and Jon Pammett. 1986. *Absent Mandate: The Politics of Discontent in Canada*. Toronto, ON: Gage.

Clarkson, Stephen. 2002. *Uncle Sam and Us: Globalization, Neoconservatism and the Canadian State*. Toronto: University of Toronto Press.

Clement, Wallace, and Glen Williams (eds.). 1989. *The New Canadian Political Economy*. Montreal and Kingston: McGill-Queen's University Press.

Cleverdon, Catherine L. 1975. [1950] *The Woman Suffrage Movement in Canada*. 2nd ed. Toronto: University of Toronto Press.

Coleman, William D. 1988. *Business and Politics: A Study of Collective Action*. Montreal and Kingston: McGill-Queen's University Press.

Coleman, William D., and Grace Skogstad. 1990. "Policy Communities and Policy Networks: A Structural Approach." In William D. Coleman and Grace Skogstad (eds.), *Policy Communities and Public Policy: A Structural Approach*. Mississauga: Copp Clark Pitman. 14-33.

Collier, Ruth Berins, and David Collier. 1991. *Shaping the Political Arena: Critical Junctures, the Labor Movement, and Regime Dynamics in Latin America*. Princeton: Princeton University Press.

Conway, Janet M. 2004. *Identity, Place, Knowledge: Social Movements Contesting Globalization*. Halifax: Fernwood.

Cortner, Richard C. 1968. "Strategies and Tactics of Litigants in Constitutional Cases." *Journal of Public Law* 17. 287-307.

Dahl, Robert A. 1957. "Decision-Making in a Democracy: The Supreme Court as a National Policy-Maker." *Journal of Public Law* 6: 279-95.

Dahl, Robert A. 1961. *Who Governs?: Democracy and Power in an American City*. New Haven: Yale University Press.

Dale, Stephen. 1996. *McLuhan's Children: The Greenpeace Message and the Media* Toronto: Between the Lines.

Dickason, Olive. 2002. *Canada's First Nations: A History of Founding Peoples from Earliest Times*. Don Mills: Oxford University Press.

Dobrowolsky, Alexandra. 2000a. "Political Parties, Teletubby Politics, the Third Way, and Democratic Challenger(s)." In Glen Williams and Mike Whittington (eds.), *Canadian Politics in the 21st Century*. Scarborough: Nelson. 131-58.

Dobrowolsky, Alexandra. 2000b. *The Politics of Pragmatism: Women, Representation, and Constitutionalism in Canada*. Don Mills: Oxford University Press.

Docherty, David. 1997. *Mr. Smith Goes to Ottawa: Life in the House of Commons*. Vancouver: University of British Columbia Press.

Doran, Charles F., and Gregory P. Marchildon. 1994. *The NAFTA Puzzle: Political Parties and Trade in North America*. Boulder: Westview.

Drache, A.B.C., with F.K. Boyle. 1998. *Charities, Public Benefit and the Canadian Income Tax System: A Proposal for Reform*. Toronto: Kahanoff Nonprofit Sector Research Initiative.

Dubinsky, Karen. 1985. *"Lament for a 'Patriarchy Lost'"?: Anti-Feminism, Anti-Abortion and R.E.A.L. Women in Canada*. Ottawa: Canadian Research Institute for the Advancement of Women.

Duverger, Maurice. 1967. *Political Parties: Their Organization and Activity in the Modern State*. New York: Wiley.

Dymond, Bill, Michael Hart, and Colin Robertson. 1994. *Decision at Midnight: Inside the Canada-US Free Trade Negotiations*. Vancouver: University of British Columbia Press.

Easton, David. 1965. *A Framework for Political Analysis*. Englewood Cliffs, NJ: Prentice-Hall.

Eisenstein, Hester. 1996. *Inside Agitators: Australian Femocrats and the State*. Philadelphia: Temple University Press.

Epp, Charles R. 1998. *The Rights Revolution: Lawyers, Activists and Supreme Courts in Comparative Perspective*. Chicago: University of Chicago Press.

Epstein, Lee. 1985. *Conservatives in Court*. Knoxville: University of Tennessee Press.

Errington, Jane. 1993. "Pioneers and Suffragists." In Sandra Burt, Lorraine Code, and Lindsay Dorney (eds.), *Changing Patterns: Women in Canada*. Toronto: McClelland and Stewart. 59-91.

Esping-Andersen, Gøsta. 1985. *Politics against Markets: The Social Democratic Road to Power*. Princeton: Princeton University Press.

Fagan, Drew. 2004. "Liberal Support Hovers on Verge of Majority Status." *Globe and Mail* (May 20): A3.

Farr, James. 1995. "Remembering the Revolution: Behavioralism in American Political Science." In James Farr, John S. Dryzek, and Stephen T. Leonard (eds.), *Political Science in History: Research Programs and Political Traditions*. Cambridge: Cambridge University Press.

Findlay, Sue. 1987. "Facing the State: The Politics of the Women's Movement Reconsidered." In Heather Jon Maroney and Meg Luxton (eds.), *Feminism and Political Economy: Women's Work, Women's Struggles*. Toronto: Methuen. 31-50.

Finkel, Alvin. 1989. *The Social Credit Phenomenon in Alberta*. Toronto: University of Toronto Press.

Flanagan, Thomas. 1998. *Game Theory and Canadian Politics*. Toronto: University of Toronto Press.

Franks, C.E.S. 1987. *The Parliament of Canada*. Toronto: University of Toronto Press.

Fraser Institute. 1999. *Challenging Perceptions: Twenty-Five Years of Influential Ideas*. Vancouver: The Fraser Institute.

Fraser, Nancy. 1995. "From Redistribution to Recognition? Dilemmas of Justice in a 'Postsocialist' Age." *New Left Review* 212 (July/August): 68-93.

Freeman, Aaron. 2004. "Supreme Court Decision Democratizes Interest Group Participation in Elections by Limiting Wealthy Interests." *Ottawa Citizen* (May 19).

Fudge, Judy. 2001. "The Canadian Charter of Rights: Recognition, Redistribution and the Imperialism of the Courts." In Tom Campbell, K.D. Ewing, and Adam Tomkins (eds.), *Sceptical Essays on Human Rights*. Oxford: Oxford University Press. 335-58.

Gaventa, John. 1982. *Power and Powerlessness*. Urbana and Chicago: University of Illinois Press.

Giddens, Anthony. 1984. *The Constitution of Society: Outline of a Theory of Structuration*. Cambridge: Polity Press.

Giddens, Anthony. 1994. *Beyond Left and Right: The Future of Radical Politics*. London: Polity.

Gill, Stephen. 1995. "Globalisation, Market Civilization, and Disciplinary Neoliberalism." *Millennium* 23(3): 399-423.

Glasbeek, Harry J. 1989. "Some Strategies for an Unlikely Task: The Progressive Use of Law." *Ottawa Law Review* 91(9): 387-418.

Gotell, Lise. 2002. "Toward a Democratic Practice of Feminist Litigation?: LEAF's Changing Approach to Charter Equality." In Radha Jhappan (ed.), *Women's Legal Strategies in Canada*. Toronto: University of Toronto Press. 135-74.

Gramsci, Antonio. 1992 [1932]. *Prison Notebooks*. New York: Columbia University Press.

Granatstein, J.L. 1998. *The Ottawa Men: The Civil Service Mandarins, 1935-1957*. Toronto: University of Toronto Press.

Green, Joyce. 2001. "Canaries in the Mines of Citizenship: Indian Women in Canada." *Canadian Journal of Political Science* 34(4): 715-38.

Greene, Ian, Carl Baar, Peter McCormick, George Szablowski, and Martin Thomas. 1998. *Final Appeal: Decision-Making in Canadian Courts of Appeal*. Toronto: Lorimer.

Greer, Allan. 1993. *The Patriots and the People: The Rebellion of 1837 in Rural Lower Canada*. Toronto: University of Toronto Press.

Gusfield, Joseph R. 1963. *Symbolic Crusade: Status Politics and the American Temperance Movement*. Urbana: University of Illinois Press.

Harrison, Kathryn. 2003. "Passing the Environmental Buck." In François Rocher and Miriam Smith (eds.), *New Trends in Canadian Federalism*. Peterborough, ON: Broadview Press. 313-52.

Harrison, Trevor. 1995. *Of Passionate Intensity: Right-wing Populism and the Reform Party of Canada*. Toronto: University of Toronto Press.

Harper v. Canada (Attorney General), [2004] 1 SCR 827.

Hattam, Victoria C. 1993. *Labor Visions and State Power: The Origins of Business Unionism in the United States*. Princeton: Princeton University Press.

Hein, Gregory. 2000. "Interest Group Litigation and Canadian Democracy." *Choices* 6(2) March: 3-31.

Held, David. 1995. *Democracy and the Global Order: From the Modern State to Cosmopolitan Governance*. Stanford: Stanford University Press.

Henderson, James Youngblood. 1994. "Empowering Treaty Federalism." *Saskatchewan Law Review* 58(2): 241-332.

Heron, Craig. 1984. "Labourism and the Canadian Working Class." *Labour/Le Travail* 13 (Spring): 45-76.

Hiebert, Janet. 2002. *Charter Conflicts: What is Parliament's Role?* Montreal and Kingston: McGill-Queen's University Press.

Hirschl, Ran. 2004. *Toward Juristocracy: The Origins and Consequences of the New Constitutionalism*. Cambridge, MA: Harvard University Press.

Howe, R. Brian. 1991. "Human Rights in Hard Times: The Post-War Canadian Experience." *Canadian Public Administration* 35(4): 26-40.

Howe, R. Brian. 1993. "Incrementalism and Human Rights Reform." *Journal of Canadian Studies* 28(3): 29-42.

Hunt, Alan. 1990. "Rights and Social Movements: Counter-Hegemonic Strategies." *Journal of Law and Society* 17(3) Autumn: 309-28.

Inglehart, Ronald. 1997. *Modernization and Postmodernization: Cultural, Economic and Political Change in Forty-Three Societies*. Princeton: Princeton University Press.

Innis, Harold A. 1954 [1940]. *The Cod Fisheries: The History of an International Economy*. Toronto: University of Toronto Press.

Innis, Harold A. 1970 [1930]. *The Fur Trade in Canada: An Introduction to Canadian Economic History*. Toronto: University of Toronto Press.

Jenkins, J. Craig. 1993. "Resource Mobilization Theory and the Study of Social Movements." *American Review of Sociology* 9: 527-53.

Jenson, Jane. 1989. "Paradigms and Political Discourse: Protective Legislation in France and the United States Before 1914." *Canadian Journal of Political Science* 22(2): 1-28.

Jenson, Jane, and Susan D. Phillips. 1996. "Regime Shift: New Citizenship Practices in Canada." *International Journal of Canadian Studies* 14: 111-35.

Juillet, Luc. 1998. "Les politiques environnementales canadiennes." In Manon Tremblay (ed.), *Les politiques publique canadiennes*. Québec: Les Presses de L'Université Laval. 161-204.

Katz, Robert. 2001. "The Problem of Candidate Selection and Models of Party Democracy." *Party Politics* 7: 277-96.

Keck, Margaret, and Kathryn Sikkink. 1998. *Activists Beyond Borders: Advocacy Networks in International Politics*. Ithaca: Cornell University Press.

Kernaghan, Kenneth, Brian Marson, and Sanford Borins. 2000. *The New Public Organization*. Toronto: Institute of Public Administration of Canada.

Kinsman, Gary, Dieter K. Buse, and Mercedes Steedman. 2000. *Whose National Security? Canadian State Surveillance and the Creation of Enemies*. Toronto: Between the Lines.

Knopff, Rainer, and F.L. Morton. 1992. *Charter Politics*. Scarborough: Nelson Canada.

Koch, John. 1990. "Making Room: New Directions in Third Party Intervention." *University of Toronto Faculty of Law Review* 48 (Winter): 151-67.

Kome, Penney. 1983. *The Taking of Twenty-Eight: Women Challenge the Constitution*. Toronto: Women's Press.

Korpi, Walter. 1983. *The Democratic Class Struggle*. London: Routledge and Kegan Paul.

Kwavnick, David. 1975. "Interest Group Demands and the Federal Political System." In A. Paul Pross (ed.), *Pressure Group Behaviour in Canadian Politics*. Toronto: McGraw-Hill. 69-86.

Ladner, Kiera L. 2003. "Governing Within an Ecological Context: Creating an AlterNative Understanding of Blackfoot Governance." *Studies in Political Economy* 70 (Spring): 125-52.

Laghi, Brian. 2003. "Liberals Could Lose Same-Sex Free Vote." *Globe and Mail* (August 14): A1.

Langille, David. 1987. "The Business Council on National Issues." *Studies in Political Economy* 24 (Autumn): 78-95.

Larner, Wendy. 2000 "Neo-liberalism: Policy, Ideology, Governmentality." *Studies in Political Economy* 63: 5-25.

Laxer, James L. 1989. *Open for Business: The Roots of Foreign Ownership in Canada.* Toronto: Oxford University Press.

Laycock, David. 2001. *The New Right and Democracy in Canada: Understanding Reform and the Canadian Alliance.* Don Mills: Oxford University Press.

Levine, Sharon. 1993. "Advocating Values: Public Interest Intervention in Charter Litigation." *National Journal of Constitutional Law* 2: 27-62.

Levitt, Kari. 1970. *Silent Surrender: The Multinational Corporation in Canada.* Toronto: Macmillan.

Lindblom, Charles E. 1977. *Politics and Markets: The World's Political Economic Systems.* New York: Basic Books.

Lindblom, Charles E. 1995 [1957]. "The Science of 'Muddling' Through." In Stella Theodoulou and Matthew Can (eds.), *Public Policy: The Essential Readings.* New York: Prentice Hall. 113-27.

Lipset, S.M. 1950. *Agrarian Socialism: The Co-operative Commonwealth Federation in Saskatchewan.* Berkeley: University of California Press.

Lockwood, Glenn J. 1993. "Temperance in Upper Canada as Ethnic Subterfuge." In Cheryl Krasnick Warsh (ed.), *Drink in Canada: Historical Essays.* Montreal and Kingston: McGill-Queen's University Press. 43-69.

Lukes, Stephen. 1974. *Power: A Radical View.* London: Macmillan.

Macdonald, Laura. 2003. "Gender and Canadian Trade Policy: Women's Strategies for Access and Transformation." In Claire Turenne Sjolander, Heather A. Smith, and Deborah Stienstra (eds.), *Feminist Perspectives on Canadian Foreign Policy.* Don Mills: Oxford University Press. 40-54.

Mahon, Rianne. 1977. "Canadian Public Policy: The Unequal Structure of Representation." In Leo Panitch (ed.), *The Canadian State: Political Economy and Political Power.* Toronto: University of Toronto Press. 165-98.

Majury, Diana. 2002. "Women's (In) equality Before and After the Charter." In Radha Jhappan (ed.), *Women's Legal Strategies in Canada.* Toronto: University of Toronto Press. 101-34.

Mallory, J.R. 1954. *Social Credit and the Federal Power in Canada.* Toronto: University of Toronto Press.

Mandel, Michael. 1994. *The Charter of Rights and the Legalization of Politics in Canada.* Revised, updated and expanded ed. Toronto: Thompson.

Manfredi, Christopher P. 1993. *Judicial Power and the Charter: Canada and the Paradox of Liberal Constitutionalism.* Toronto: McClelland and Stewart.

Manfredi, Christopher P. 2004. *Feminist Activism in the Supreme Court: Legal Mobilization and the Women's Legal Education and Action Fund.* Vancouver: University of British Columbia Press.

Manley, John F. 1983. "Neo-Pluralism." *American Political Science Review* 77: 368-89.

March, James G. and Johan P. Olsen. 1989. *Rediscovering Institution: The Organizational Basis of Politics.* Boston: Free Press.

Marchak, Patricia. 1985. "Canadian Political Economy." *Canadian Review of Sociology and Anthropology* 22(5): 673-709.

Mayer, Margit. 1995. "Social Movement Research in the United States: A European Perspective." In Stanford M. Lyman (ed.), *Social Movements: Critiques, Concepts, Case-Studies*. London: Macmillan. 168-95.

Mayer, Margit. 2003. "The Onward Sweep of Social Capital: Causes and Consequences for Understanding Cities, Communities and Urban Movements." *International Journal of Urban and Regional Research* 27(1): 110-32.

McAdam, Doug. 1982. *Political Process and the Development of Black Insurgency, 1930-1970*. Chicago: University of Chicago Press.

McBride, Stephen. 2001. *Paradigm Shift: Globalization and the Canadian State*. Halifax: Fernwood.

McCormack, A. Ross. 1977. *Rebels, Reformers and Revolutionaries*. Toronto: University of Toronto Press.

McIvor, Heather. 1996. "Do Canadian Political Parties Form a Cartel?" *Canadian Journal of Political Science* 29(2): 317-33.

McKeen, Wendy, and Anne Porter. 2003. "Politics and Transformation: Welfare State Restructuring in Canada." In Wallace Clement and Leah Vosko (eds.), *Changing Canada: Political Economy as Transformation*. Montreal: McGill-Queen's University Press. 109-134.

McKenzie, Judith I. 2002. *Environmental Politics in Canada: Managing the Commons into the Twenty-First Century*. Don Mills: Oxford University Press.

McMahon, Kevin J. 2004. *Reconsidering Roosevelt on Race: How the Presidency Paved the Road to Brown*. Chicago: University of Chicago Press.

McNeil, Kent. 2001. *Emerging Justice: Essays on Indigenous Rights in Canada and Australia*. Saskatoon: Native Law Centre, University of Saskatchewan.

Melucci, Alberto. 1996. *Challenging Codes: Collective Action in the Information Age*. Cambridge: Cambridge University Press.

Miller, J.R. 2000. *Skyscrapers Hide the Heavens: A History of Indian-White Relations in Canada*. Toronto: University of Toronto Press.

Milner, Henry (ed.). 1999. *Making Every Vote Count*. Peterborough, ON: Broadview.

Monière, Denis, 1977. *Le développement des idéologies au Québec: des origines à nos jour*. Montréal: Editions Québec-Amérique.

Moore, Barrington. 1966. *Social Origins of Dictatorship and Democracy: Lord and Peasant in the Making of the Modern World*. Boston: Beacon Hill.

Moore, Christopher. 1998. *1867: How the Fathers Made a Deal*. Toronto: McClelland and Stewart.

Morton, W.L. 1950. *The Progressive Party in Canada*. Toronto: University of Toronto Press.

Naylor, Tom. 1972. "The Commercial Empire of the St. Lawrence." In Gary Teeple (ed.), *Capitalism and the National Question in Canada*. Toronto, University of Toronto Press. 1-36.

Nevitte, Neil. 1993. "New Politics, the Charter and Political Participation." In Herman Bakvis (ed.), *Representation, Integration and Political Parties in Canada*. Toronto and Oxford: Dundurn Press. 355-417.

Nevitte, Neil. 1996. *The Decline of Deference*. Peterborough, ON: Broadview Press.

New York Times (editorial). 2004. "Disney's Craven Behavior." (May 6). <http://www.nytimes.com/2004/05/06/opinion/06THU4.html?ex=1085 198400&en=eb357cf36dabf730&ei=5070>.

Niskanen, William A. 1994. *Bureaucracy and Public Economics*. London: E. Elgar.

Noel, Jan. 1995. *Canada Dry: Temperance Crusades Before Confederation*. Toronto: University of Toronto Press.

Offe, Claus. 1985. "New Social Movements: Challenging the Boundaries of Institutional Politics." *Social Research* 52(4): 817-68.

Olson, Mancur. 1971 [1965]. *The Logic of Collective Action: Public Goods and the Theory of Groups*. Cambridge, MA: Harvard University Press.

Olson, Mancur. 1982. *The Rise and Decline of Nations: Economic Growth, Stagflation and Structural Rigidities*. New Haven: Yale University Press.

Olson, Susan M. 1990. "Interest Group Litigation in Federal District Court: Beyond the Political Disadvantage Theory." *Journal of Politics* 52: 854-76.

Orsini, Michael. 2002. "The Politics of Naming, Blaming and Claiming: HIV, Hepatitis C and the Emergence of Blood Activism in Canada." *Canadian Journal of Political Science* 35(3): 1-21.

Ostry, Bernard. 1960. "Conservatives, Liberals and Labour in the 1870s." *Canadian Historical Review* 41(June): 93-127.

Ostry, Bernard. 1961. "Conservatives, Liberals and Labour in the 1880s." *Canadian Journal of Economic and Political Science* 27(2) May: 141-61.

Pal, Leslie A. 1993. *Interests of State: The Politics of Language, Multiculturalism and Feminism in Canada*. Montreal and Kingston: McGill-Queen's University Press.

Pal, Leslie A. 2001. *Beyond Policy Analysis: Public Issue Management in Turbulent Times*. 2nd ed. Scarborough: Nelson Thompson.

Pal, Leslie A., and R. Kent Weaver. 2003. "The Politics of Pain." In Leslie A. Pal and R. Kent Weaver (eds.), *The Government Taketh Away: The Politics of Pain in the United States and Canada*. Washington, DC: Georgetown University Press. 1-40.

Pammett, Jon H., and Lawrence LeDuc. 2003. *Explaining the Turnout Decline in Canadian Federal Elections: A New Survey of Non-Voters*. Ottawa: Elections Canada.

Panitch, Leo. 1995. "Elites, Classes, and Power in Canada." In Michael S. Whittington and Glen Williams (eds.), *Canadian Politics in the 1990s*. Toronto: Nelson. 152-75.

Patten, Steve. 1999. "The Reform Party's Re-imagining of the Canadian Nation." *Journal of Canadian Studies* 34(1): 1-23.

Phillips, Susan D. 2001a. "SUFA and Citizen Engagement: Fake or Genuine Masterpiece?" *Policy Matters* 2(7): 1-36.

Phillips, Susan D. 2001b. "From Charity to Clarity: Reinventing Federal Government-Voluntary Sector Relationships." In Leslie A. Pal (ed.), *How Ottawa Spends 2001-2002: Power in Transition*. Don Mills: Oxford University Press. 145-76.

Pierson, Paul. 1993. "When Effect Becomes Cause: Policy Feedback and Political Change." *World Politics* 45 (July): 595-628.

Pierson, Paul, and Theda Skocpol. 2002. "Historical Institutionalism in Contemporary Political Science." In Ira Katnelson and Helen V. Milner (eds.), *Political Science: The State of the Discipline*. New York and London: W.W. Norton. 693-721.

Pierson, Paul, and Miriam Smith. 1993. "Bourgeois Revolutions? The Policy Consequences of Resurgent Conservatism." *Comparative Political Studies* 25(4) January: 487-520.

Piva, Michael J. 1979. "The Toronto District Labour Council and Independent Political Action: Factionalism and Frustration, 1900-1921." *Labour/Le Travailleur* 4: 115-30.

Polsby, Nelson W. 1963. *Community Power and Political Theory*. New Haven: Yale University Press.

Presthus, Robert. 1973. *Elite Accommodation in Canadian Politics*. Cambridge: Cambridge University Press.

Pross, A. Paul (ed.). 1975. *Pressure Group Behaviour in Canadian Politics*. Scarborough: McGraw-Hill Ryerson.

Pross, A. Paul. 1992. *Group Politics and Public Policy*. 2nd ed. Toronto: Oxford University Press.

Putnam, Robert. 1988. "Diplomacy and Domestic Politics: The Logic of Two-level Games." *International Organization* 42(3): 427-60.

Rayside, David. 2001. "The Structuring of Sexual Minority Activist Opportunities in the Political Mainstream: Britain, Canada, and the United States." In Mark Blasius (ed.), *Sexual Identities, Queer Politics*. Princeton: Princeton University Press. 23-55.

Razack, Sherene. 1991. *Canadian Feminism and the Law: The Women's Legal Education and Action Fund and the Pursuit of Equality*. Toronto: Second Story Press.

Richardson, R. Jack. 1992. "Free Trade: Why Did It Happen?" *Canadian Review of Sociology and Anthropology* 29: 307-29.

Ripley, Randall. 1988. *Congress: Process and Policy*. New York: W.W. Norton.

Roach, Kent. 1993. "The Role of Litigation and the Charter in Interest Advocacy." In F. Leslie Seidle (ed.), *Equity and Community: The Charter, Interest Advocacy and Representation*. Montreal: Institute for Research on Public Policy. 159-88.

Robin, Martin. 1968. *Radical Politics and Canadian Labour*. Kingston: Industrial Relations Centre, Queen's University.

Rosenberg, Gerald N. 1991. *The Hollow Hope: Can Courts Bring About Social Change?* Chicago: University of Chicago Press.

Rouillard, Jacques. 1989. *Histoire du syndicalisme Québécois*. Montréal: Boréal.

Russell, Peter H. 1983. "The Political Purposes of the Charter" *Canadian Bar Review* 61: 30-54.

Russell, Peter H. 1992. *Constitutional Odyssey: Can Canadians Become a Sovereign People?* Toronto: University of Toronto Press, 1992.

Saint-Martin, Denis. 2000. *Building the New Managerialist State*. Oxford: Oxford University Press.

Savoie, Donald J. 1999. *Governing from the Centre: The Concentration of Power in Canadian Politics*. Toronto: University of Toronto Press.

Savoie, Donald J. 2003. *Breaking the Bargain: Public Servants, Ministers and Parliament*. Toronto: University of Toronto Press.

Scheingold, Stuart. 1974. *The Politics of Rights: Lawyers, Public Policy, and Political Change*. New Haven and London: Yale University Press.

Scheingold, Stuart. 1989. "Constitutional Rights and Social Change: Civil Rights in Perspective." In Michael W. McCann and Gerald L. Houseman (eds.), *Judging the Constitution: Critical Essays on Judicial Lawmaking*. Glenview, IL: Scott, Forseman. 73-91.

Schultz, Richard. 1977. "Interest Groups and Intergovernmental Negotiation: Caught in the Vise of Federalism." In Peter Meekison (ed.), *Canadian Federalism: Myth or Reality*. Toronto: Methuen. 79-90.

Scott, James C. 1998. *Seeing Like a State: How Certain Schemes to Improve the Human Condition Have Failed*. New Haven: Yale University Press.

Seidman, Steven. 2004. *Contested Knowledge: Social Theory Today*. 3rd ed. Oxford: Blackwell.

Sheldrick, Byron M. 2003. "Judicial Review and the Allocation of Health Care Resources in Canada and the United Kingdom." *Journal of Comparative Policy Analysis* 5: 149-66.

Sheldrick, Byron M. 2004. *Perils and Possibilities: Social Activism and the Law*. Halifax: Fernwood.

Shepard, Benjamin. 2002. "Introductory Notes on the Trail From ACT UP to the WTO." In Benjamin Shepard and Ronald Hayduk (eds.), *From Act Up to the WTO: Urban Protest and Community-Building in the Era of Globalization*. London: Verso. 11-20.

Sigurdson, Richard. 1993. "Left- and Right-Wing Charterphobia in Canada: A Critique of the Critics." *International Journal of Canadian Studies* 7-8 (Spring-Fall): 95-116.

Simeon, Richard. 1972. *Federal-Provincial Diplomacy: The Making of Recent Policy in Canada*. Toronto: University of Toronto Press.

Simeon, Richard, and Ian Robinson. 1990. *State, Society and the Development of Canadian Federalism*. Toronto: University of Toronto Press.

Simon, Herbert A. 1989. *Complex Information Processing: The Impact of Herbert A. Simon*. London: E. Elgar.

Simpson, Jeffrey. 2001. *The Friendly Dictatorship*. Toronto: McClelland and Stewart.

Skocpol, Theda. 1979. *States and Social Revolutions: A Comparative Analysis of France, Russia and China*. Cambridge: Cambridge University Press.

Skocpol, Theda. 1985. "Bringing the State Back In: Strategies of Analysis in Current Research." In Peter B. Evans, Dietrich Rueschmeyer, and Theda Skocpol (eds.), *Bringing the State Back In*. Cambridge: Cambridge University Press. 3-37.

Skowronek, Stephen. 1982. *Building a New American State: The Expansion of National Administrative Capacity, 1877-1920*. Cambridge: Cambridge University Press.

Small, Peter. 2004. "Lobbyist List Debated." *Toronto Star* (January 22): B7.

Smiley, Donald V. 1976. *Canada in Question: Federalism in the Seventies*. 2nd ed. Toronto: McGraw-Hill Ryerson.

Smith, Miriam. 1999. *Lesbian and Gay Rights in Canada: Social Movements and Equality-Seeking, 1971-1995.* Toronto: University of Toronto Press.

Smith, Miriam. 2002. "Ghosts of the JCPC: Group Politics and Charter Litigation in Canadian Political Science," *Canadian Journal of Political Science* 35(1) March: 3-29.

Soysal, Yasmin. 1994. *Limits of Citizenship: Migrants and Postnational Membership in Europe.* Chicago: University of Chicago Press.

Stanbury, William T. 1991. *Money in Politics: Financing Federal Parties and Candidates in Canada.* Ottawa: Supply and Services Canada, 1991.

Stevenson, Garth. 1993. *Ex Uno Plures: Federal-Provincial Relations in Canada, 1867-1896.* Montreal and Kingston: McGill-Queen's University Press.

Sutherland, Sharon. 1991. "The Al-Mashat Affair: Administrative Accountability in Parliamentary Institutions" *Canadian Public Administration* 34(4): 573-603.

Taras, David. 2001. *Power and Betrayal in the Canadian Media.* Peterborough, ON: Broadview Press.

Tarrow, Sidney. 1998. *Power in Movement: Social Movements, Collective Action and Politics.* 2nd ed. Cambridge: Cambridge University Press.

Thelen, Kathleen, and Sven Steinmo. 1992. "Institutionalism in Comparative Politics." In Sven Steinmo, Kathleen Thelen, and Frank Longstreth (eds.), *Historical Institutionalism in Comparative Analysis.* Cambridge: Cambridge University Press. 1-32.

Thomas, Paul G. 2001. "Caucus and Representation in Canada." In Hugh G. Thorburn and Alan Whitehorn (eds.), *Party Politics in Canada.* 8th ed. Toronto: Pearson Educational. 221-30.

Thorburn, Hugh. 1985. *Interest Groups in the Canadian Federal System.* Toronto: University of Toronto Press.

Touraine, Alain. 1981. *The Voice and the Eye: An Analysis of Social Movements.* Cambridge: Cambridge University Press.

Truman, David B. 1951. *The Governmental Process: Political Interests and Public Opinion.* New York: Alfred A. Knopf.

Tully, James. 2000. "A Just Relationship between Aboriginal Peoples and Canadians." In Curtis Cook and Juan Lindau (eds.), *Aboriginal Rights and Self-Government: The Canadian and Mexican Experience.* Montreal: McGill-Queens University Press. 39-71.

Valverde, Mariana. 1991. *The Age of Light, Soap and Water.* Toronto: McClelland and Stewart.

VanNijnatten, Debora L., and Douglas MacDonald. 2003. "Reconciling Energy and Climate Change Policies: How Ottawa Blends." In G. Bruce Doern (ed.), *How Ottawa Spends 2003-2004: Regime Change and Policy Shift.* Don Mills: Oxford University Press. 72-88.

Vickers, Jill, Pauline Rankin, and Christine Appelle. 1993. *Politics as if Women Mattered: A Political Analysis of the National Action Committee on the Status of Women.* Toronto: University of Toronto Press.

Vosko, Leah. 2000. *Temporary Work: The Gendered Rise of a Precarious Employment Relationship.* Toronto: University of Toronto Press.

Walker, Jack L. Jr. 1991. *Mobilizing Interest Groups in America: Patrons, Professions, and Social Movements.* Ann Arbor: University of Michigan Press.

Warner, Tom. 2002. *Never Going Back: A History of Queer Activism in Canada*. Toronto: University of Toronto Press.

Warsh, Cheryl Krasnick. 1993. "'John Barleycorn Must Die': An Introduction to the Social History of Alcohol." In Cheryl Krasnick Warsh (ed.) *Drink in Canada: Historical Essays*. Montreal and Kingston: McGill-Queen's University Press. 3-26.

Watkins, Mel. 1977. "The Staples Theory Revisited." *Journal of Canadian Studies* 12(5): 83-95.

Wearing, Joseph. 1988. *Strained Relations: Canadian Parties and Voters*. Toronto: McClelland and Stewart.

Weir, Lorna. 1993. "Limitations of New Social Movement Analysis." *Studies in Political Economy* 40: 73-102.

Weir, Margaret, and Theda Skocpol. 1985. "State Structures and the Possibilities for 'Keynesian' Responses to the Great Depression in Sweden, Britain, and the United States." In Peter B. Evans, Dietrich Rueschmeyer, and Theda Skocpol (eds.), *Bringing the State Back In*. Cambridge: Cambridge University Press. 107-68.

Whitehorn, Alan. 1985. "An Analysis of the Historiography of the CCF-NDP: The Protest Movement Becalmed Tradition." In J. William Brennan (ed.), *"Building the Co-operative Commonwealth": Essays on the Democratic Socialist Tradition in Canada*. Regina: University of Regina Press. 1-24.

Williams, Robert J. 2001. "The Ontario Party System and the Common Sense Revolution: Transformation or Transient Turmoil." In Hugh G. Thorburn and Alan Whitehorn (eds.), *Party Politics in Canada*. 8th ed. Toronto: Pearson Educational. 335-50.

Wilson, Jeremy. 1992. "Green Lobbies: Pressure Groups and Environmental Policy." In Robert Boardman (ed.), *Canadian Environmental Policy: Ecosystems, Politics and Process*. Toronto: Oxford University Press. 109-25.

Wilson, John. 1968. "Politics and Social Class in Canada." *Canadian Journal of Political Science* 1(3, September): 397-412.

Wood, Lesley J., and Kelly Moore. 2002. "Target Practice: Community Activism in a Global Era." In Benjamin Shepard and Ronald Hayduk (eds.), *From Act Up to the WTO: Urban Protest and Community-Building in the Era of Globalization*. London: Verso. 21-34.

Young, Claire F.L. 1994. "Taxing Times for Lesbians and Gay Men: Equality at What Cost?" *Dalhousie Law Journal* 17(2): 534-59.

Young, Lisa. 2000. *Feminists and Party Politics*. Vancouver: University of British Columbia Press.

Young, Walter. 1969. *Portrait of a Party: The National CCF, 1932-1961*. Toronto and Buffalo: University of Toronto Press.

Zakuta, Leo. 1964. *A Protest Movement Becalmed: A Study of Change in the CCF*. Toronto and Buffalo: University of Toronto Press.

Index